A Photographic History of
English Football

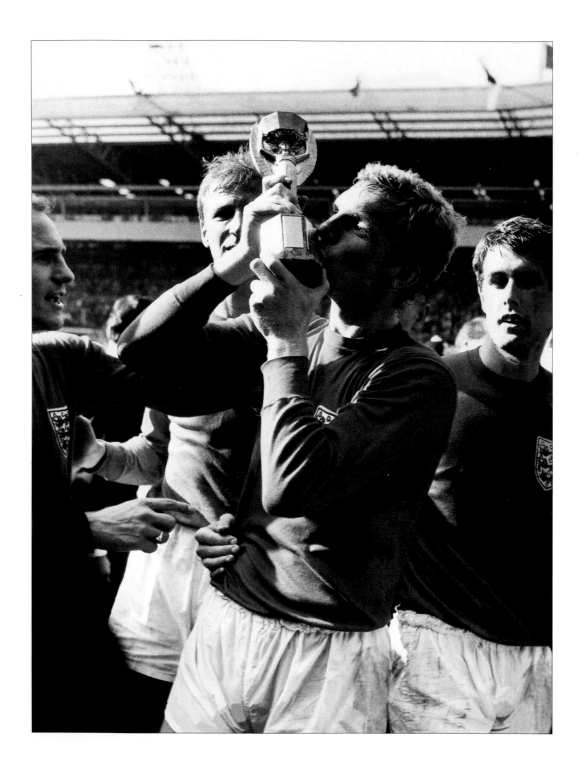

A Photographic History of
English Football

Tim Hill

Photographs by the

Daily Mail

p

For Laura and Jenny

This is a Parragon Book
This edition published in 2005

Parragon
Queen Street House
4 Queen Street
Bath, BA1 IHE, UK

All photographs © Associated Newspapers Archive
Text © Parragon

Produced by Atlantic Publishing Ltd
Origination by Croxons PrePress
Designed by John Dunne

A catalogue record for this book is available from the British Library.

ISBN 1-40545-682-5

Printed in Indonesia

Contents

Introduction

The People's Game

In the mid-19th century, a few English 'football clubs' came up with a novel idea: playing the game purely with the feet! Association Football formally made its bow in a London tavern in 1863. The early champions of the new game were men from the great public schools and universities, but within a generation all that had changed. The inaugural FA Cup took place in 1872 and the Football League was founded in 1888; by then football had become the People's Game.

Other countries eventually caught up, and with the glorious exception of 1966, England hasn't ruled the footballing world as it did in those heady early days. And yet in places as far afield as Africa, China and Scandinavia, English football is followed as passionately as it is at home.

Lavishly illustrated using over 400 photographs from the archives of the *Daily Mail*, many of which have never been previously published, *A Photographic History of English Football* charts all the key events in the 140-year history of the game, from the time when players wore knickerbockers, balls had laces and goals lacked crossbars, to the game we know today. There are statistics and profiles, controversies and shocks, developments in tactics and rules. But mostly it is about the great teams and great players of the country that gave football to the world.

The Origins of the Game

The beginnings of football cannot be dated exactly. A rudimentary form of the game was played in China as early as 200 BC, and the ancient Greeks and Romans also had their own versions. Suffice to say that throughout history inflated animals' bladders, indeed any spherical objects that would serve the purpose, have been kicked, thrown and headed in the name of sporting endeavour.

Britain was just one of many countries that absorbed football into its cultural fabric. It is said that after the Anglo-Saxons repelled an attack by the Danes in the early Middle Ages, a celebratory game of football was played using the head of one of the vanquished as a ball. Entire villages would participate in long attritional sporting battles with their neighbours, often on Shrove Tuesday or other public holidays. One such took place between the Derbyshire villages of All Saints and St Peter's and gave rise to the expression "local derby". Several monarchs, including Edward III and Richard II, attempted to ban football, fearing that their subjects were spending too much time honing their ball skills at the expense of their dexterity with the longbow. The Puritans were equally concerned, regarding football as a form of revelling that the country could well do without. Needless to say, all these efforts came to nought.

Public schools and universities lead the way

It wasn't until the 19th century that a number of games which could all be loosely united under the umbrella of "football" finally spread their wings and stood alone. Diversification was the new Zeitgeist, and it was not achieved without a degree of acrimony.

The game of football in the eighteenth and early nineteenth centuries was championed by the elite

A recent re-enactment of the famous occasion in 1823 when William Webb Ellis decided to pick up the ball and run with it. In 1839 Queen Adelaide, widow of William IV, visited Rugby School and watched a game on the famous sporting field. The boys had been given a tasselled cap to commemorate the visit, and some of them wore the headgear on the field of play. That didn't catch on, but the idea of presenting caps as a way of honouring international appearances did.

educational institutions. Thomas Arnold, the headmaster of Rugby School in the 1830s, took the progressive view that football ought to be positively encouraged, not suppressed. He felt that exercising both mind and body were equally important, and football was far preferable to drinking and gambling as a leisure pursuit. Many other public schools and universities took the same view, and it was here that the game flourished, although each institution developed its own version of the game.

William Webb Ellis "disregards the rules"

Ironically, a fictitious event at Rugby School a decade before Arnold took up his post remains a key date in the annals of sport. In 1823 William Webb Ellis is supposed to have shown "a fine disregard for the rules of football" by picking up the ball and running with it. This landmark event is almost certainly nothing more than an apocryphal tale, but it did usher in a period in which a number of distinct sports emerged from a plethora of broadly similar ball games.

Contrary to the view expressed in the William Webb Ellis commemorative plaque, which speaks of his celebrated exploit "originating the distinctive feature of the rugby game", it was those who wanted to play only a dribbling, kicking game who were the real innovators. All the other football-derived sports - including Australian Rules, American football and hurling, as well as rugby

An illustration dating from the 1860s shows a group of boys playing "football". Public schools such as Eton and Winchester had taken up the game but each team played according to its own set of rules making competition almost impossible.

itself - embraced handling as a key element. It was these sports which represented a link with the past. In the mid-19th century, it was Association football that was the brand new package on offer, although the term itself had not yet been coined.

Hacking becomes the key issue

It wasn't simply a case of a handling game versus a dribbling game, however. Proponents of the latter, including those at Eton and Charterhouse, wanted to do away with hacking - kicking an opponent's shins. This was the issue of greatest concern. The hacking that went on at that time made the on-field misdemeanours of the modern era seem tame by comparison. Broken limbs were commonplace, and fatalities not unknown. Etonians and Carthusians were in the vanguard of those who wanted a game in which the ball - and only the ball - was kicked. There were many who harrumphed at the idea; the aggression that was central to the game of rugby football was the stuff on which Great Britain had built her empire. A more "civilised" game, so the argument ran, risked the country's pre-eminence as a military power.

Football Association formed

Above: Richmond rugby team pictured in the 1890s. In 1863 eleven southern clubs formed the Football Association. Blackheath refused to accept the majority decision and left the FA to form the Rugby Football Union.
Below: An early advertisement for boots mentions both rugby and 'association', but a clear distinction between the two games was not properly made until the second half of the 19th century.

When Old Etonians of the 1840s moved on to Cambridge University, they continued to express their opposition to the version of football as played at Rugby School. The battle lines were drawn, and the battle itself would be fought over the rules. In 1848 some of the proponents of the dribbling game drew up the Cambridge Rules, which were forerunners of those of Association Football. This was a key event, despite the fact that these rules were not widely taken up. Even within the walls of Rugby School itself there had been no standard set of rules. There were no intercollegiate fixtures, and so the students themselves could make up and amend rules on a whim. A revised version of the Cambridge Rules was drafted in 1862. The time was fast approaching when the rival camps would have to face each other and thrash the issue out once and for all.

Historic decision

On 26 October 1863 representatives from eleven leading football clubs met at the Freemasons' Tavern, Great Queen Street, London. Of the dribbling game's champions in academia, only Charterhouse School was represented. The decision to form a new body, the Football Association, was uncontroversial. Some six weeks later, at the fifth meeting, the laws of the game were up for discussion and the temperature rose. The majority view favoured outlawing handling the ball and hacking. A vocal minority, led by

Blackheath FC, would not countenance what they perceived as a bastardisation of their beloved game. Once again, the objectors were more concerned over the abandonment of hacking than they were at the prospect of seeing running with the ball in hand outlawed. Having lost the vote 13-4, Blackheath's representatives resigned and withdrew, hardly realising the historic significance of their decision.

The "new" dribbling game

There were many clubs who chose to follow Blackheath and stick with the traditional handling game. But these were far outnumbered by those who subscribed to the "new" kicking and dribbling sport. And so, ironically, the traditional roughhouse working man's game of rugby lost out in the popularity stakes to a perceived less manly code whose champions had been public schoolboys! Association football quickly established itself as the sport of the masses, while rugby became something of an elitist pursuit. In a remarkably short space of time, orthodoxy had been stood on its head.

Hybrid games still common

Football in 1863 still retained many of the elements of rugby. Hacking had gone, but handling the ball was still permissible, and a kick at goal could be won by touching down over the opposition's goal-line. Nor did the formation of the FA have an immediate unifying effect on the game that was played up and down the country. Many clubs played "soccer" - a word coined from Association football - others played rugby, while it was common to see games that were a hybrid of the two codes. When the FA was formed, Sheffield FC had already been in existence for at least five years. But this club had devised its own rules and when it sought FA membership, the Association did not even deign to reply. Notts County, established in 1862, thus became the oldest club among the founding members of the Football League. That was still a long way off, however. During the 1860s and 1870s the FA's priorities were consolidation and standardisation, amending the laws and, in 1871, establishing a cup competition.

Rule changes

Rule changes that made the game far more recognisable as the one we know today included the introduction of goal kicks (1869) and corner kicks (1872). Offside was integrated into the laws, with three defenders required between the attacking player and the goal. In the mid-1860s tape was stretched between the posts at a height of 8 feet; a decade later it was replaced by a crossbar. In 1871 the term "goalkeeper" made its first appearance in the game's legislative framework, and sealed the end of handling the ball for the outfield players. 11-a-side games became the norm and the rules were enforced by an umpire. Thus, by the time the Rugby Football Union was formed in 1871, the two codes had diverged dramatically.

Not every match was played according to the regulations but the rules of the game gradually expanded from the 14 agreed upon by the FA in 1863. In 1865 the height of the tape which formed the crossbar of the goal was set at 8 feet although nets were not compulsory until 1891. Goalkeepers were first mentioned in the rules in 1871 and the penalty kick was introduced in 1891.

The birth of the FA Cup

One of the key events in this period was not a change in the way the game was played but an administrative appointment. Charles Alcock was an Old Harrovian who, along with his elder brother James, had helped to found the Forest club. Forest was among those clubs represented at the historic meeting at the Freemasons' Tavern, although Alcock himself was not present. James Alcock became an FA Committee member when it was first constituted, but within three years Charles had replaced him and it was he who became one of the most influential figures of the day. Alcock was a driving force in the effort to establish a unified game throughout the land. In 1870 he was appointed Secretary to the FA, a position he held for 25 years. His greatest contribution came just one year into that appointment, when he was the prime mover in the birth of the FA Cup.

15 clubs enter inaugural FA Cup

It was at an FA Committee meeting on 20 July 1871 that Alcock proposed the following motion: "That it is desirable that a Challenge Cup should be established in connection with the Association, for which all clubs belonging to the Association should be invited to compete". The idea was probably based on the inter-house competitions he had participated in during his time at Harrow.

As there were no league matches at this time, fixtures were an ad hoc mish-mash cobbled together between club secretaries with varying degrees of success. A Cup competition suddenly gave football a focal point, and it quickly caught the imagination of the clubs. By this time some fifty of them were affiliated to the FA, yet logistical problems meant that only 15 entered the inaugural competition, held in the 1871-72 season. There was an overwhelming southern bias, 13 of the entrants coming from that region, including eight from the environs of the capital. Donington Grammar School in Lincolnshire was England's most northerly participant, while Queen's Park ignored a daunting travel schedule and flew the flag for Scotland. With the aid of two byes and a walk-over - after Donington scratched - Queen's Park found themselves in the semi-finals without having kicked a ball! They funded their trip to London to play the Wanderers from public subscription. The game ended in a goalless draw, and as the Scottish club's resources wouldn't stretch to a replay, it was the Wanderers who went on to contest the Final.

> "It is desirable that a Challenge Cup should be established in connection with the Association, for which all clubs belonging to the Association should be invited to compete".

Cambridge University football team in 1894. Until the 1880s football was dominated by the gentlemen-amateur teams coming mainly from the public schools and universities of the south. In 1881 Old Etonians played Old Carthusians for the Cup, the last time two amateur sides appeared in the final.

Milestones to 1899

1848 Cambridge Rules drawn up at Cambridge University and form a basis for the rules later adopted by the FA

1855 Sheffield FC founded by members of Sheffield Cricket club and becomes the oldest football club in the world

1856 Sheffield FC publishes the "Sheffield Rules"

1862 The world's oldest league club, Nottingham (Notts) County is founded

1863 October 26th, the Football Associated formed at a meeting at Freemasons' Tavern in London

1867 The Wednesday founded. The team would later become Sheffield Wednesday in 1929. Wednesday refers to the day of the week in Sheffield which was set aside for workers' recreation.

1870 Eleven players becomes the standard size for a football team

1872 First FA Cup Final between Wanderers and the Royal Engineers at the Kennington Oval sees Wanderers winning 1-0

England's first international fixture is a game against Scotland resulting in a 0-0 draw

1874 Cricketers at the Villa Cross Wesleyan Chapel in Aston, Birmingham found Aston Villa Football Club

First mention of umpires in the game's laws

Shin-guards first introduced by England and Nottingham Forest player Sam Widdowson

1875 A Crossbar replaces the previous method of using tape strung between the goalposts

Blackburn Rovers formed by ex-Public School boys - it turned professional in 1880

Birmingham City founded by cricketers of the Trinity Church, Bordesley

1878 Referee uses a whistle for first time during a game at Nottingham Forest

Everton founded as Domingo FC which later changed its name to Everton after the region of Liverpool in which it was based

Floodlights first used in a game at Bramall Lane, the home of Sheffield United

1879 England beats Wales 2-1 in their first international fixture

Preston North End cricket club forms a football team of the same name

1881 Referees given power to order players off the field

Newcastle United founded as Stanley FC in the Byker district of Newcastle; the club went on to be known as Newcastle East End before finally settling on the current name in 1893

1882 The English National side secured its greatest-ever win, beating Ireland 13-0 in Belfast

1883 New rules require throw-ins to be two-handed

1884 Preston North End uses professionals in the FA Cup and is expelled as a result

Blackburn wins the FA Cup at the start of a run in which it would win the trophy five times over the following decade

1885 The Football Association legalises professionalism

1886 Arsenal Football Club founded by workers of the Royal Arsenal in Woolwich, London

1888 William McGregor, a director of Aston Villa suggests a football league, which is established with twelve teams

1889 Preston North End wins the first League Championship

1891 The old system of using referees and umpires to monitor games is replaced with referees and linesmen

Introduction of Goal Nets

The Penalty Kick was introduced at the request of William McCrum of the Irish FA, as it was considered that a free kick was not adequate enough for fouls which prevented almost certain goals

1892 A second division of the Football League is formed

1894 Manchester City is formed following financial difficulties of Ardwick, the club which had preceded it

The FA Amateur Cup is played for the first time

1895 Crystal Palace Stadium is first used to host the FA Cup Final between Aston Villa and West Bromwich Albion; the stadium would go on to hold the event twenty times

The FA Cup is stolen from a Birmingham shop window where it was on display after being won by Aston Villa

1897 A Players' Trade Union formed

Aston Villa secure the "Double" by winning the FA Cup and the league

1898 Teams can now be promoted and relegated between the football leagues

By the 1880s the game was more structured. Rules were recognised nationally and the FA Cup was a well-established competition. In 1888 William McGregor, a director of Aston Villa, took the initiative and invited 11 teams to join his club in the formation of a league.

Wanderers win the first Cup Final

The captain of the Wanderers was none other than Charles Alcock himself. Alcock had founded the club, which had no ground of its own and played its home matches at Battersea Park. That meant early kick-offs in winter, as the park closed its gates at 4.00 p.m.!

The Wanderers' opponents in the inaugural Cup Final were the Royal Engineers, the latter being installed as warm favourites. The match took place at Kennington Oval on 16 March 1872 in front of a 2000-strong crowd who had paid a shilling each for the privilege. The Wanderers upset the odds and ran out 1-0 winners. The goal was scored by Matthew Betts, who had been a registered member of the Harrovian Chequer club which had scratched earlier in the competition. He turned out for the Wanderers under an assumed name, a clear breach of the regulations. The first FA Cup Final thus saw the deciding goal scored by a player who really shouldn't have been on the pitch. If that weren't bad enough, the Royal Engineers had been handicapped by the fact that one of their players, Lieutenant Cresswell, was nursing a broken collarbone for most of the match. Nearly a hundred years before the era of substitutes, players had to be made of stern stuff.

Clash with the Boat Race

Wanderers went on to win the Cup four more times in the 1870s, although this was not a feat that could be compared to the modern era. In 1873, for example, the club was given a bye to the Final as cup holders. That match, in which Wanderers beat Oxford University 2-0, took place at 11.00 a.m. to avoid a clash with the Boat Race. For all the strides football had made, the latter remained a much more prestigious event in the sporting calendar.

Of more significance was the fact that gentlemen-amateurs, the leisured classes, dominated the competition in the early years. The Wanderers had the cream of the players from the public school and university systems. Old Etonians appeared in five Finals in that first decade, finally winning the trophy in 1879. Oxford University beat Royal Engineers to lift the Cup in 1874 and were also beaten finalists in 1873 and 1877. Clearly football in the elite educational institutions was still strong enough to get the better of the teams from the industrial Midlands and North. One of the stars of the day was Arthur Kinnaird, who was said to have been a dynamic, skilful performer in any position on the field. He appeared in nine FA Cup Finals, picking up winners' medals with Old Etonians in 1879 and 1882, and adding three more victories to his tally with Wanderers in 1873, 1877 and 1878.

In the late 19th century football teams sprang up all over the country. Some of these, such as Bolton, Southampton, Wolves and Everton, originally called St Domingo's, were established by churches. Others, like Spurs and the two Sheffield sides, were offshoots from cricket clubs. Newton Heath, later re-named Manchester United, began life as a works team started by employees of the Lancashire and Yorkshire Railway Company.

The rise of professionalism

In 1879 Lancashire side Darwen almost produced an upset of seismic proportions. In their 4th-round match against Old Etonians at Kennington Oval they came back from 5-1 down to force a draw. Darwen were in the ascendancy at the end of the match, and the Old Etonians' captain hastily declined the offer to play extra time. There was no question of the Old Etonians heading north for a replay, so Darwen had to make another trip to the capital. That game finished level too, and although Old Etonians prevailed in the third clash, it was clear that dominance of the gentlemen-amateurs was under threat.

End of the road for the gentleman-amateur

The pendulum swung after 1881, when Old Carthusians beat Old Etonians in the last all-amateur Final. By then, many future illustrious clubs had been formed. Some had their roots in church schools, including Aston Villa, Woverhampton Wanderers and Everton. Others, such as Newton Heath and Stoke City sprang up as works teams. Sheffield Wednesday and Preston North End were among those formed as offshoots of existing sports clubs, often ones for which cricket was the chief

> Some had their roots in church schools, including Aston Villa, Woverhampton Wanderers and Everton. Others, such as Newton Heath and Stoke City sprang up as works teams.

pursuit. But it was the town of Blackburn which ushered in the new era. Rovers reached the Cup Final in 1882, with Old Etonians providing the opposition. Blackburn boasted several classy Scottish players and, like many other clubs, was covertly organised along professional lines. One of the players' fathers was so confident of the result that he bet a row of houses on a Blackburn victory. It was an expensive gamble, for Old Etonians won the match 1-0. But the writing was on the wall. This would be the last time that an amateur club would lift the trophy.

The Cup goes north

The following year, Blackburn Olympic took the Cup north for the first time. The backbone of the team was made up of weavers and spinners, plumbers and sheet-metal workers. It also included players who appeared to earn their living purely from football, professionals in all but name. Olympic had a player-manager, Jack Hunter, who used advanced methods to prepare the team, including taking the players away to Blackpool to get them into peak physical and mental condition for the Final, in which they were up against the holders. Blackburn won the match 2-1 after extra time. For Old Etonians, a sixth Final appearance in twelve years was to be their last. They, together with the other clubs spawned from academia and the military, represented the old guard. And the shift in footballing power was not just away from the gentleman-amateur to artisans and professionals; it was also from the Home Counties to the industrial heartlands of the Midlands and the North. In the next 37 years the Cup would return to the south-east just once.

West Bromwich Albion appeared in the Cup Final on five occasions between 1886 and 1895, winning once against Preston in 1888 and later defeating Aston Villa in 1892.

English FA Cup Winners
1872 - 1899

1872	Wanderers	1878	Wanderers	1884	Blackburn Rovers	1890	Blackburn Rovers	1896	Sheffield Wednesday
1873	Wanderers	1879	Old Etonians	1885	Blackburn Rovers	1891	Blackburn Rovers	1897	Aston Villa
1874	Oxford University	1880	Clapham Rovers	1886	Blackburn Rovers	1892	West Bromwich Albion	1898	Nottingham Forest
1875	Royal Engineers	1881	Old Carthusians	1887	Aston Villa	1893	Wolves	1899	Sheffield United
1876	Wanderers	1882	Old Etonians	1888	West Bromwich Albion	1894	Notts County		
1877	Wanderers	1883	Blackburn Olympic	1889	Preston North End	1895	Aston Villa		

"Shamateurism"

By the 1870s it was clear that what would later be dubbed "shamateurism" was rife. Teams were vying for the best players, and it was inevitable that inducements would be offered. There was a game of cat-and-mouse between the clubs and the Football Association. The clubs found all manner of means to reward their players. These included giving nominal jobs which required little, if any, work to be done; putting money into players' boots on match days; and having phoney sets of accounts which would suggest to any enquiring eyes that everything was above board.

For a time the FA stood firm. In 1882 the Association reaffirmed its commitment to an amateur game, with payments strictly limited to out-of-pocket expenses. While the clubs made it difficult for the authorities to prove any underhand dealings, they did sometimes slip up. One of the victims was Accrington, who were thrown out of the FA after being found guilty of paying one of their players. Another was Preston, who were disqualified from the FA Cup after brazenly admitting to a misdemeanour that virtually every club was guilty of. The same issue was affecting rugby, and along the same geographical lines. In the case of the handling code, the rival camps became so entrenched that many northern clubs eventually broke away and established a new professional game; Rugby League was born.

FA relents

Football came close to suffering the same kind of split which divided rugby down the middle. Manual workers at that time might have earned one or two pounds a week, and although more liberal employment laws had been introduced, for many Saturday was still just another working day. Matters came to a head in October 1884, when a number of northern clubs banded together with a view to setting up a professional football league. In July the following year the FA relented. The administrators initially tried to impose caveats and restrictions, imposing a two-year residence rule to prevent clubs from importing star players for Cup matches. But the door was now ajar and it was soon fully opened. The age of the professional footballer had officially begun.

England's first international

The 1870s also saw international football take off. Five England-Scotland matches were staged between 1870 and 1872, but these took the form of London-based players from north and south of the border taking part in representative fixtures. Once again it was Charles Alcock who was the driving force behind these encounters. The first international proper between the two countries took place on 30 November 1872. Alcock initially set a midweek date for the match, rearranging it for a Saturday when he realised that Scottish players and spectators might not have the same independent means that he and his team enjoyed.

Manual workers at that time might have earned one or two pounds a week. For many Saturday was still just another working day.

The match took place at the West of Scotland cricket ground, Partick. At that time cricket enjoyed a higher profile than football in Scotland and the formation of the SFA was still a year away. One of the country's leading clubs, Queen's Park, thus took responsibility for organizing the team to take on England. A crowd of just over 2000 paid a shilling apiece to watch the match, which ended in a goalless draw. The embryonic state of Scottish football was illustrated by the fact that the photographer who was due to record the event wanted a guarantee that he would be able to sell his prints. No guarantee was forthcoming and the photographer thus withdrew, seeing little market for such pictures. Nevertheless, the game created a lot of interest in Scotland. It wasn't long before football, which could be played on almost any patch of ground, supplanted cricket as both a participation and spectator sport.

12 teams that founded the league in 1888

Accrington Stanley	Bolton Wanderers	Everton	Stoke City
Aston Villa	Burnley	Notts County	West Bromwich Albion
Blackburn Rovers	Derby County	Preston North end	Wolverhampton Wanderers

Scots influence English game

The Scots came to the Oval for a return match on 8 March 1873. Alexander Bonsor, who played for Old Etonians and the Wanderers, wrote his name into the history books as the scorer of England's first international goal. England won the game 4-2, and it became a fixture on the sporting calendar thereafter.

As well as promoting the game in their own country, the top Scotttish players of the day influenced the development of English football too. Dribbling was a feature of the English game, a legacy of the public schools and universities, which concentrated on individual skills rather than teamwork. It was the Scots who saw the advantage of playing a passing game. Many were recruited by clubs in the north of England, a practice that had gone on long before the FA embraced professionalism. They were usually the star players. Fergus Suter and James Love, the leading lights in the Darwen team that had given Old Etonians such a scare, were prime examples of this trend. It was the influence of Suter, Love and their ilk which made English clubs realise that packing a team with dribblers was not the way forward.

Villa man proposes league football

By the late 1880s professional footballers were playing international matches and clubs were competing for the FA Cup. Rule changes had given the game all its distinctive features. The last big piece of the jigsaw was league competition.

At the time fixtures were often anything but "fixed". Shambolic was a more apposite description. Postponements or cancellations were commonplace, and the game was crying out for organised fixture lists, not least because spectators who turned up to find there was no game were bound to feel aggrieved. Regular matches were also vital to meet a club's overheads, which now included players' wages. The establishment of a competitive league was the brainchild of William McGregor, a Scot who had relocated from Perthshire to Birmingham and ran a draper's shop. McGregor had no track record as a player, but his decision to join the board of his local club, Aston Villa, was to have a profound effect on the game.

12 teams contest new league competition

On 2 March 1888 McGregor wrote to Blackburn, Bolton, Preston and West Bromwich Albion about the prospect of forming a league, and naturally he also sounded out his own club on the idea. Throughout the spring of 1888 a series of meetings took place to thrash out the details and agree a name for the new body: the Football League. 12 teams were incorporated as founder members. These were the original five clubs that McGregor contacted, together with Accrington, Burnley, Everton, Derby County, Notts County, Wolverhampton Wanderers and Stoke. Other clubs, including Nottingham Forest, had also been keen to join, but the dates set aside for the matches, which were to be held on a home and away basis, meant that only 12 teams could be accommodated. Teams would be awarded two points for a win and one for a draw, a system which was to endure for almost a hundred years. McGregor became the Football League's first president, and the opening matches were played on 8 September 1888.

> *At the time fixtures were often anything but "fixed". Shambolic was a more apposite description.*

Right: The original FA trophy.

"Invincibles" of Preston set the standards

Preston set the standards in the early years, winning the league in the first two seasons and finishing runners-up in the following three campaigns. The inaugural season, 1888-89, was the most remarkable, Preston remaining unbeaten on their way to the championship, and not conceding a goal in the FA Cup, which they won by defeating Wolves 3-0 in the Final. Quite justifiably they were dubbed the "Invincibles". The team's star striker was a Scot, John Goodall. Goodall had previously shone for Great Lever, and representatives from Deepdale all but kidnapped him to acquire his services. Apart from his goalscoring feats, Goodall was also noteworthy for the fact that despite his roots he played international football for England by dint of residence. Goodall left to join Derby after Preston's Double-winning campaign.

Rise of Sunderland

Supremacy passed from Preston to Sunderland. The Wearside club had replaced founder-members Stoke in the 1890-91 season and finished in mid-table in their first campaign. They would have finished fifth but had two points deducted for fielding 'keeper Ned Doig before his move from Arbroath was sanctioned. In the next four years Sunderland lifted the title three times and were runners-up once. Of the 116 games played during those four campaigns the "team-of-all-talents" won 81, drew 13 and were beaten just 22 times. Their success was based on a phenomenal home record; the team lost just once in six years on their own ground.

The first of Sunderland's championships came in 1891-92, when the league was also extended to 14 clubs. Stoke were back, and Darwen were admitted. These clubs occupied the bottom two places, and Darwen had the dubious honour of becoming the first-ever team to suffer relegation to the newly-formed Second Division. The following year saw the league expanded again, to 16 clubs. Nottingham Forest were finally admitted, and ended their debut season in mid-table. The other debutants didn't fare quite so well. Newton Heath, the team that would eventually be reconstituted as Manchester United, propped up the table five points adrift of their nearest rivals.

Promotion and relegation

Promotion and relegation were not automatic, however; a series of "test matches" was held between the bottom three clubs of Division One and the top three in the new Second Division to decide the issue. Newton Heath survived that year but weren't so lucky the next. After finishing bottom in 1893-94 too, Newton Heath went down 2-0 to Division Two champions Liverpool, and the two teams swapped places. For Liverpool it meant promotion to the top flight at the first time of asking. Having had considerable success in the Lancashire League, the club had applied for a place in the Second Division after hearing that Accrington Stanley had resigned. Another club which achieved league status in the same year was Woolwich Arsenal. The Gunners had been formed in 1886, turned professional in 1891 and had already undergone three name changes. The team didn't quite have the same impact as the men from Anfield, but they had the honour of becoming the first southern club to be elected to the Football League.

Villa win the Cup - and lose it

In 1893-94 Aston Villa prevented Sunderland from making it a hat-trick of league titles, finishing six points ahead of the Wearside club. Villa went on to win the championship four more times in the next six seasons. They added the FA Cup to their trophy cabinet in 1895 and 1897, and were also runners-up in 1892. By completing the Double in 1896-97, Villa matched Preston's feat of eight years earlier. The Midlanders did lose four league games that season, yet still equalled Preston's achievement of finishing 11 points clear of the field. A thrilling 3-2 win over Everton completed the Double, an achievement that would prove elusive for the next 64 years.

Villa were also involved in a major off-field drama. Following the club's 1-0 FA Cup win over West Bromwich Albion in 1895, the trophy was put on display at a Birmingham bootmaker's shop belonging to William Shillcock. It was stolen on 11 September and never recovered. As a result, the FA fined Villa £25 and put the money towards a replacement trophy.

Townley the hat-trick hero

Following their three successive FA Cup wins in the mid-1880s, Blackburn Rovers notched two more successes at the start of the next decade. In 1890 Blackburn thumped Sheffield Wednesday 6-1, the biggest margin of the 19 finals that had taken place thus far. Blackburn had finished third in the championship and were hot favourites to beat Wednesday, despite the fact that the Yorkshire club had taken three league scalps in previous rounds.

The Gunners had been formed in 1886, turned professional in 1891 and had already undergone three name changes.

Blackburn winger William Townley hit three of the goals, becoming the first player to score a hat-trick in the final.

The following year Notts County thought they had a better chance of beating Blackburn, having just thrashed them 7-1 on their own ground in the league. But three first-half goals at the Oval meant that the Lancashire club lifted the trophy for the fifth time in eight years.

Opposite: 1895 works team Woolwich Arsenal was founded in 1886 as Dial Square FC and played their home matches on Plumstead Common. In 1893 it was admitted to the newly-formed Second Division becoming the first southern club to be admitted to the league.

Below: In 1895 Aston Villa won the FA Cup for the second time. While on display in Birmingham the trophy was stolen and is believed by some to have been melted down to be made into counterfeit coins. Three more trophies have been used since this time, the most recent being introduced in the early 1990s.

Cup Final moves north to Goodison

West Bromwich Albion put Rovers out in 1892 and went on to beat their much-fancied neighbours Aston Villa in the Final. There was another upset in 1893, when Wolves beat Everton 1-0. This match took place at Fallowfield, Manchester, after Surrey County Cricket Club expressed concerns that the Oval might not be able to cope with the huge numbers that the Cup Final now regularly attracted. Wolves' first victory prompted the club to award miniature replicas of the trophy to the players. This proved

Manchester City and Glossop were the first beneficiaries of the new two-up, two-down system.

very handy two years later after the Cup was stolen; it meant that an identical replacement could be made.

1893-94 was a bitter-sweet year for Notts County. Having been relegated the previous year, the team won through to face Division One side Bolton in the final, which was staged at Goodison Park. County were unhappy about the choice of venue, feeling that it favoured their opponents. They needn't have worried as they ran out 4-1 winners, with Jimmy Logan grabbing a hat-trick to equal William Townley's feat of four years earlier. Notts County failed to make it a Cup-promotion double, though. Having finished third in Division Two, they were beaten 4-0 by Preston in the play-off.

Glory for Sheffield clubs

The Cup Final returned to the capital in 1895, Crystal Palace hosting the clash between Aston Villa and WBA. It was the third time in nine years that these two clubs had met in the Final, both having registered a win each. There was no upset this year. Form side Villa won 1-0, the goal scored by the captain John Devey after just 40 seconds. This remains the fastest goal ever scored in an FA Cup Final.

The city of Sheffield briefly enjoyed a spell in the limelight in the late 1890s. Wednesday beat Wolves by the

odd goal in the 1896 Cup Final, neither club having set the league alight. The following year United finished as championship runners-up to Villa in the latter's Double-winning season. The Blades went one better in 1897-98, becoming only the fifth club to win the title. Their league form slumped dramatically in the next campaign, and they narrowly avoided relegation. But they made it to the Cup Final, where they faced Derby County, whose side boasted goal ace Steve Bloomer. United managed to shackle him, although they did find themselves a goal down at half-time. A storming second half saw the Blades hit four goals without reply for a famous victory. Full-back Harry Thickett was the hero of the hour, having played the game out with two broken ribs.

Automatic promotion and relegation

The "test match" system was scrapped at the end of the 1897-98 season. A suspicious play-off prompted the Football League to adopt automatic promotion and relegation. Stoke and Burnley, who had finished bottom of Division One and top of Division Two respectively, played out a tame goalless draw which saw both teams secure top-flight status the following season. At the end of the 1898-99 season, Manchester City and Glossop were the first beneficiaries of the new two-up, two-down system, with Bolton and Sheffield Wednesday becoming the first clubs to suffer the drop without the lifeline of a play-off.

The popularity of football among the masses had grown rapidly. By the turn of the century an estimated 7 million spectators watched league matches each year and in the 1890s the first newspaper devoted to sport was published. At the same time manufacturers saw the opportunity to make money by producing football equipment and began to advertise their products.

A new century dawns

As the new century dawned, the interest in football continued to grow exponentially. An aggregate of seven million people turned out to watch two 18-strong leagues battle it out for supremacy. And in less than thirty years the FA Cup had grown into one of the pre-eminent events of the sporting calendar. A record 73,833 crowd watched Sheffield United's win over Derby in 1899; attendances would soon comfortably exceed the six-figure mark. It was the showpiece event of the people's game, and had come a long way since the day it was moved to accommodate the Boat Race.

Football League 1888-1899
Top 10 League Positions

	1888-89			1891-92			1894-95			1897-98	
1	Preston	40	1	Sunderland	42	1	Sunderland	47	1	Sheffield United	42
2	Aston Villa	29	2	Preston	37	2	Everton	42	2	Sunderland	37
3	Wolverhampton W.	28	3	Bolton Wanderers	36	3	Aston Villa	39	3	Wolverhampton W.	35
4	Blackburn Rovers	26	4	Aston Villa	30	4	Preston	35	4	Everton	35
5	Bolton Wanderers	22	5	Everton	28	5	Blackburn Rovers	32	5	The Wednesday	33
6	West Bromwich Albion	22	6	Wolverhampton W.	26	6	Sheffield United	32	6	Aston Villa	33
7	Accrington	20	7	Burnley	26	7	Nottingham Forest	31	7	West Bromwich Albion	32
8	Everton	20	8	Notts County	26	8	The Wednesday	28	8	Nottingham Forest	31
9	Burnley	17	9	Blackburn Rovers	26	9	Burnley	26	9	Liverpool	28
10	Derby County	16	10	Derby County	24	10	Bolton Wanderers	25	10	Derby County	28

	1889-90			1892-93			1895-96			1898-99	
1	Preston	33	1	Sunderland	48	1	Aston Villa	45	1	Aston Villa	45
2	Everton	31	2	Preston	37	2	Derby County	41	2	Liverpool	43
3	Blackburn Rovers	27	3	Everton	36	3	Everton	39	3	Burnley	39
4	Wolverhampton W.	25	4	Aston Villa	35	4	Bolton Wanderers	37	4	Everton	38
5	West Bromwich Albion	25	5	Bolton Wanderers	32	5	Sunderland	37	5	Notts County	37
6	Accrington	24	6	Burnley	30	6	Stoke	30	6	Blackburn Rovers	36
7	Derby County	21	7	Stoke	29	7	The Wednesday	29	7	Sunderland	36
8	Aston Villa	19	8	West Bromwich Albion	29	8	Blackburn Rovers	29	8	Wolverhampton W.	35
9	Bolton Wanderers	19	9	Blackburn Rovers	29	9	Preston	28	9	Derby County	35
10	Notts County	17	10	Nottingham Forest	28	10	Burnley	27	10	Bury	35

	1890-91			1893-94			1896-97	
1	Everton	29	1	Aston Villa	44	1	Aston Villa	47
2	Preston	27	2	Sunderland	38	2	Sheffield United	36
3	Notts County	26	3	Derby County	36	3	Derby County	36
4	Wolverhampton W.	26	4	Blackburn Rovers	34	4	Preston	34
5	Bolton Wanderers	25	5	Burnley	34	5	Liverpool	33
6	Blackburn Rovers	24	6	Everton	33	6	The Wednesday	31
7	Sunderland	23	7	Nottingham Forest	32	7	Everton	31
8	Burnley	21	8	West Bromwich Albion	32	8	Bolton Wanderers	30
9	Aston Villa	18	9	Wolverhampton W.	31	9	Bury	30
10	Accrington	16	10	Sheffield United	31	10	Wolverhampton W.	28

1900-1919
The National sport

Football in the Edwardian era continued to provide rich entertainment for very little outlay. Sixpence was the typical entrance fee, and working men in their droves flocked to matches. Lifelong allegiances were developed, passions aroused. These sometimes manifested themselves in ways that earned rebuke. An over-exuberant crowd invaded the pitch in a Cup-tie between Spurs and Villa in 1904, causing the match to be abandoned. The FA ordered a replay at Villa Park and fined the London club £350. Some years later, when Europe was plunged into war, politicians expressed concern that munitions workers were preoccupied by football when their minds should have been on the war effort.

Left: At the end of the 19th century, Sunderland, dubbed "team of all the talents" was the most successful club in the north east. However by 1900 Newcastle United began to make its mark. Like its neighbour, the Newcastle team contained many Scottish players. In the 1901-2 season Sunderland regularly fielded 9 Scots.

Opposite: Supporters of Everton and Sheffield had a long way to travel for the 1907 Cup Final at Crystal Palace. Here supporters are going past St Paul's as they make their way to South London. 84,000 fans watched Wednesday win the match 2-1.

Meredith leads players' challenge against maximum wage

Burgeoning interest inevitably meant that football was no longer simply sport and entertainment but also big business. Some of the top clubs started to show extremely healthy balance sheets, and it wasn't long before players began to demand a bigger slice of the cake. In April 1901 a new maximum wage of £4 a week was introduced. This compared favourably with other skilled tradesmen of the day, but players began to recognise their worth and started to express dissatisfaction. Matters came to a head in 1907 with the formation of a Players' Union. The league and FA were worried about footballers becoming organised, possibly even affiliating to the Trades Union movement. They threatened to impose a ban on players who took up union membership. Manchester United star Billy Meredith was one of a vociferous group unwilling to be browbeaten. While many players lost their nerve and fell into line, Meredith led a group of players who threatened to withdraw all their labour. Prior to the 1909-10 season they began training independently under the banner of The Outcasts. Just before the season got under way the

authorities caved in. The maximum wage was subsequently increased to £5 a week. The principle of player power was established.

First £1000 transfer

Another manifestation of the way in which football was now a huge enterprise was in the transfer market. 1905 saw Sunderland and England inside-forward Alf Common join Middlesbrough for £1000, the first four-figure fee. This landmark deal polarised opinion. Boro fans were jubilant after Common helped the club finish clear of relegation. But to some the buying and selling of players in such a way smacked of human trafficking, something that was morally questionable. The game's administrators may not have taken such an extreme view, but they were apprehensive. In 1908 the league tried to impose a £350 cap on transfers. It lasted just four months. The authorities realised that the ruling was unenforceable. Pragmatism won the day, as it had over the issue of professionalism some 20 years earlier.

Billy Meredith
"The Welsh Wizard"

Billy Meredith, "the Welsh Wizard", is widely regarded as the game's first superstar. Meredith came from Welsh mining stock, and he himself was working underground by the age of 12. His parents were eventually persuaded to allow him to pursue a career in football and Meredith joined Manchester City in 1894. He quickly established himself as a skilful, free-scoring winger, and became known for the fact that he never took to the field without a toothpick to chew on.

By 1904 30-year-old Meredith was City's captain, and scored the only goal of the game in that year's FA Cup Final win over Bolton. Meredith was banned for eight months after allegedly attempting to bribe an Aston Villa player before a vital league match in April 1905. He denied the charge and when the ban was lifted he moved across the city to join Manchester United. He helped United to win the FA Cup in 1909 and the championship in 1910-11. He rejoined Manchester City in 1921 as a player-coach. He finally hung up his boots three years later, when he was four months short of his 50th birthday. His swansong came in City's 1924 FA Cup semi-final defeat by Newcastle. He had played 48 times for Wales between 1895 and 1920, winning the last of his caps when he was 45.

Meredith was at the forefront of a campaign to end the £4 maximum wage that was in force in the early 1900s. That figure was increased to £5 as a result, and the roots of the PFA can be traced back to the Welshman's early efforts to establish a Players' Union.

Billy Meredith, a tough, talented and controversial player who captained Wales and played for both Manchester City and Manchester United in a 30-year career which ended in 1924. Instrumental in setting the foundations for a Players' Union, he was also banned for a season for reportedly attempting to bribe an Aston Villa player in a match-fixing scandal.

Newcastle dominant

On the field of play one team stood out in the early years of the new century: Newcastle United. In the 13 seasons 1899-1900 to 1911-12 Newcastle finished in the top 6 eleven times and won the championship on three occasions, in 1905, 1907 and 1909. Their Cup record was, if anything, even more remarkable. Between 1905 and 1911 they reached the Final five times. In 1909 the team went down to Manchester United in the semis, so 1907 was the only year in which the club failed to reach the last four. And that season of "failure" was dramatic indeed - a home defeat by Crystal Palace, then a Southern League outfit.

Unfortunately, Newcastle's record after reaching the Final was not so impressive. Crystal Palace, the venue for each of them, was not a happy hunting ground. Newcastle failed to record a single victory in five attempts. Their best effort came in 1910, when they managed a 1-1 draw with Second Division Barnsley before beating the Yorkshire side in a replay at Goodison Park.

Villa thwart Double hopes

1904-05 saw Newcastle come agonisingly close to the Double. Aston Villa spoiled the party in the Cup Final. Villa were not quite the force they'd been in the 1890s, but spearheaded by new young striking sensation Harry Hampton they ran out 2-0 winners. Hampton scored both goals. Newcastle picked themselves up and won 3-0 at Middlesbrough on the last day of the season, enough to pip Everton for the championship by a point.

A scene from the 1907 Cup Final between Everton and Sheffield Wednesday. Just one year earlier Everton were 1-0 victors over Newcastle, but on this occasion were beaten 2-1 by Wednesday. The middle years of the decade were highly successful for both Merseyside teams. Alec Young's goal gave Everton the FA Cup in 1906 and Liverpool's Scottish centre-half Alex Raisbeck helped them secure victory in the league in the same year.

Rise of Liverpool and Manchester United

Liverpool and Manchester United also made their mark in this period, winning the title four times between them. Liverpool had come a long way since their League baptism in 1893. Just six years later they were on course for the Double, but were hammered 5-0 by Villa in a title showdown, then lost an FA Cup semi-final to Sheffield United. That was the year that Liverpool changed their colours from blue-and-white quarters to red. It didn't help them then, but two years later, 1900-01, the title went to Anfield for the first time. On that occasion, instead of riding high then falling away, as they had done two years earlier, the team went on a tremendous late run which included nine wins and three draws in 12 games. A 1-0 victory at relegated West Bromwich Albion clinched the championship.

Raisbeck stars at Anfield

Liverpool's star was Alex Raisbeck. In his third season at the club, the Scottish international was tigerish in the tackle and outstanding in the air, despite standing only 5ft. 9in. tall. Raisbeck was still the linchpin when Liverpool won their second title five years later, 1905-06. The intervening period had been something of a rollercoaster, the club having been relegated in 1903-04. But they made their mark in the record books by winning the Second and First Division championships in consecutive seasons. 1905-06 was also noteworthy for the fact that Everton beat Newcastle in the FA Cup Final; Liverpool's journalists made much capital out of their city's footballing supremacy that year.

Spectators climb trees to watch the 1912 Cup Final between Barnsley and West Bromwich Albion, that ended in a no-score draw. Second Division Barnsley finally defeated West Brom by a single goal scored during extra time in the replay. Three successive drawn Cup Finals convinced the FA to change the rules of the competition to allow extra time to be played should the first match be tied.

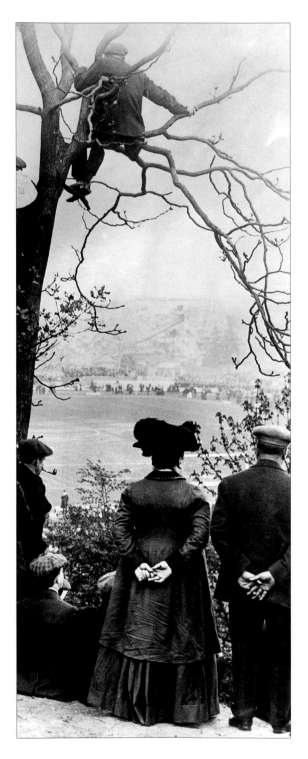

League Division One 1900-1919

Top 10 League Positions

1899-1900

1	Aston Villa	50
2	Sheffield United	48
3	Sunderland	41
4	Wolverhampton W	39
5	Newcastle United	36
6	Derby County	36
7	Manchester City	34
8	Nottingham Forest	34
9	Stoke	34
10	Liverpool	33

1900-01

1	Liverpool	45
2	Sunderland	43
3	Notts County	40
4	Nottingham Forest	39
5	Bury	39
6	Newcastle United	38
7	Everton	37
8	The Wednesday	36
9	Blackburn Rovers	33
10	Bolton Wanderers	33

1901-02

1	Sunderland	44
2	Everton	41
3	Newcastle United	37
4	Blackburn Rovers	36
5	Nottingham Forest	35
6	Derby County	35
7	Bury	34
8	Aston Villa	34
9	The Wednesday	34
10	Sheffield United	33

1902-03

1	The Wednesday	42
2	Aston Villa	41
3	Sunderland	41
4	Sheffield United	39
5	Liverpool	38
6	Stoke	37
7	West Bromwich Albion	36
8	Bury	35
9	Derby County	35
10	Nottingham Forest	35

1903-04

1	The Wednesday	47
2	Manchester City	44
3	Everton	43
4	Newcastle United	42
5	Aston Villa	41
6	Sunderland	39
7	Sheffield United	38
8	Wolverhampton W	36
9	Nottingham Forest	31
10	Middlesbrough	30

1904-05

1	Newcastle United	48
2	Everton	47
3	Manchester City	46
4	Aston Villa	42
5	Sunderland	40
6	Sheffield United	40
7	Small Heath	39
8	Preston	36
9	The Wednesday	33
10	Woolwich Arsenal	33

1905-06

1	Liverpool	51
2	Preston	47
3	The Wednesday	44
4	Newcastle United	43
5	Manchester City	43
6	Bolton Wanderers	41
7	Birmingham City	41
8	Aston Villa	40
9	Blackburn Rovers	40
10	Stoke	39

1906-07

1	Newcastle United	51
2	Bristol City	48
3	Everton	45
4	Sheffield United	45
5	Aston Villa	44
6	Bolton Wanderers	44
7	Woolwich Arsenal	44
8	Manchester United	42
9	Birmingham City	38
10	Sunderland	37

1907-08

1	Manchester United	52
2	Aston Villa	43
3	Manchester City	43
4	Newcastle United	42
5	The Wednesday	42
6	Middlesbrough	41
7	Bury	39
8	Liverpool	38
9	Nottingham Forest	37
10	Bristol City	36

1908-09

1	Newcastle United	53
2	Everton	46
3	Sunderland	44
4	Blackburn Rovers	41
5	The Wednesday	40
6	Woolwich Arsenal	38
7	Aston Villa	38
8	Bristol City	38
9	Middlesbrough	37
10	Preston	37

1909-10

1	Aston Villa	53
2	Liverpool	48
3	Blackburn Rovers	45
4	Newcastle United	45
5	Manchester United	45
6	Sheffield United	42
7	Bradford City	42
8	Sunderland	41
9	Notts County	40
10	Everton	40

1910-11

1	Manchester United	52
2	Aston Villa	51
3	Sunderland	45
4	Everton	45
5	Bradford City	45
6	The Wednesday	42
7	Oldham	41
8	Newcastle United	40
9	Sheffield United	38
10	Woolwich Arsenal	38

1911-12

1	Blackburn Rovers	49
2	Everton	46
3	Newcastle United	44
4	Bolton Wanderers	43
5	The Wednesday	41
6	Aston Villa	41
7	Middlesbrough	40
8	Sunderland	39
9	West Bromwich Albion	39
10	Woolwich Arsenal	38

1912-13

1	Sunderland	54
2	Aston Villa	50
3	The Wednesday	49
4	Manchester United	46
5	Blackburn Rovers	45
6	Manchester City	44
7	Derby County	42
8	Bolton Wanderers	42
9	Oldham	42
10	West Bromwich Albion	38

1913-14

1	Blackburn Rovers	51
2	Aston Villa	44
3	Oldham	43
4	Middlesbrough	43
5	West Bromwich Albion	43
6	Bolton Wanderers	42
7	Sunderland	40
8	Chelsea	39
9	Bradford City	38
10	Sheffield United	37

1914-15

1	Everton	46
2	Oldham	45
3	Blackburn Rovers	43
4	Burnley	43
5	Manchester City	43
6	Sheffield United	43
7	The Wednesday	43
8	Sunderland	41
9	Bradford PA	41
10	West Bromwich Albion	40

WHAT A CLINKER

FA Cup Finals

1900	Bury	v	Southampton	4-0
1901	Tottenham H.	v	Sheffield United	3-1
1902	Sheffield United	v	Southampton	2-1
1903	Bury	v	Derby County	6-0
1904	Manchester City	v	Bolton Wanderers	1-0
1905	Aston Villa	v	Newcastle United	2-0
1906	Everton	v	Newcastle United	1-0
1907	Sheffield W.	v	Everton	2-1
1908	Wolverhampton W	v	Newcastle United	3-1
1909	Manchester Utd	v	Bristol City	1-0
1910	Newcastle United	v	Barnsley	2-0
1911	Bradford City	v	Newcastle United	1-0
1912	Barnsley	v	West Bromwich A.	1-0
1913	Aston Villa	v	Sunderland	1-0
1914	Burnley	v	Liverpool	1-0
1915	Sheffield United	v	Chelsea	3-0
1916-1919		no competition		

Steve Bloomer

Steve Bloomer was the most prolific marksman of his day. An inside-forward with a deadly accurate shot, Bloomer began his career as an 18-year-old with Derby in 1892. He ended his career at the age of 40 in 1914 at the same club, although he did have a four-year spell at Middlesbrough along the way. These 22 years yielded a remarkable 352 League goals in 598 appearances. It was not until the 1936-37 season that Dixie Dean set a new mark, and only a handful of players have outscored him since. Bloomer's record 28 goals in just 23 games for England stood even longer, until the 1950s. The FA presented him with a portrait of himself when he won his 21st cap, which was a record at the time. After hanging up his boots, Bloomer took up a coaching job in Germany and was interned for the duration of the First World War.

The 1911 Cup Final played at Crystal Palace ended in a 2-2 draw forcing a mid-week replay at newly-completed Old Trafford. Newcastle were unlucky again being defeated by Bradford by one goal to nil. The Tyneside team had reached the Final 5 times in the last 7 years but had only lifted the trophy once - in 1910.

During the 1909-10 season Manchester United took up residence at Old Trafford and Arsenal's new stadium at Highbury was completed in 1913.

Newton Heath reformed as Manchester United

Manchester United also scaled the heights after some lean times at the turn of the century. By 1901 the Newton Heath club was in a parlous state, both on and off the field. The team was languishing in the Second Division and facing crippling debts. A winding-up order was issued and the team had to rely on fund-raising through bazaars and the like in order to fulfil its fixtures. In 1902 things improved dramatically when some wealthy local businessmen pumped much-needed funds into the club. The Phoenix-like revival prompted a call for a new name. Manchester Celtic and Manchester Central were considered; Manchester United was settled upon.

Mangnall masterminds title win

Legendary manager Ernest Mangnall arrived the following year, and after three top six finishes in Division Two, United won promotion in 1905-06 and made their debut in the top flight the following season. The team that was promoted already boasted Charlie Roberts, one of the outstanding half-backs of his day. Apart from his dominance on the pitch, Roberts was noted for bucking the usual trend regarding length of shorts, preferring to wear his well above the knee. This act of rebelliousness, together with his vocal support of the Players' Union, was said to be one of the reasons why he won only three caps.

Mangnall knew he had to strengthen the team for an assault on the championship. He signed Billy Meredith from neighbours Manchester City, one of the transfer coups of the period. Meredith, who had scored the goal which beat Bolton in the 1904 Cup Final was an established star but arived at United under a cloud. There had been allegations of illegal payments at Manchester City and Meredith himself was implicated in a bribery scandal. All that was forgotten two years later when Manchester United became champions for the first time. Ten straight wins early in the 1907-08 season, including a 6-1 thrashing of defending champions Newcastle, gave United a lead that proved decisive. As champions, United took part in the inaugural Charity Shield match, in which they faced Southern League winners Queen's Park

Rangers. The match took place at Stamford Bridge, United winning 4-0 after a replay.

United relocate to Old Trafford

The following season was disappointing as far as the league went, but it brought a first FA Cup success. In the Final United beat mid-table side Bristol City 1-0, but along the way they had accounted for Newcastle, Everton and Blackburn, who occupied three of the top four places in the league that year.

1909-10 saw United finish empty-handed but it was noteworthy as the season in which the club took up residence at Old Trafford. The move to the new stadium, which cost £60,000 and could hold 100,000, was timely; for as United played host to Liverpool on 19 February 1910 to mark the beginning of a new era, part of the old Bank Street ground collapsed in a gale. In 1910-11, United's first full season at Old Trafford, they were crowned champions for the second time.

Teams from the Midlands and the North continued to dominate. Sunderland, Sheffield Wednesday, Blackburn and Everton were the other clubs which won league titles between 1900 and 1915. In that final campaign before war brought a 4-year hiatus, one of Lancashire's lesser lights very nearly made it to the top of the tree. Oldham would have won the championship had they beaten Liverpool in their final match; they lost and Everton snatched the title by a point.

A record crowd of over 120,000 gather outside the Crystal Palace ground for a view of the 1913 FA Cup Final between Aston Villa and Sunderland.

Spurs set new record

The 1914 Cup Final in which Burnley defeated Liverpool by one goal scored in the 58th minute. This was the fourth year in succession that the Final had ended with a 1-0 scoreline.

For the emerging teams from the South success was sporadic. However, in 1901 it was a London team which created a record that will surely remain unequalled. Spurs, then in the Southern League, won the FA Cup, the only non-league side ever to win the trophy. They disposed of three Division One sides en route, Preston, West Bromwich Albion and holders Bury. They faced Sheffield United in the final, and most observers thought they were on the receiving end of a bad decision when 'keeper Clawley was adjudged to have made a save behind his line. A goal was given and the game ended 2-2. A 3-1 victory in the replay at Bolton meant that any error hadn't been too costly. Sandy Brown was the Spurs' hero, netting a record 15 times during the Cup run, including three in the two Finals. 110,000 watched the first encounter at Crystal Palace, a record that has been beaten only twice since. Some commentators did note that the team consisted entirely of players from the provinces and Scotland, and as such the victory could hardly be regarded as a revival of the capital's footballing fortunes. Spurs were elected to the league in 1908, winning promotion to Division One at the first attempt.

Arsenal's rise was more steady. It wasn't until 1904-05 -11 years after becoming a League club - that the Gunners made it into the top flight. Several seasons of consolidation followed before the club was relegated in 1912-13. This proved to be a blessing in disguise, as it precipitated Chairman Henry Norris's decision to relocate to Highbury. New neighbours Spurs were none too pleased with the decision, creating a rivalry that continues unabated.

Chelsea win league status in five months

Chelsea's entry into the league was remarkable in itself. At the start of 1905 the club didn't exist, yet just five months later it was elected to Division Two. Founder Gus Mears was behind this amazing rise up the ladder. He acquired the Stamford Bridge Athletic ground, signed a group of players and then, in May, saw the club's application to join the Second Division accepted. Both divisions were expanded from 18 to 20 clubs, and Chelsea joined the ranks with a club that would have rather less of an impact on the game, Clapham Orient. Chelsea finished third in their debut season, while Clapham Orient propped up the table. Chelsea were promoted to the First Division the following year.

"Khaki Final"

In 1914-15 Chelsea finished second from bottom in the league but reached their first Cup Final. They failed to reproduce their best form, however, and went down 3-0 to Sheffield United. The Yorkshire club hoisted a brand-new trophy aloft, the third in the competition's history. The design of the previous cup had been copied by a regional competition, and the FA decided to present it to Lord Kinnaird for his services to the game and have a new one made.

The Chelsea-Sheffield United match was dubbed "The Khaki Final" because of the number of uniformed spectators present. Football had come in for a lot of criticism for completing the 1914-15 programme, hostilities having broken out the previous August. Questions had been asked in the House of Commons over the issue, but the game did serve as an effective recruiting sergeant. Rousing speeches were made at matches, and both players and supporters enlisted in droves, long before conscription was introduced. At the end of the Khaki Final Lord Derby gave a speech, saying: "You have played with one another and against one another for the Cup. Play with one another for England now".

Brief moment in the limelight

The period immediately prior to World War One saw some unheralded clubs enjoy a brief moment in the spotlight. Apart from Oldham's agonising experience in the 1914-15 championship race, Bradford City and Barnsley also tasted success. In 1910-11 Bradford finished 5th in the league and beat Newcastle in the Cup Final. Division Two side Barnsley made it to two Finals in three seasons, losing to Newcastle in 1910 and beating West Brom in 1912. Between those two appearances the club had finished 19th in Division Two and been forced to apply for re-election.

Both of Barnsley's Cup appearances and Bradford's 1911 victory had gone to replays, prompting the FA to institute extra time from 1913. It wasn't needed that year - a 1-0 win for Villa over Sunderland - or the next, when Burnley ran out 1-0 winners over Liverpool. That 1914 Final marked the first time that a reigning monarch attended football's showpiece. King George V handed Burnley's skipper Tommy Boyle the Cup and at the same time rang down the curtain on the Crystal Palace as a final venue.

> *Football served as an effective recruiting sergeant. Rousing speeches were made at matches, and both players and supporters enlisted in droves.*

Tottenham Hotspur, winners of the FA Cup 1901, the only non-league side to win the trophy since the league was founded in 1888. In the first years of the new century the northern clubs still dominated league and Cup football. The 'great eight' comprised Everton, Sheffield Wednesday, Newcastle, Sunderland, Liverpool, Aston Villa and both Manchester clubs. Arsenal was the first southern side to be admitted to the First Division in the 1903-4 season with Chelsea following on in 1907.

Decline of gentlemen-amateurs

Until the early 1900s the England side invariably included a number of amateurs. The cream of the public school and university systems could still hold their own against the professionals. Players such as Charles Burgess Fry and Gilbert Oswald Smith were outstanding performers. The latter was rated a better goalscorer than the legendary Steve Bloomer.

Many of the top gentlemen-amateurs turned out for Corinthians, who regularly beat the top league sides they came up against. In 1900 Corinthians put eight past Wolves and in 1904 thrashed Cup holders Bury 10-3. In March 1902 England fielded just one amateur in the side that drew with Wales in Wrexham. In April 1905 Spurs' centre-forward Vivian Woodward was the sole amateur in the side which beat Scotland 1-0 at Crystal Palace. The decline of the amateur international was hastened in 1907, when the FA sought to bring all players under their jurisdiction. The amateurs demurred and formed the Amateur Football Association. This marked a parting of the ways, and as top sides such as Corinthians were now prevented from testing themselves against league opposition, they soon lost their edge and a proud tradition was consigned to the history books.

Ibrox disaster

On the international front this period is remembered chiefly for a tragedy. When Scotland and England met at Ibrox Park on 5 April 1902, 25 people were killed when a section of the stand collapsed. The game eventually continued and ended 1-1 but the result was later expunged from the record books.

Among the crowd at the 1914 Cup Final was King George V, the first monarch ever to attend the event. The route between Buckingham Palace and Crystal Palace was lined with cheering crowds. Ironically, the public schools that had done so much to develop the game of football had now adopted rugby as their sport and football was the passion of the working classes.

Milestones 1900-1919

1901 A maximum wage for footballers introduced

1902 Sheffield United's Alf Common is transferred to Sunderland for £500

A stand collapses at a Scotland v England match at Ibrox Park killing 25 people

Manchester United founded when brewer John Davies bought up a bankrupt team, Newton Heath. The team did not enter the league until 1904

1904 FIFA, Federation of International Football Associations is formed with seven members

1905 England joins FIFA

Alf Common is transferred from Sunderland to Middlesbrough for a fee of £1000

Billy Meredith of Manchester City is suspended after attempting to bribe Aston Villa's captain to help his team win the league

After Fulham turned down an offer to buy Stamford Bridge the owners decided to create Chelsea FC to play there

Despite being created by staff at the Royal Exhibition in 1861, Crystal Palace did not turn professional until 1905 because the FA opposed the idea that a team could play an FA Cup Final on their home ground, which was used as the location for FA Cup Finals at the time

1906 Prevention of Corruption Act passed making bribery and match fixing a punishable offence

1908 England plays Austria in Vienna; its first international against foreign opposition

Football was first introduced as an Olympic sport at the London Olympics in White City. England went on to win the gold medal beating Denmark 2-0

First FA Charity Shield match played; the idea for a match between the winners of the FA Cup and the league for charity was that of Charles Clegg the then Vice President of the FA

1909 Walter Tull becomes the first black outfield player in the First Division, playing for Tottenham Hotspur.

1912 It becomes illegal for goalkeepers to handle the ball outside the penalty area

Danny O'Shea of West Ham is transferred to Blackburn Rovers for £2000

The Stockholm Olympics sees England take their second gold by beating Denmark 4-2 in the final

1913 Woolwich Arsenal moves from South-East to North London in a bid to gain more supporters amid financial difficulties

1915 Football League games suspended for the duration of the war, although a limited regional programme introduced later

FA Cup Final still played and won by Sheffield United. The event became known as the Khaki Cup Final on account of the large number of servicemen in the crowd

1919 Leeds City is expelled from the football league for allegedly making illegal payments to players. The club was replaced with Leeds United

Football League enlarged to hold 44 clubs

The 1913 Cup Final brought together two of the most successful clubs in the league: Aston Villa and Sunderland. In the 1912-13 season both sides had the potential of winning the Double, which Aston Villa had succeeded in doing in 1896-7. In the event, Sunderland took the league title and Villa won the Cup, defeating Sunderland by one goal to nil in front of a record crowd of over 120,000. The scores might have been higher since the Birmingham team were without their keeper for part of the second half and Villa's Charlie Wallace missed a penalty, only the second ever awarded in an FA Cup Final.

Football becomes Olympic sport

International football was still largely confined to fixtures against the other home nations. But in 1908 football made its official debut as an Olympic sport. An England side was chosen to represent the United Kingdom and took the gold medal. England retained the Olympic crown in 1912; on both occasions the beaten finalists were Denmark.

FIFA founded

Bohemia had sought entry into the 1912 Olympic tournament but had been unable to compete since the country was not a member of FIFA. The Federation International de Football Association had been formed in Paris on 21 May 1904. France, Belgium, Switzerland, Denmark, the Netherlands, Sweden and Spain were the founding members of world football's new governing body, England joining the following year.

Over 70,000 people officially attended the Cup Final in 1914 but many preferred to spectate from vantage points outside the ground. This was the last time that Crystal Palace was to play host to the Final, the first time being in 1895 when Aston Villa's John Devey scored a goal forty seconds into the game.

The 1915 Cup Final was a subdued affair, held in Manchester on a damp afternoon before a crowd of only 50,000, many of whom were servicemen displaying signs of the injuries sustained in battle.

Football in the trenches

As the 1914-15 season drew to a close it was clear that football could not continue. The decision to suspend the League and Cup competition came as no surprise, and the global conflict brought forth the heroic and less seemly side of the footballing fraternity. The unsavoury element occurred in a game between Manchester United and Liverpool on 2 April 1915. The political uncertainties prompted a number of players to conspire and rig the result - a 2-0 win for United - and make a killing at the bookmaker's. Suspicions were aroused and the subsequent inquiry resulted in eight players receiving life bans. After the war the Football League took a more charitable view of those who had fought for their country. The exception was Manchester United's Enoch "Knocker" West, whose ban remained in force after he continued to deny all charges.

Greater nobility was shown in the famous Christmas Day truce of 1914, when German and British soldiers played an impromptu game in No-Man's-Land. And even in the height of battle football was often used as a morale booster. Members of some regiments invoked the names of their beloved clubs as they advanced, and even dribbled balls onto the battlefield. Back in England, regional football replaced the traditional competitions between 1915 and 1918. These were low-key affairs and fixtures were organised so as not to interfere with the war effort. After Armistice Day on 11 November 1918 the appetite of both clubs and supporters to reinstate the official programme was huge. There was even talk of getting a truncated FA Cup competition off the ground immediately. In the end the authorities decided in favour of starting afresh the following season, and 1919-20 thus became the first postwar campaign.

1920-1929
Expanding the Game

Once the Great war was over, the appetite to quickly reinstate the league and Cup competitions proper was huge. The early months of 1919 saw all the clubs take stock. After a four-year interruption they had to assess their playing staffs and effect repairs to their stadiums. The administrators were also busy. Divisions One and Two were immediately expanded to 22 clubs, and within two years two regional Third Divisions had been formed. This meant that the Football League in 1921-22 comprised 86 clubs compared with just 40 prior to World War One.

A typical band of Cup-tie enthusiasts who paraded the streets on their way to Stamford Bridge plentifully bedecked with rosettes and ribbons, and keeping up their spirits with rattles and other noisy instruments. Stamford Bridge, an impressive stadium built in 1904 by Chelsea with a capacity of 100,000 was to be the venue for the postwar Cup Finals until Wembley Stadium was completed in 1923.

Controversy as 5th-placed Arsenal gain promotion

The way in which Division One was expanded in 1919-20 got the new era off to a controversial start. The expectation was that the top two Second Division sides from the 1914-15 season, Derby and Preston, would simply be promoted. But the Football League decided that Arsenal would go up too. The Gunners had finished only 5th in that final pre-war season, and Chairman Henry Norris was said to have engaged in some feverish behind-the-scenes lobbying in order to get the club elected to the top table. Three promoted teams meant that a First Division club had to go. Tottenham had finished bottom in 1914-15 and they were the obvious candidates. It took Spurs just one season to bounce back, but the circumstances in which they had swapped places with their north London rivals did nothing to promote harmony between the two clubs.

Below: Aston Villa play Huddersfield in the 1920 Cup Final. Villa's winning goal was scored by Kirton who had joined the Birmingham side from Leeds City after the club had been forced to sell off its entire squad.
Above: Aston Villa collect the Cup at Stamford Bridge in 1920.

Leeds expelled over illegal payments

The early drama of the 1919-20 campaign took place off the field, when Second Division side Leeds City were expelled from the league for making illegal payments. City, managed by Herbert Chapman, had won the Northern regional championship in 1918 and seemed to be a team on the up. After the allegations were made Chapman chose to put a match to the club's books rather than submit them for scrutiny. He was suspended and Port Vale took over Leeds' fixtures. For Chapman and Leeds it was the parting of the ways, though both would rise again after a brief period in the wilderness. In 1920 the club reconstituted itself as Leeds United and returned to the fold. That same year Chapman, after a short spell with an engineering firm, also returned to the game. Over the next 14 years, first with Huddersfield Town and then with Arsenal, Chapman would take club management into a different realm.

Above: Supporters of both Aston Villa and Huddersfield seemed full of confidence on their way to the 1920 Cup Final. Villa, who eventually won a closely fought contest 1-0 after extra time, had now won the Cup six times. They would only win the competition once more in the twentieth century - beating Manchester United in 1957.

Below left: Cantrell, the Spurs centre-forward, and Bliss (right) inside-left, battling with defenders in the Wolves' goalmouth during the 1921 Cup Final.

Below right: Bliss gets past Woodward as the defender slips on the muddy surface. Heavy rain had created poor playing conditions and spectators were disappointed that the quality of the football suffered. Spurs' 1-0 win was the first southern victory in the Cup since 1901 when the London club last won the trophy.

The rise of Huddersfield

In 1920 Huddersfield were in dire straits. The club was the poor relation to the town's rugby league side, and had even contemplated relocating lock, stock and barrel to Leeds. Things improved after the club acquired several of the players auctioned off by Leeds City. Huddersfield then made the most important signing of all: Herbert Chapman himself. In 1920 Huddersfield won promotion to the top flight for the first time and also made it to the FA Cup final, in which they went down 1-0 to Aston Villa. This was no flash in the plan; the best was yet to come. Chapman set to work using his uncanny knack for buying the right player at the right time and moulding individuals into a formidable unit. Probably the key acquisition was Villa's inside-forward Clem Stephenson, who arrived in March 1921 in a £4000 deal. Many

thought 30-year-old Stephenson's best years were behind him, but Chapman made him captain and in the autumn of his career he enjoyed a golden period as he led Huddersfield on an extraordinary run of success. The first silverware came in 1922, when the Yorkshire club lifted the FA Cup. It was a dour affair, with Preston providing the opposition. The only goal came from the penalty spot after Huddersfield winger Billy Smith was brought down. Preston seemed to have a legitimate case that the foul had been committed outside the box, but the referee waved this away and Smith himself stepped up to score. This game marked the last of three postwar finals to be contested at Stamford Bridge. By the following April the new Wembley Stadium would be ready.

Mathematicians needed to determine championship
In the next six seasons Huddersfield finished no lower than third in the league, and the club's remarkable run included a famous hat-trick of championships starting in 1923-24. This first league title was also the most dramatic.

Herbert Chapman (back row, left) pictured with Huddersfield Town in 1921. Chapman is one of a select group of managers who have won the league championship with different clubs: Huddersfield Town in 1924 and 1925, Arsenal in 1931 and 1933.

At the end of the season Huddersfield and Cardiff both had 57 points. Huddersfield's goals column read 60-33, Cardiff's 61-34. This was an era in which goal average decided such issues and Huddersfield's was superior by a wafer-thin 0.024. Cardiff would not have needed to trouble the mathematicians had they converted a last-minute penalty in their final match at Birmingham. But a nervous Len Davies fired wide, the game ended in a goalless draw and Cardiff had to settle for the runners-up spot. Under the modern goal difference system, of course, the placings would have been reversed, Cardiff having scored one more goal than their rivals.

Chapman moves to Arsenal

Huddersfield retained their title in 1924-25, conceding just 28 goals all season. No club had ever won the championship with a better defensive record than that. Wednesday had been equally miserly in 1903-04 but that was in the days of a 34-match season.

Herbert Chapman laid the foundations for Huddersfield's hat-trick of league titles but before the third crown had been claimed he had taken up a new challenge. It would take him longer to shape his new club, Arsenal, into a championship-winning side, but by the end of the decade the Gunners would be setting the standards all other clubs had to measure themselves by.

Above: Going for goal: Decades before Denis Law perfected the art Bliss executes an overhead kick for Tottenham in the Cup Final against Wolverhampton Wanderers. Later in the game he tries a more conventional shot at goal.

Left: With his rosettes and cockerel, Tottenham's emblem, this fan left no doubt as to which side he supported.

Opposite above: Stamford Bridge 1922: The Duke of York shakes hands with the Huddersfield team with Prince George and Wilson, the Huddersfield captain, behind him. Chapman's most important addition to his new team was Aston Villa's inside-forward Clem Stephenson for whom he paid £4000.

Opposite below: W.H. Smith of Huddersfield scores the winning goal from a disputed penalty in the 1922 final. Smith had been brought down by the Preston defence but it was generally agreed that the action took place outside the box.

Rise and fall of West Brom and Burnley

Huddersfield apart, no club enjoyed a sustained period of success in the 1920s. West Bromwich Albion won the first postwar championship, 1919-20, for the only time in their history. Long before the decade was out the Midlands club was languishing in the Second Division. Burnley had finished runners-up to West Brom, and they took over the mantle in 1920-21. A 30-match unbeaten run - 21 wins and 9 draws - between early September and late March carried the Lancashire club to its first title. But once again decline quickly set in. After six seasons in the bottom half of the table Burnley finally suffered the drop in 1929-30.

Scott marshals mean Liverpool defence

Liverpool were the only club apart from Huddersfield to win two championships in this period. The team's success was built on a resilient defence, with the huge Irish goalkeeper Elisha Scott performing heroics and establishing himself as an Anfield legend. In 1921-22 Liverpool found the net just 63 times. Six teams had bettered that but none could match the 36 in the Goals Against column. The following year Liverpool held off the challenge of a skilful Sunderland side to retain their crown, and this time their defence was even more impenetrable: only 31 goals conceded in their 42 games, a new record. Liverpool didn't suffer the same fate as West Bromwich Albion and Burnley thereafter, but their form for the rest of the 1920s was erratic and they didn't mount another serious title challenge.

Gallacher becomes toast of Tyneside

Huddersfield then took charge, and their vice-like grip on the league was not broken until Newcastle claimed their 4th title in 1926-27. Their star was diminutive Scottish striker Hughie Gallacher, widely regarded as the greatest finisher of his era. Gallacher, who had joined Newcastle from Airdrie for £5500, hit 36 of the team's 96 league goals. Having missed four matches, this very nearly gave him a scoring ratio of a goal a game.

A panoramic photograph of the last Cup Final at Stamford Bridge before the move to Wembley. Smith's winning penalty kick for Huddersfield was the first to decide a Cup Final. Preston's goalkeeper, James Mitchell, had tried to distract Smith as he prepared to take the kick by moving about on the goal line. Following this incident, the rule was brought in which required the goalkeeper to remain still until the ball was kicked.

Herbert Chapman

Herbert Chapman was the most successful manager of the 1920s and early 1930s, his influence on the game continuing long after his death in 1934. He had had an undistinguished playing career at Northampton, Sheffield United and Spurs, standing out more for his trademark yellow boots than for the quality of his play. He made his name during the First World war as manager of Leeds City, but in 1919 he was suspended over financial irregularities. He took over an ailing Huddersfield Town side in 1920 and within four years he transformed the club into championship winners. After retaining the title, Chapman moved to Highbury in 1925. Along with veteran inside-forward Charlie Buchan, Chapman reacted to a change in the offside law by introducing a fluid WM system, replacing the rigid 2-3-5 formation that most teams played. This involved the centre-half dropping into a purely defensive role, abandoning his usual role of providing the link between defence and attack. That "schemer's" job was filled by an inside forward, which meant a revolutionary 3-3-4 formation.

Chapman had an uncanny knack for spotting potential. He signed Cliff Bastin and paid a world record £10,890 for David Jack. It is said that when he met his opposite number at Bolton to discuss Jack's transfer, he arranged for the hotel waiter to to keep the drinks coming - but instructed that his own glass should contain nothing alcoholic. By the time the men got down to business the atmosphere was very convivial. Bolton did get a world record fee but Chapman still thought his underhand tactic had given him the better of the deal.

Alex James was acquired for slightly less than Jack, but it was his arrival from Preston in 1929 that sparked a phenomenal run of success.

With James playing that key schemer's role, Arsenal went on to win the championship three times in four years, and finished runners-up to Everton in 1931-32. There was also an FA Cup victory over Chapman's former club, Huddersfield, in 1930.

Chapman died just before Arsenal confirmed their third championship, but all the pieces were in place for further success. The Gunners' league titles of 1935 and 1938, together with another FA Cup victory in 1936, also owed much to the groundwork Chapman laid. His influence also spread to the international side, notably when England beat Italy in November 1934. Chapman's Arsenal provided seven of the players who beat the reigning world champions 3-2.

Above: Herbert Chapman made his name as manager of Leeds City during the First World War. After transforming Huddersfield he went on to even greater success at Arsenal.

Below: Frank Barson was one of the game's best-known characters. He played 353 league games for five clubs, most notably for Aston Villa and Manchester United. He was considered one of the first "hard" men in football and was often sent off and suspended. As a commanding centre-half who liked to go forward he was powerful in the air. On Boxing Day in 1921 he scored with a header from almost 30 yards to give Aston Villa victory over Sheffield United.

New offside law brings goal avalanche

Newcastle's record of 96 goals scored and 58 conceded in 1926-7 made for an interesting comparison with Huddersfield's performance two years earlier. In their second championship-winning season the Yorkshire club's goals column read 69-28, their defence proving even meaner than Liverpool's. For Newcastle to have scored 27 more goals but let in 30 more suggests a cavalier approach. But the chief reason for the surge in goalscoring was a change in the offside law which had been brought in in 1925.

Since the 1870s three players were required between the attacker and the goal for him to be onside. Over that 50-year period defences had got the offside trap down to a fine art. Newcastle themselves were arch-exponents. It is said that when one visiting team pulled into the city's train station and heard a guard's whistle, a wag chimed: "Blimey! Offside already!"

Under the new law only two players were now required between the attacking player and the goal for him to be onside. As most teams played the traditional 2-3-5 formation, forwards could now be onside with just the two full-backs to beat. There was a goal avalanche, which was exactly what the FA had wanted. On 29 August 1925 the first matches took place under the new system and the effect was immediate and dramatic. Villa beat Burnley 10-0, and in the following weeks there was a plethora of high-scoring games. 1703 goals were scored in Division One in 1925-26, an increase of over 500 on the previous season. Sterile, negative play might have been eliminated but not everyone was thrilled by the goal-fest. Some felt that goalscoring had become devalued and that the ingenuity and skill required to find the back of the net before the rule change was somewhat lacking under the revised system.

Villa beat Burnley 10-0, and in the following weeks there was a plethora of high-scoring games. 1703 goals were scored in Division One in 1925-26.

The 1923 Cup Final, played at the new Empire Stadium at Wembley between West Ham United and Bolton Wanderers, attracted the largest crowd ever seen at a football match in the country. The King was present and was one of the most keenly interested spectators. Here the nearest fans are seen cheering as the National Anthem is played.

60-goal Dean fires Everton to title

Everton rattled in 102 goals on their way to the 1927-28 championship. They weren't the first team to hit the magic ton mark, but it was a record-breaking campaign for one man: Dixie Dean. When Everton went into their final league fixture, a home clash with Arsenal, they were already confirmed as champions. Nevertheless, a vast crowd turned up to see if Dean, who had hit 57 goals, could break the individual scoring record. That was held by George Camsell, who had hit 59 for Second Division champions Middlesbrough a year earlier. Dean got the hat-trick he needed, ending the campaign with a phenomenal 60 goals to his name. Herbert Chapman wanted Dean to spearhead the Arsenal side he was building and asked Everton to name their price. Unsurprisingly, the Merseyside club was in no hurry to part with its prized asset.

Everton slipped to 18th the following season, and the decade ended with Wednesday on top of the pile. Having finished 16th and 14th in the two previous campaigns, Wednesday edged out Leicester and Villa to claim their third championship. It was to be their last appearance under the Wednesday banner; by the time they began the defence of their title in the summer of 1929 the club had officially been renamed Sheffield Wednesday.

Dixie Dean
1907 – 1980

Middlesbrough's George Camsell is unfortunate that his name is not better known in footballing circles. Camsell scored 59 goals for Boro in 1926-27 as they won the Division Two title. His record lasted just one year. William "Dixie" Dean hit 60 for Everton the following season, a record which stands to this day.

Dean moved to Goodison Park for £3000 in 1925, having scored 27 goals in as many games for Tranmere Rovers. Everton were languishing in mid-table at the time, but Dean's phenomenal strike rate soon changed all that. Everton already had the championship sewn up when Arsenal came to Goodison on the last day of the 1927-28 season. 48,000 turned up to see if their 21-year-old goal machine, who had netted 57 times, could beat Camsell's record. Dean scored a hat-trick, the third goal, fittingly, coming from a towering far-post header eight minutes from time. He was imperious in the air, despite the fact that he stood just 5ft 10in tall.

Dean also hit 44 goals as Everton won the league title in 1931-32. He ended his career with 473 goals from 502 appearances in all competitive matches. 379 of those came in the league, putting him second to Arthur Rowley on the all-time list.

His 18 games for England yielded 16 goals. He ended his career at Notts County, then went to play in Ireland, but Everton was his greatest love. Dean died after watching his beloved team play Liverpool at Goodison Park on 1 March 1980.

International Caps	16
International Goals	18
Total appearances	502
Total Goals	473

Dixie Dean: his record 60 goals in a season still stands today.

F A Cup moves to Wembley

The first three postwar FA Cup competitions were staged at Stamford Bridge. This was not a popular venue and in 1919-20 nearly proved embarrassing for the FA as Chelsea won through to the semi-finals. Villa saved the authorities from the headache of having one of the finalists playing at home. They beat Chelsea and went on to score a 1-0 win over Huddersfield in the Final. It was the Midland club's 6th win, a record for the competition. The next two Finals, won by Spurs and Huddersfield respectively, were uninspiring affairs which were also decided by a single goal. By the time Bolton met West Ham on 28 April 1923 the new Wembley Stadium was ready.

Below: Storming the turnstiles - a vivid glimpse of the invasion in progress. The crowd is seen clambering over the turnstiles and 'making tracks' for the arena, while a solitary policeman looks on helplessly.
Above: Bolton's David Jack and Pym the goalkeeper (facing the camera) are among the players waiting on the pitch while the police push the people back. Officially the gate was 126,000 but the actual number was closer to 200,000. Police reinforcements were sent for and the game kicked off 45 minutes late.
Opposite below: A crowded street scene in Wembley which was to host the F A Cup Final for the rest of the century.
Opposite above: 'The Cup Draw' was already part of tradition by the 1920s.

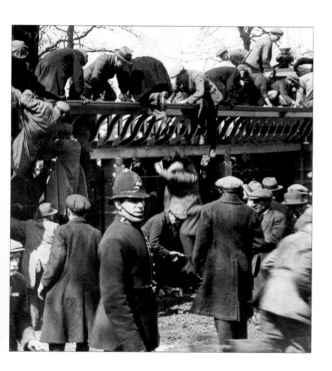

200,000 see first Wembley final

With a capacity of 127,000, Wembley was capable of holding 70,000 more fans than had turned up to watch the previous year's showpiece. Few thought there would be a problem. But West Ham were a popular Second Division side and the occasion captured the public's imagination. Estimates vary as to how many flooded into Wembley that day, the figure put anywhere from 150,000 to 200,000-plus. The official gate of 126,047 didn't take into account the thousands who poured into the stadium by climbing walls and shinning up drainpipes. The game was held up for 45 minutes as fans spilled onto the pitch. PC George Scorey and his white horse Billy were in the thick of things trying to restore order and duly took their place in the annals of the sport. A grateful FA gifted the officer complimentary tickets for subsequent finals but Scorey, who was not a football fan, never took up the offer.

Left: A spectacular aerial view of PC George Scorey and his white horse, Billy, trying to restore order. Admission by ticket was not even considered because it was thought there was room for all. Ever since the showpiece game has been an all-ticket affair. With the postwar expansion of the leagues and the ever-increasing popularity of the game, the FA wanted a prestigious stadium to host national and Cup games. After rejecting the idea of developing Crystal Palace the decision was made to move to Wembley. Work didn't commence until January 1922 but the stadium was ready for the legendary 1923 Final.

Above: A Bolton player heads the ball at a critical moment following a corner forced by West Ham. Within two minutes of the late kick-off David Jack put Bolton ahead and Smith scored their second early in the second half. Bolton went on to win the Cup twice more before the end of the decade - in 1926 and 1929.

Hughie Gallacher

Hughie Gallacher stood barely 5ft. 6in. tall, yet he is rated as one of the best centre-forwards of all time. He played for Queen of the South and Airdrie before heading south to join Newcastle for £5500 in 1926. He quickly established himself as an idol on Tyneside after firing Newcastle to the championship in 1926-27, his first full season with the club. He hit 36 goals in 38 games during the campaign, which remains a club record. Gallacher was a complete striker and amazingly powerful in the air considering his lack of inches. He was capped 23 times for Scotland, scoring 22 goals. Gallacher's private life was more turbulent. He ended his days in straitened circumstances and threw himself under a train in 1957.

1923: The White Horse Final

Bolton Wanderers 2 - West Ham United 0

West Ham, in contention for promotion to Division One, played exciting, fast-moving football and their 5-2 defeat of Derby in the Cup semi-final enhanced this reputation. However, once the match got underway, it was only two minutes before Bolton's Jack opened the scoring and from then on West Ham never regained their stride. The game was disrupted after 11 minutes when the crowd surged back onto the pitch and after order was restored, the police rode along the touchline to prevent a recurrence. Just minutes after half-time, during which the teams were unable to leave the field, Bolton's J.R. Smith headed the ball, hitting the underside of the West Ham crossbar. The ball bounced inside the goal then back onto the field and although West Ham protested, the goal was given. The match ended in a 2-0 victory for Bolton whose keeper, Pym, was scarcely tested during the contest. Smith, scorer of the second goal, completed a personal 'double' having already won a Scottish Cup medal. Jack's contribution to his club's Cup run had been crucial to their success; he was the only man to score in four of their matches leading up to the Final and his early goal at Wembley set Bolton on their way.

Left: Seymour setting the seal on Newcastle United's victory in the 1924 Cup Final just before the final whistle. Although the Cup Final was between Newcastle and Aston Villa, the most successful club of the middle part of the decade was Herbert Chapman's Huddersfield Town who topped the league in 1924, 1925 and 1926. Huddersfield had been on the verge of bankruptcy after the war and narrowly escaped a forced merger with Leeds United.
Overleaf: A sea of umbrellas as a shower of rain falls during the opening ceremony of the 1925 Cup Final.

Future Cup Finals to be all-ticket

The West Ham camp were rather less enamoured with Billy and the other police horses on duty that day in 1923. The Hammers claimed the pitch was badly churned up as a result, something which didn't suit their nimble forwards. Bolton's attackers seemed to cope well enough, however. David Jack scored Wembley's first-ever goal and Bolton ran out 2-0 winners. After the game the FA quickly realised that only good fortune had prevented a catastrophe. Cup Finals thereafter became all-ticket affairs to prevent a recurrence of the 1923 situation.

Bolton went on to lift the Cup in 1926 and 1929. Amazingly, in those three triumphs over a seven-year spell only 17 players were used. In 1926 Manchester City were the beaten side. City went on to lose their last league match at Newcastle the following week and were relegated. It was the first time that a club had had that particular double disappointment.

Above: Sheffield United's goalkeeper, Sutcliffe, punches clear.
Top right: Cardiff's goal under siege. Thousands of Welsh fans flocked to London in 1925 to support Cardiff City's bid to bring the FA trophy back with them to Wales. Strong defences on both sides meant that the final score was 1-0 and Sheffield United won the cup for the fourth time in their history.

David Jack

David Jack was 29 years old when Herbert Chapman targeted him as the man to replace Charlie Buchan after the latter retired at the end of the 1927-28 season. Jack had already had a glittering career at Bolton, with whom he won two FA Cup winners' medals. An inside-forward with terrific ball skills and a keen eye for goal, Jack scored the first-ever goal in a Wembley showpiece, the famous "White Horse Final" in which Bolton beat West Ham 2-0.

Chapman caused a stir when he paid £10,890 to bring Jack to Highbury, doubling the previous transfer record. It proved an astute move, however, as Jack was a key figure in the all-conquering Arsenal side of the 1930s. He picked up three championship medals and also made it a hat-trick of Cup successes when Arsenal beat Huddersfield in the 1930 final.

Above: David Jack watches the ball soar into the net as he scores the goal that won the Cup for Bolton Wanderers in 1926.
Below: England's Billy Walker scores against Scotland in the last international match of the 1924 season played at Wembley before 65,000 spectators. Harper, Scotland's goalkeeper rushes out in an attempt to save. The game finished all square at 1-1. Scotland's next visit to Wembley 4 years later ended in a famous 5-1 victory.

Above: An aerial photograph of the crowded Wembley Stadium during the Cup Final in which Bolton defeated Manchester City by 1-0 watched by 92,000 people. Despite reaching the Cup Final and scoring 89 goals in the 1925-6 season, Manchester City were relegated to the Second Division along with Notts County and Leeds.

A change in the offside rule came into effect in the 1925-6 season. Three defenders between the attacker and the goal were no longer necessary to remain onside, two would suffice. The tally of goals scored soared at the beginning of the season until defenders learned to cope with the change.

Milestones 1920-1929

1920 A Third Division of the football league is formed

England resigns from FIFA unable to tolerate dealing with former enemies only to rejoin in 1924

1921 Third Division divided into the Third Division South and the Third Division North

The English FA bans women's football

1922 Syd Puddefoot becomes the first player to be transferred for a fee of £5000 in a move from West Ham to Falkirk

The maximum wage for professional footballers is reduced from £9 to £8 per week

1923 Wembley hosts the FA Cup for the first time when Bolton beat West Ham 2-0

The football pools is introduced

1925 The Offside rule is updated to allow only two players, not the previous three, to be between the player with the ball and the goal

1926 BBC broadcast the FA Cup Final over radio for the first time

Huddersfield wins the league title three years in a row becoming the first team to do so

1927 A game between Arsenal and Sheffield United at Highbury becomes the first game to be broadcast live by the BBC on the radio

The FA Cup goes out of England for the first time when it is won by Cardiff City

1928 David Jack is sold to Arsenal from Bolton for £10,890

Arsenal and Chelsea become the first teams to choose to wear numbers on the back of shirts for league matches

England leaves FIFA for a second time over a dispute over Amateur Status in the Olympic Games

Everton's Bill 'Dixie' Dean scores 60 goals in a First Division season

Bolton and Jack again

The 1926 Cup Final between Lancashire sides Bolton and Manchester City kept the crowds on tenterhooks right until the last minutes of the game. Bolton had the better of the match and the Manchester side seemed to be nervous at the outset. But Pym, the Bolton keeper was called upon to make many saves during the afternoon, most spectacularly when he stopped a dangerous header from Manchester's Johnson in the second half. With just minutes to go, David Jack, standing in front of the Manchester goal, received the ball from Vizard. Jack grasped the opportunity and launched the ball into the back of the net, scoring his second goal in an FA Cup Final and winning the trophy for Bolton.

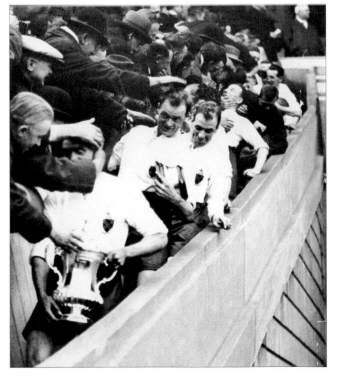

Above: Goalmouth action. A late goal gave Bolton the Cup for the second time in three years.
Right: The heroes of the day receive boisterous congratulations as they leave the Wembley grandstand with the FA Cup.

"Wembley Wizards" thrash England

International football in the 1920s began on a sour note. The FA withdrew from FIFA over the question of rejoining competition with the defeated Axis powers, a rift that rumbled on until 1924. The late 1920s saw the England team suffer two reverses which became milestones in the record books. The first came on 31 March 1928, when Scotland came to Wembley and handed England a 5-1 thrashing. Alex Jackson, Alex James and Hughie Gallacher were among the stars who would go down in history as the "Wembley Wizards".

Continental football on the rise

Perhaps an even more significant defeat came on 15 May the following year. England went to Madrid and lost 4-3 to Spain, their first-ever defeat at the hands of a foreign side. This didn't surprise everyone. There were already rumblings from some commentators, who argued that English teams would do well to look to their continental cousins, who put greater emphasis on coaching and training. This was an era in which many English coaches were adherents of the "ball starvation" philosophy, denying players too much ball-work during the week so that they would be hungry for it on match days.

Above: England's goalkeeper, Brown, clearing from a corner kick in the international match with Wales at Wrexham in 1927. The game finished in a 3-3 draw.
Below: 1928: Blackburn's Roscamp charges towards Mercer, the Huddersfield keeper, and seconds later scored when Mercer lost the ball. The 1928 Cup Final brought fewer surprises and upsets than that held the previous year when Cardiff City defeated Arsenal and carried the cup to Wales, but Roscamp's first goal scored in the opening minutes of the match was an exciting start. Huddersfield were outplayed by the Blackburn team, losing the match by three goals to one.

Above: Ours again. Blackburn players show off the Cup from a motor-coach as the team leave Wembley.
Right: Portsmouth goalkeeper Gilfillan makes a good save under pressure from a Bolton attacker in the 1929 Cup Final. His outstanding performance, however, couldn't stop Bolton running out 2-0 winners.

FA Cup leaves England

One of the big Cup stories of the decade came in 1926-27. Arsenal and Cardiff were both mid-table sides when they won through to the Wembley Final. Cardiff boasted eight internationals, all of whom were well known to Gunners' 'keeper Dan Lewis, who had also been capped by Wales. The game was settled when Lewis fumbled a speculative shot by Cardiff centre-forward Hugh Ferguson. It rolled agonisingly over the line and the FA Cup left England for the only time in its history. Lewis later blamed the slippery sheen on his new jersey for the blunder, and thereafter Arsenal always made sure that new kit was washed before it was worn.

Bolton's third triumph in six years

1929 was a remarkable year for Bolton Wanderers who appeared in their third Cup Final since the fixture had first been staged at Wembley in 1923. The game, against Portsmouth, ended in 2-0 victory for the northern team and Pym, the Bolton keeper, kept a clean sheet for the third time in the final. This victory in 1929 brough Lancashire's tally of Cup wins to 17 since the competition was established in 1871.

However, the trophy didn't leave the capital straight away because the team, taking the Cup with it, attended a concert at the London Palladium before returning. In response to calls from the audience, Bolton's captain Seddon came up on to the stage so that the crowd would have a better view.

Above: The Portsmouth team is introduced to the Prince of Wales before the start of the 1929 Cup Final. Bolton are without their 29-year-old star player David Jack on this occasion having agreed to sell him to Arsenal for the record sum of £10,890.
Opposite top: Thirteen minutes before the final whistle Gilfillan, the Portsmouth goalkeeper, stumbles when he rushes out to intercept a shot and the ball is deflected off his team-mate Mackie and crosses the line. Here, Mackie is trying to control the spinning ball but can't prevent the goal.
Opposite below: Bolton's goalkeeper Pym stops a shot by Weddle, the Portsmouth centre-forward.
Right: Eddie Hapgood, a key defender in Herbert Chapman's Arsenal side who were to dominate the next decade.

Arsenal's first major honour

Fittingly, the 1930 FA Cup Final saw Huddersfield take on Arsenal, the team of the 1920s against the team which would dominate the 1930s. By now Herbert Chapman had forged a side capable of beating his former club. Arsenal won the match 2-0, Highbury's first major honour. Since Chapman's arrival five years earlier, Arsenal had spent much of the time in mid-table, saving their best form for the Cup. That was all about to change.

League Division One 1920-1929

1919-1920

1	West Bromwich Albion	60
2	Burnley	51
3	Chelsea	49
4	Liverpool	48
5	Sunderland	48
6	Bolton Wanderers	47
7	Manchester City	45
8	Newcastle United	43
9	Aston Villa	42
10	The Arsenal	42
11	Bradford PA	42
12	Manchester United	40
13	Middlesbrough	40
14	Sheffield United	40
15	Bradford City	39
16	Everton	38
17	Oldham	38
18	Derby County	38
19	Preston	38
20	Blackburn Rovers	37
21	Notts County	36
22	The Wednesday	23

1920-21

1	Burnley	59
2	Manchester City	54
3	Bolton Wanderers	52
4	Liverpool	51
5	Newcastle United	50
6	Tottenham Hotspur	47
7	Everton	47
8	Middlesbrough	46
9	The Arsenal	44
10	Aston Villa	43
11	Blackburn Rovers	41
12	Sunderland	41
13	Manchester United	40
14	West Bromwich Albion	40
15	Bradford City	39
16	Preston	39
17	Huddersfield	39
18	Chelsea	39
19	Oldham	33
20	Sheffield United	30
21	Derby County	26
22	Bradford PA	24

1921-22

1	Liverpool	57
2	Tottenham Hotspur	51
3	Burnley	49
4	Cardiff	48
5	Aston Villa	47
6	Bolton Wanderers	47
7	Newcastle United	46
8	Middlesbrough	46
9	Chelsea	46
10	Manchester City	45
11	Sheffield United	40
12	Sunderland	40
13	West Bromwich Albion	40
14	Huddersfield	39
15	Blackburn Rovers	38
16	Preston	38
17	The Arsenal	37
18	Birmingham City	37
19	Oldham	37
20	Everton	36
21	Bradford City	32
22	Manchester United	28

1922-23

1	Liverpool	60
2	Sunderland	54
3	Huddersfield	53
4	Newcastle United	48
5	Everton	47
6	Aston Villa	46
7	West Bromwich Albion	45
8	Manchester City	45
9	Cardiff	43
10	Sheffield United	42
11	The Arsenal	42
12	Tottenham Hotspur	41
13	Bolton Wanderers	40
14	Blackburn Rovers	40
15	Burnley	38
16	Preston	37
17	Birmingham City	37
18	Middlesbrough	36
19	Chelsea	36
20	Nottingham Forest	34
21	Stoke	30
22	Oldham	30

1923-24

1	Huddersfield	57
2	Cardiff	57
3	Sunderland	53
4	Bolton Wanderers	50
5	Sheffield United	50
6	Aston Villa	49
7	Everton	49
8	Blackburn Rovers	45
9	Newcastle United	44
10	Notts County	42
11	Manchester City	42
12	Liverpool	41
13	West Ham United	41
14	Birmingham City	39
15	Tottenham Hotspur	38
16	West Bromwich Albion	38
17	Burnley	36
18	Preston	34
19	The Arsenal	33
20	Nottingham Forest	32
21	Chelsea	32
22	Middlesbrough	22

1924-25

1	Huddersfield	58
2	West Bromwich Albion	56
3	Bolton Wanderers	55
4	Liverpool	50
5	Bury	49
6	Newcastle United	48
7	Sunderland	48
8	Birmingham City	46
9	Notts County	45
10	Manchester City	43
11	Cardiff	43
12	Tottenham Hotspur	42
13	West Ham United	42
14	Sheffield United	39
15	Aston Villa	39
16	Blackburn Rovers	35
17	Everton	35
18	Leeds United	34
19	Burnley	34
20	The Arsenal	33
21	Preston	26
22	Nottingham Forest	24

1925-26

1	Huddersfield	57
2	The Arsenal	52
3	Sunderland	48
4	Bury	47
5	Sheffield United	46
6	Aston Villa	44
7	Liverpool	44
8	Bolton Wanderers	44
9	Manchester United	44
10	Newcastle United	42
11	Everton	42
12	Blackburn Rovers	41
13	West Bromwich Albion	40
14	Birmingham City	40
15	Tottenham Hotspur	39
16	Cardiff	39
17	Leicester City	38
18	West Ham United	37
19	Leeds United	36
20	Burnley	36
21	Manchester City	35
22	Notts County	33

1926-27

1	Newcastle United	56
2	Huddersfield	51
3	Sunderland	49
4	Bolton Wanderers	48
5	Burnley	47
6	West Ham United	46
7	Leicester City	46
8	Sheffield United	44
9	Liverpool	43
10	Aston Villa	43
11	The Arsenal	43
12	Derby County	41
13	Tottenham Hotspur	41
14	Cardiff	41
15	Manchester United	40
16	The Wednesday	39
17	Birmingham City	38
18	Blackburn Rovers	38
19	Bury	36
20	Everton	34
21	Leeds United	30
22	West Bromwich Albion	30

1927-28

1	Everton	53
2	Huddersfield	51
3	Leicester City	48
4	Derby County	44
5	Bury	44
6	Cardiff	44
7	Bolton Wanderers	44
8	Aston Villa	43
9	Newcastle United	43
10	Arsenal	41
11	Birmingham City	41
12	Blackburn Rovers	41
13	Sheffield United	40
14	The Wednesday	39
15	Sunderland	39
16	Liverpool	39
17	West Ham United	39
18	Manchester United	39
19	Burnley	39
20	Portsmouth	39
21	Tottenham Hotspur	38
22	Middlesbrough	37

1928-29

1	The Wednesday	52
2	Leicester City	51
3	Aston Villa	50
4	Sunderland	47
5	Liverpool	46
6	Derby County	46
7	Blackburn Rovers	45
8	Manchester City	45
9	Arsenal	45
10	Newcastle United	44
11	Sheffield United	41
12	Manchester United	41
13	Leeds United	41
14	Bolton Wanderers	40
15	Birmingham City	40
16	Huddersfield	39
17	West Ham United	39
18	Everton	38
19	Burnley	38
20	Portsmouth	36
21	Bury	31
22	Cardiff	29

FA Cup Finals

1920	Aston Villa	v	Huddersfield Town	1-0	
1921	Tottenham H.	v	Wolverhampton W.	1-0	
1922	Huddersfield T.	v	Preston N.E.	1-0	
1923	Bolton Wanderers	v	West Ham United	2-0	
1924	Newcastle United	v	Aston Villa	2-0	
1925	Sheffield United	v	Cardiff City	1-0	
1926	Bolton Wanderers	v	Manchester City	1-0	
1927	Cardiff City	v	Arsenal	1-0	
1928	Blackburn Rovers	v	Huddersfield Town	3-1	
1929	Bolton Wanderers	v	Portsmouth	2-0	

Football takes to the airwaves

The excitement of domestic football continued to draw huge crowds. The minimum entrance fee had been raised from sixpence to one shilling, but football remained cheap entertainment for the masses. Inevitably, it also attracted the new broadcast media. 22 January 1927 saw the first radio commentary of a football match, a clash between Arsenal and Sheffield United. To enable the listeners to visualise proceedings, a pitch divided into numbered squares was published in *Radio Times*. As the commentators described the play they also reported in which square the action was taking place.

Right: Part of the excited crowd at the 1929 Cup Final. Football remained cheap entertainment and now commentary could be followed on the radio.
Above: The Prince of Wales presents the cup to Seddon, the captain of Bolton Wanderers in 1929.

1930-1945
A Shift in Power

English football in the 1930s was dominated by one club: Arsenal. The Gunners won the championship five times, and only once, in 1929-30, did they fail to finish in the top six. There were also three FA Cup Final appearances, two of them victorious, and five wins in the Charity Shield. Under Herbert Chapman Arsenal took professional football to a new level, and even after the legendary manager's death the Gunners continued to set the pace in the domestic game.

Cameras at Highbury

Fittingly, the team of the decade became the first to be filmed for television. In 1937, a decade after radio coverage of football had been established, the cameras rolled for a practice match at Highbury. With the age of television still in its infancy, and the ownership of a set a rarity, it is doubtful whether those present that day realised the role that televised football would come to play in the nation's cultural landscape.

Opposite: Four of the Arsenal players named for the England team to meet world champions Italy at Highbury in November 1934. L-R; Copping, Hapgood, Moss and Bowden. The contest, later dubbed "The Battle of Highbury" ended in a 3-2 win for England but commentators were critical of the Italians' behaviour. Copping, Drake, Moss and Bastin all needed treatment for injuries incurred and Hapgood's nose was broken when he was hit in the face.

Above: 1931: West Bromwich Albion v Birmingham: Pearson, the Albion goalkeeper, dashes across to meet a shot that went past the post. West Brom had the better of the Final with Richardson scoring both goals. Despite a quick equaliser scored by Bradford and Gregg's early disallowed goal, Birmingham never looked in contention to win.

Right: Eddie Hapgood was Arsenal's powerful full-back who led his team to five championship medals and two F A cup victories. He also captained England 21 times in the thirties.

Championship goes south for the first time

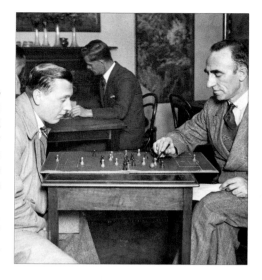

In 1930-31 Arsenal not only won the championship for the first time but also became the first southern club to do so since the inception of the league 43 years earlier. The team lost just four games and notched 66 points, a record that would stand for 38 years. In only one of their 42 league fixtures did they fail to score. Interestingly, the Gunners' home and away records were identical: Won 14, Drew 5, Lost 2. Jack Lambert top-scored with 38 goals, but all the forwards made handsome contributions. David Jack hit 31 goals, while the brilliant wingers Cliff Bastin and Joe Hulme scored 28 and 14 respectively.

An aggregate 127 goals was not quite enough to set a new record, however. That honour went to runners-up Aston Villa, for whom Tom "Pongo" Waring netted 49 times. Villa scored 128 goals in that campaign, which remains a record in English football's premier division.

Hard-fought Villa-Blues Derby

Opposite: Some of the large crowd that watched the hard-fought contest between Aston Villa and Birmingham at Villa Park in October 1930. The game provided an abundance of thrills and ended in a draw, each side scoring in the first half.

Below: Victory – and the Cup. West Brom captain Glidden, surrounded by his elated team mates, carries the Cup after defeating their neighbours Birmingham 2-1. Second Division West Brom were the first team to win promotion and the FA Cup in the same year. Aston Villa also entered the record book in 1931, finishing the season with 128 goals, 49 of which were attributed to Pongo Waring, the season's top marksman.

Above: Would-be referees take a practical examination using chess pawns to represent players before they appear in front of the Essex County FA Referees Committee.

Promotion and Cup "double" for West Brom

That season's Cup Final was an all-Midlands affair. Second Division side West Bromwich Albion came out on top against Division One strugglers Birmingham City, becoming the first club to win promotion and the Cup in the same season.

West Brom went up after finishing runners-up to Everton. The following season, 1931-32, the Liverpool club continued an extraordinary run of fluctuating fortunes. Champions in 1928, relegated in 1930, promoted in 1931, Everton lifted the title again in their first season back in the top flight. In winning the Second and First Division championships in successive seasons Everton emulated the achievement of their city rivals Liverpool between 1904 and 1906. Unsurprisingly, the key to Everton's revival was their goalscoring hero Dixie Dean, whom the club had managed to hold on to despite suffering the drop. Dean couldn't quite match his feat of 1927-28, but his 44 goals were enough to make him the number one marksman once again.

Dixie Dean top scorer again

Officials of the Football Association meet at their headquarters in Lancaster Gate to make the draw for the fourth round of the FA Cup.

December 1932: Viennese goalkeeper Hiden stops an attack on the Austrian goal by England's Jimmy Hampson at Stamford Bridge. Austria, coached by ex–Bolton player Jimmy Hogan, and recognised as one of the most impressive teams in Europe, were defeated by 4 goals to 3 in an exciting contest. Had Herbert Chapman had his way, Austrian keeper Rudi Hiden would have joined Arsenal in 1930 but the Ministry of Labour refused to allow his transfer from Wiener Sportklub to protect the jobs of British goalkeepers.

FIFA unveils World Cup

The main event in international football in the interwar period was the establishment of a World Cup competition. In 1930, when the inaugural tournament was staged in Uruguay, the prevailing attitude in England was that the country which had given football to the world remained its pre-eminent exponent. The defeat by Spain in 1929 was dismissed as an aberration, and a 7-1 win over the same opposition in 1931 seemed to confirm that view. A few lone voices suggested that English football could learn a thing or two from overseas opposition, but when FIFA unveiled its new tournament, none of the home countries was champing at the bit to be included.

England beat the Scots

Right: England's goalkeeper, Pearson, keeping out a determined attack from Scotland's forwards in the 1932 Wembley international. England won the game 3-0. Even though England had not competed in the inaugural World Cup, most spectators considered English football to be the best in the world.
Below: 50,000 fans packed into Highbury to watch the league champions.

England side run by committee

England certainly lagged behind some of the Continental sides regarding the employment of a manager for the national team. While other countries saw the value in having a single supremo responsible for international team affairs, the England side was still chosen by the International Selection Committee, which had been formed in 1888. The vagaries of this unwieldy system included political manoeuvrings. Committee members who favoured a particular player would try to garner support for their man, and some horse-trading undoubtedly went on. There was little consistency, and in the 1930s nearly a hundred players were capped, although many of these may have played just once or twice before being discarded.

Herbert Chapman becomes England's first manager.

Herbert Chapman was quick to recognise the shortcomings of this system and he persuaded the FA to allow him to take charge of the England side which toured Italy and Switzerland in May 1933. Chapman thus became the international side's only pre-war manager. England drew with Italy and beat Switzerland, but it would be another decade before the authorities took the idea on board seriously.

Newcastle's controversial victory

At the end of the 1931-32 season Arsenal fans were left to reflect on what might have been. Having faded in the league and seen their crown pass to Everton, the Gunners also lost in the FA Cup Final, and in highly controversial circumstances. Bob John put Arsenal 1-0 up against Newcastle United but it was the equalising goal which provided the game's talking point. The Arsenal defenders momentarily stopped as Jimmy Richardson crossed from the right, the ball appearing to have gone well over the bye-line. Jack Allen pounced to score and the referee allowed the goal to stand. Allen went on to hit the winner 20 minutes from time. Photographic evidence subsequently showed that Arsenal had been hard done by but that was scant consolation. At one point the Gunners looked like becoming the first twentieth-century team to achieve the coveted Double; in fact, Chapman's men ended the campaign empty-handed.

Below: The 'over the line' Final: Jack, the Arsenal inside-right, gets his head to the ball in front of the Newcastle goal, but McInroy is ready to save the shot. The 1932 Cup Final was a battle between the North and the South remembered for Newcastle's equaliser which came in the 42nd minute after John had put Arsenal ahead. Arsenal defenders thought the ball had crossed the bye-line before Allen scored for Newcastle but referee Mr W.P. Harper thought otherwise and the goal was given. Allen scored again in the 71st minute and Newcastle took the Cup for the first time since 1924.

Everton beat
nervous Manchester City

Right: Play around Manchester City's goal in the 1933 Cup Final. 93,000 people watched as Everton defeated a nervous-looking Manchester City by 3 goals to nil. The 1930s was a successful period in the history of Everton; having been promoted back into Division One in the 1931-2 season the Merseyside team finished the year at the top of the league pushing Arsenal into second place.

Below: Sagar, the Everton goalkeeper, makes a remarkable save in the 1933 Cup Final. Creswell, in white, is nearest the camera, behind him is White and on the left is Herd, Manchester City's centre-forward. This was the first Cup Final in which players wore numbers on the backs of their shirts. Everton was allocated numbers 1 – 11, printed in black on their white shirts, and Manchester City was given 12 – 22, written in white on red shirts.

Alex James

Alex James was the outstanding player of Herbert Chapman's mighty Arsenal side of the 1930s. Probably the most complete player of his generation, James was equally adept in the scheming role or as a finisher. Chapman paid Preston £8750 for his services in 1929. It proved to be money well spent. Over the next eight years James was the orchestrator-in-chief in a phenomenally successful spell which included four championships and two FA Cup victories. James was a wayward star, however, and that contributed to the fact that he won a meagre eight caps for Scotland. One of those came in March 1928, when Scotland took on England at Wembley. James was outstanding, scoring twice in a 5-1 victory and cementing his place in the annals as one of the famous "Wembley Wizards".

A spectacular view of Wembley just over ten years after it hosted the 1923 Cup Final. Gate receipts had now risen to £25,000. Of this, one third went to the Football Association and one third to each of the competing teams.

Arsenal follow Huddersfield into record books

The following three seasons saw Arsenal - and Chapman - equal Huddersfield's achievement of the previous decade. The Gunners' record over those three championship-winning campaigns was impressive: they won 73 of their 126 league matches, were beaten just 24 times and scored over 300 goals.

Chapman's sudden death in January 1934 meant that he did not see the triumphant completion of the hat-trick with either club. Yet no one was in any doubt as to who masterminded both achievements. Chapman was known for his attention to detail, and it was typical of the man that he insisted on watching his juniors play, despite the adverse conditions and the fact that he was already running a temperature. He contracted pneumonia and succumbed to the illness on 6 January. He was 62 years old.

Chapman the visionary manager

Chapman's legacy stretched far beyond another domestic championship for the Gunners. He was a prescient manager and many of the ideas he championed came to fruition long after his death. These included the advent of night matches under floodlights, the use of numbered shirts and even the Champions League!

In many ways Chapman's Arsenal side played in the modern style. The team was well schooled in the art of absorbing pressure, then quickly turning defence into attack. Swift counter-attacking football is one of the hallmarks of the modern era, yet to the fans in the 1930s it often seemed that the Gunners won matches when they appeared to be on the back foot. This gave rise to the "Lucky Arsenal" jibe which stuck for so long.

Chapman's Arsenal were quick to turn defence into attack.

Chapman was also ahead of his time as far as transfer dealings were concerned. In 1930 he signed goalkeeper Rudi Hiden from Wiener Sportklub for £2600. International transfers of this type were almost unheard of, and this one sparked a row which is all too familiar more than 70 years later. The Ministry of Labour refused to sanction Hiden's entry into the country, on the grounds that he would put a British goalkeeper out of work.

City Swift to react

Opposite above: Frank Swift, Manchester City's 19-year-old goalkeeper clears from a corner kick in the 1934 Final at Wembley. After Cup Final nerves disrupted their performance in last year's tie, Manchester City defeated Portsmouth 2-1 in a dramatic game. Portsmouth led until almost the last 15 minutes of the match when Allen was knocked unconscious in the penalty area. While he recovered Tilson scored two goals in quick succession for City.

Opposite below: 1934: Arsenal's first practice match of the season. Arsenal were the most successful team of the era. League champions in 1930-1 and 1932-33 and narrowly missing winning the Double in 1932 when they came second in the league and were runners-up in the Cup. However, disaster struck on 6 January when Herbert Chapman, manager and driving force behind their achievements, died suddenly. Director George Allison took on management duties and Arsenal finished the season on top of the First Division. Allison continued Chapman's work in strengthening the side, signing centre-forward Ted Drake and wing-halves Crayston and Copping.

Referees under fire

Left: During a game against Chelsea at Stamford Bridge in 1934, Blackburn players appeal to the referee after a goal was given against them - proving that some aspects of the game remain unchanged even 70 years later.

Walsall in giant-killing act

Almost inevitably, fans of rival clubs envied and resented Arsenal's success in equal measure. Any ill-feeling was not simply down to the club's dominance on the pitch. This was a period of depression and high unemployment, and while the industrial heartlands of the Midlands and the North were hit hard, Highbury epitomised the affluence of a capital which seemed impervious to the economic climate.

Thus, in 1933 there was a widespread feeling of schadenfreude as Arsenal fell victim to one of the great giant-killing acts of all time. The team was weakened by the loss of several players through illness and injury, but no one expected an upset when mighty Arsenal went to

Walsall for a third round FA Cup-tie. There were three new faces in the Gunners' line-up and each of them had a nightmare. One of the trio, defender Tommy Black, gave away the penalty which resulted in the Third Division side going 2-0 up. That was how it finished. Black had no chance to make amends; he was transfer-listed immediately.

Chapman's successor was George Allison, a club director who was best known as a radio commentator. He had no playing experience, but the organisation at Highbury was so well established that this hardly proved a handicap, at least not in the short term. Allison had the benefit of inheriting Tom Whittaker as his right-hand man. Whittaker was an excellent coach and also a top physiotherapist. His methods meant that injured players were back in action in days rather than weeks, another factor in the club's success.

Young Gunner

Opposite: Arsenal stars (r-l) Alex James, goalkeeper Frank Moss and Eddie Hapgood admire the juvenile prowess of Hapgood's son, Tony. All three players had international experience: Hapgood and Moss with England and James representing Scotland. Of the three, Hapgood was most capped, making 30 appearances during 1933-9. Moss's recurring shoulder injury forced him to retire in 1937 to take up the post of manager of Heart of Midlothian in Edinburgh.

Highbury Lock-out

Above: Amazing scenes were witnessed at Arsenal with huge numbers of people hoping to attend the clash between Spurs and Arsenal in January 1934. In the background is the vast crowd who were unable to get into the game. In 1936 a new East Stand was opened at Highbury which provided seating for a further 8000 spectators.

Right: An aerial picture of Maine Road taken when Manchester City played Sheffield Wednesday in March 1934.

Playing by the Rules

Above: An instructor takes a class with the aid of a miniature football field as the London Society of Referees commences courses for the training of new referees at the Feathers Hotel in Westminster.

Top: The scene at the Bristol City ground when spectators surged onto the pitch.

Opposite above: Crowds look at the "Ground Full" notice outside the turnstiles at Stamford Bridge when Chelsea met Arsenal in 1934. Arsenal won their third league title in the 1934-5 season by a margin of four points over Sunderland and new signing Ted Drake was the season's top scorer with 42 goals.

Opposite below: Even with Gallacher in the strike force Scotland couldn't score and went down 3-0 at Wembley in 1934.

Right: Well-known referee J.M. Wiltshire from Dorset during the Brentford - Wolverhampton match in 1937.

Pools disrupted

By the mid-1930s, fans were not only interested in their own team's performance; football was also hugely popular as a means of having a flutter. The Football Pools had been launched by Littlewoods in 1923, and in barely a decade filling in the coupon was for many a weekly ritual. There were those who were unhappy about the promotion of gambling on such a widespread scale, and

in 1936 even the Football League itself began to have reservations. The memories of match-fixing were still relatively fresh, and the league took the draconian decision to withhold fixture lists to the last possible moment in order to disrupt the pools companies' operations. It was a short-lived experiment. There was an outcry as fans demanded to know who their team was playing against in good time. Normal service was quickly resumed and the public carried on checking their coupons to see if they'd hit the jackpot.

Drake keeps Gunners on top

Allison had mixed fortunes in the transfer market as he sought to keep Arsenal at the top of the pile. He told a young Len Shackleton that he wouldn't make the grade, and it was Sunderland and Newcastle who would benefit from the services of one of the great inside-forwards of the postwar era. If Allison made a long-term mistake with Shackleton, he certainly made an inspired signing shortly after Chapman's death. The acquisition of Ted Drake from Southampton undoubtedly helped maintain the club's supremacy. In 1934-35, his first full season at Highbury, Drake hit 42 league goals, making him the First Division's top marksman. In December 1935 Drake hit all seven of Arsenal's goals when they won 7-1 at Villa Park, and he also scored the goal which beat Sheffield United in the 1936 Cup Final.

Wednesday win goal feast

Above: West Brom attack the Sheffield Wednesday goal in the 1935 FA Cup Final. It was a six-goal thriller, the highest goal tally in the showpiece since Bury's 6–0 win over Derby County in 1903. The crowd had hardly settled after kick-off before Wednesday took the lead, while Rimmer's final goal for the Midlands team came in the last minute. Sheffield Wednesday won 4–2.

Top: Albion's Pearson punches clear a dangerous free kick. The scores were level at half-time, 2-2.

Left: Enthusiastic Sheffield Wednesday supporters trying to touch the Cup as the team coach drives away from the stadium.

Opposite above: While the other members of the team are in Brighton preparing for their FA Cup-tie with Bolton Wanderers, George Hunt (left) and Ted Drake remain at Highbury for treatment. They are seen in the electrical room where Drake is receiving infra-red rays. Hunt played with Arsenal for just one season, coming from Spurs in October 1937 for a fee of £7500 and transferring to Bolton for £4000 in March 1938.

Opposite below: A disputed goal at the Burnley end of the field when Sheffield Wednesday met Burnley in the semi-final of the FA Cup at Villa Park in 1935. Sheffield went on to win by 3 goals to nil having defeated Arsenal in the previous round.

FA Cup Finals

1930	Arsenal	v	Huddersfield Town	2-0
1931	West Bromwich A.	v	Birmingham	2-1
1932	Newcastle United	v	Arsenal	2-1
1933	Everton	v	Manchester City	3-0
1934	Manchester City	v	Portsmouth	2-1
1935	Sheffield Wed.	v	West Bromwich Albion	4-2
1936	Arsenal	v	Sheffield United	1-0
1937	Sunderland	v	Preston North End	3-1
1938	Preston North End	v	Huddersfield	1-0
1939	Portsmouth	v	Wolverhampton Wanderers	4-1
1940-45			No competition	

Manchester City on the rise

Below: Manchester City playing Portsmouth at Maine Road in January 1936. City finished ninth that season but went on to win the league the following year, losing only seven times.

Opposite above: Cheering crowds lined the streets to greet the Sheffield Wednesday team on their arrival home with the Cup. Wednesday had last won the Cup in 1907 but the West Bromwich team had come to Wembley in 1935 with high hopes of repeating their success in the 1931 Final when they defeated their Birmingham neighbours.

Opposite below: Action around the Spurs goal in the 1935 Cup tie between Spurs and Bolton Wanderers. Bolton narrowly missed out on a place in the final losing to West Brom in the replay of the semi-final. In the 1934–5 season there were still only 4 southern teams in Division One: Arsenal, Chelsea, Portsmouth and Spurs.

Right: Bags containing the numbered balls to be used in the draw for the FA Cup-ties which is to be broadcast live for the first time in 1935. Match commentaries had been broadcast since 1927, beginning with Arsenal v Sheffield United on 22 January of that year.

Drake to the rescue

Left: Alex James supported by his team-mates holds the 1936 FA Cup aloft, Arsenal having overcome Sheffield United in the Final by one goal to nil. The London club's goal was scored by Ted Drake who had recently rejoined the side after a knee operation. The victorious team returned to Islington Town Hall in North London driving through two miles of cheering crowds. In response to the demands of the fans, James and Drake stood on the roof of the motor vehicle holding the cup between them.

Below: Magnall heads Millwall's first goal in the 1937 Cup tie against Manchester City. Millwall became the first Third Division team to reach the semi-final of the Cup and were eventually eliminated by winners Sunderland.

Opposite: Arsenal's Kirchen leaps to challenge Strong, the Portsmouth keeper at Highbury in April 1937. Television coverage of football began with a practice match transmitted from Highbury in 1937 but it wasn't until the 1940s that those with television sets could expect regular transmissions of games.

Sunderland hold off Gunners

It was Sunderland who halted Arsenal's run of championship successes. The Wearsiders' star was inside-forward Horatio "Raich" Carter, and he inspired the club's title-winning campaign of 1935-36, their first since 1913. Sunderland couldn't maintain their form, slipping to 8th the following season, but there was compensation in the form of a first FA Cup triumph. They came from a goal behind against Preston to win 3-1 in 1937. A Preston side including Bill Shankly made it to Wembley again the following year, with Huddersfield their opponents. A drab, goalless 90 minutes meant that this became the first Wembley final to go into extra time. It was also the first to be decided by a penalty, George Mutch scoring from the spot with the last kick of the match.

Swift is City star

Manchester City were another side that tasted both league and Cup success in the 1930s. In the 1933 FA Cup Final City were thumped 3-0 by Everton, who thus completed a remarkable treble, following their championship wins in the Second and First Divisions in the previous two seasons. The 1933 Final was unique in that the teams wore numbered shirts for the first time, but not in the familiar manner. The Everton shirts were numbered 1 to 11, City's 12 to 22.

City bounced back to reach the final the following year, and this time they got their hands on the Cup with a 2-1 win over Portsmouth. The City side boasted a fine wing-half called Matt Busby, but it was 19-year-old goalkeeper Frank Swift who made the headlines. Swift blamed himself for the goal which gave Portsmouth a half-time lead. Fred Tilson scored twice for City after the break, but when reporters behind Swift's goal began counting down the minutes, it all proved too much. At the final whistle he collapsed with nervous exhaustion. Three years later Swift helped City to win their first championship, 44 years after the club entered the league. He went on to become one of the all-time great keepers, spending his entire playing career at Maine Road. After retiring from the game he turned his hand to journalism and was among those killed in the Munich air crash in 1958.

Manchester City and Everton wear numbered shirts for the first time.

Milestones 1930-1945

1930 The first Football World Cup is won by Uruguay; England is not one of the 13 teams participating

1933 Numbers first required to be worn on the back of players' shirts for the FA Cup Final between Everton who were numbered 1 to 11 and Manchester City, numbers 12 to 22

1934 Herbert Chapman the successful manager who took Arsenal to 1930 FA Cup glory dies suddenly

Second World Cup competition takes place in Italy, again England does not compete and the host nation wins

1935 Football managers are banned from the touchline

1936 Luton Town scores a 12-0 victory over Bristol Rovers, with Joe Payne scoring 10

Football highlights shown for the first time by the BBC on a match between Arsenal and Everton

1937 The first foreign professionals enter the British game when Barrow sign two players from Argentina

1938 The first game to be broadcast live on BBC television is the FA Cup Final between Preston North End and Huddersfield, however only 10,000 people watched compared with 90,000 present in the stadium

The third World Cup is won by Italy for a second tournament running; England still did not participate

England beat Nazi Germany 6-3 the game became infamous because the English team gave a Nazi salute before the game

Aston Villa beats a German select XI the day after the national game but is jeered off the pitch for failing to follow suit and give the Nazi salute

1939 The Football League makes numbers on the back of players' shirts compulsory

The FA suspends all normal competition at the outbreak of war; although the 1939-40 season was started it was cancelled the day after the outbreak of war on September 3rd

Sunderland win their first cup

Opposite: Cup Final 1937: O'Donnell, the Preston centre-forward and scorer of their first-half goal, receives attention after an injury. Despite holding 6 league titles, it was not until 1937 that Sunderland were successful in the Cup. After being 1-0 down through the whole of the first half, the team from the north-east came back to win the match 3-1 with goals from Gurney, Carter and Burbanks.

Above: Gurney, in stripes, scores Sunderland's equaliser.

Right: Cup Final programmes from the late twenties and thirties. Most programmes gave very basic information until the 1950s.

Tommy Lawton

Celebrated by Stanley Matthews as "a brilliant header of the ball", centre-forward Tommy Lawton also had two good feet and blistering pace. When he joined Third Division Notts County in 1947, attendances at Meadow Lane soared. The affection was mutual, with Bolton-born Lawton naming Nottingham his adopted city. He collected 103 goals in 166 run-outs for the club, and was also capped for England – one of the few lower division players ever to wear the national colours. In all his career, he was never booked or sent off.

A teenage sensation at Burnley, he was quickly signed up to a bigger club, Everton, for the then remarkable fee of £6500. As part of Everton's 1938-39 championship-winning side, he scored 35 goals and seemed set to be the next Dixie Dean. But the outbreak of war prevented Lawton from playing other than unofficial internationals, and he moved to Chelsea when he was demobbed. It was a golden time: in 1946–7 he broke the club's scoring record, with 26 goals in 34 matches.

Joining Brentford as player-manager in 1952, aged 33, he admitted to finding it a struggle, but he bowed out of the Football League in fine style with a spell in dangerously good form at Arsenal. He died of pneumonia in 1996.

Facelift for Wembley

Opposite above: An aerial view of Wembley during the 1936 Cup Final where Arsenal beat Sheffield United by a Ted Drake goal.

Opposite below: In 1938 plans to enlarge the stadium move ahead. The capacity was 93,000 but the scheme aims at providing accommodation for an additional 38,000. The budgeted cost for the project is £70,000. Although Wembley's present arrangement with the F A Council still had five years to run, agreement had already been reached for a further 21 years, thus securing the Cup Final at Wembley until at least 1964.

Right: a large crowd gathered to watch Arsenal - Brentford on Good Friday morning, 1938. Arsenal won the league again that year while Brentford repeated the sixth position from the previous year's campaign.

World football catches up

England's claim to footballing supremacy was dented in the early 1930s. There were defeats against France, Czechoslovakia and Hungary, albeit all away from home. In December 1933 Hugo Meisl's much-vaunted Austrian "Wunderteam" came to Stamford Bridge. England played to their strengths and won the match 4-3, but the Austrians had displayed some dazzling skills and were on top for long periods.

A year later, 14 November 1934, Vittorio Pozzo's Italy, the newly-crowned world champions, came to Highbury to try to become the first team to win on English soil. Pozzo, like Hugo Meisl, believed in meticulous preparation. In contrast, the England players all turned out for their clubs the previous Saturday, and there were several withdrawals before the team was announced, 24 hours before the game. There was hardly any time for practice, but England at least benefited from the fact that seven Arsenal players were in the line-up.

"Battle of Highbury"

It was an ugly game, one which would go down in the annals as the "Battle of Highbury". The scene was set in the opening moments when Ted Drake clashed with Italy's centre-half Luisito Monti. The latter came off worse, breaking a bone in his foot and eventually having to leave the field. His team-mates were bent on retribution for what they regarded as a blatant foul. As the world champions took their eye off the ball - quite literally - England eased into a 3-0 lead. In the second half the visitors regained their composure and began to play. They scored twice, both from the great Giuseppe Meazza, but couldn't complete the comeback. England's record remained intact, but at a cost. Eric Brook and Eddie Hapgood had to go to hospital and there was a queue of players for the treatment table.

England hold out against Austrian "Wunderteam".

No stroll for England in Vienna

Eighteen months later, 6 May 1936, England went to Vienna and lost to Austria in circumstances which showed up the international team's lack of an overseer. On the day of the match the players accepted Hugo Meisl's "generous" offer of a walking tour of the city, and it was only after they had pounded the streets for some miles that the players realised that the hospitality was perhaps not as gracious as it first appeared. England lost the game 2-1.

In May 1938 England went to Berlin to face Germany in the Olympic Stadium. The players reluctantly agreed to perform the Nazi salute prior to the game, and although they ran out convincing 6-3 winners, the occasion was overlaid with political rather than sporting significance.

Victory over Wales

Opposite: England thwarted by the Wales goalkeeper in their international match at Middlesbrough in 1937. England went on to win the game 2-1. There were growing concerns that England needed a full-time manager in order to play a dominant role in world football.

Above: Thousands on the terraces watch as Wolverhampton's Dorsett scores in the 10th minute of the second half of the 1939 Cup Final.

Right: A Wolves supporter gets that Cup Final feeling in Trafalgar Square. Wolverhampton Wanderers performed well in the league in the 1938-9 season finishing behind Arsenal and had high hopes of taking home the Cup.

League Division One 1930-1940

1930-31

1	Arsenal	66
2	Aston Villa	59
3	Sheffield Wednesday	52
4	Portsmouth	49
5	Huddersfield	48
6	Derby County	46
7	Middlesbrough	46
8	Manchester City	46
9	Liverpool	42
10	Blackburn Rovers	42
11	Sunderland	41
12	Chelsea	40
13	Grimsby	39
14	Bolton Wanderers	38
15	Sheffield United	38
16	Leicester City	36
17	Newcastle United	36
18	West Ham United	36
19	Birmingham City	36
20	Blackpool	32
21	Leeds United	31
22	Manchester United	22

1931-32

1	Everton	56
2	Arsenal	54
3	Sheffield Wednesday	50
4	Huddersfield	48
5	Aston Villa	46
6	West Bromwich Albion	46
7	Sheffield United	46
8	Portsmouth	45
9	Birmingham City	44
10	Liverpool	44
11	Newcastle United	42
12	Chelsea	40
13	Sunderland	40
14	Manchester City	38
15	Derby County	38
16	Blackburn Rovers	38
17	Bolton Wanderers	38
18	Middlesbrough	38
19	Leicester City	37
20	Blackpool	33
21	Grimsby	32
22	West Ham United	31

1932-33

1	Arsenal	58
2	Aston Villa	54
3	Sheffield Wednesday	51
4	West Bromwich Albion	49
5	Newcastle United	49
6	Huddersfield	47
7	Derby County	44
8	Leeds United	44
9	Portsmouth	43
10	Sheffield United	43
11	Everton	41
12	Sunderland	40
13	Birmingham City	39
14	Liverpool	39
15	Blackburn Rovers	38
16	Manchester City	37
17	Middlesbrough	37
18	Chelsea	35
19	Leicester City	35
20	Wolverhampton W.	35
21	Bolton Wanderers	33
22	Blackpool	33

1933-34

1	Arsenal	59
2	Huddersfield	56
3	Tottenham Hotspur	49
4	Derby County	45
5	Manchester City	45
6	Sunderland	44
7	West Bromwich Albion	44
8	Blackburn Rovers	43
9	Leeds United	42
10	Portsmouth	42
11	Sheffield Wednesday	41
12	Stoke	41
13	Aston Villa	40
14	Everton	40
15	Wolverhampton W.	40
16	Middlesbrough	39
17	Leicester City	39
18	Liverpool	38
19	Chelsea	36
20	Birmingham City	36
21	Newcastle United	34
22	Sheffield United	31

1934-35

1	Arsenal	58
2	Sunderland	54
3	Sheffield Wednesday	49
4	Manchester City	48
5	Grimsby	45
6	Derby County	45
7	Liverpool	45
8	Everton	44
9	West Bromwich Albion	44
10	Stoke	42
11	Preston	42
12	Chelsea	41
13	Aston Villa	41
14	Portsmouth	40
15	Blackburn Rovers	39
16	Huddersfield	38
17	Wolverhampton W.	38
18	Leeds United	38
19	Birmingham City	36
20	Middlesbrough	34
21	Leicester City	33
22	Tottenham Hotspur	30

1935-36

1	Sunderland	56
2	Derby County	48
3	Huddersfield	48
4	Stoke	47
5	Brentford	46
6	Arsenal	45
7	Preston	44
8	Chelsea	43
9	Manchester City	42
10	Portsmouth	42
11	Leeds United	41
12	Birmingham City	41
13	Bolton Wanderers	41
14	Middlesbrough	40
15	Wolverhampton W.	40
16	Everton	39
17	Grimsby	39
18	West Bromwich Albion	38
19	Liverpool	38
20	Sheffield Wednesday	38
21	Aston Villa	35
22	Blackburn Rovers	33

1936-37

1	Manchester City	57
2	Charlton Athletic	54
3	Arsenal	52
4	Derby County	49
5	Wolverhampton W.	47
6	Brentford	46
7	Middlesbrough	46
8	Sunderland	44
9	Portsmouth	44
10	Stoke	42
11	Birmingham City	41
12	Grimsby	41
13	Chelsea	41
14	Preston	41
15	Huddersfield	39
16	West Bromwich Albion	38
17	Everton	37
18	Liverpool	35
19	Leeds United	34
20	Bolton Wanderers	34
21	Manchester United	32
22	Sheffield Wednesday	30

1937-38

1	Arsenal	52
2	Wolverhampton W.	51
3	Preston	49
4	Charlton Athletic	46
5	Middlesbrough	46
6	Brentford	45
7	Bolton Wanderers	45
8	Sunderland	44
9	Leeds United	43
10	Chelsea	41
11	Liverpool	41
12	Blackpool	40
13	Derby County	40
14	Everton	39
15	Huddersfield	39
16	Leicester City	39
17	Stoke	38
18	Birmingham City	38
19	Portsmouth	38
20	Grimsby	38
21	Manchester City	36
22	West Bromwich Albion	36

1938-39

1	Everton	59
2	Wolverhampton W.	55
3	Charlton Athletic	50
4	Middlesbrough	49
5	Arsenal	47
6	Derby County	46
7	Stoke	46
8	Bolton Wanderers	45
9	Preston	44
10	Grimsby	43
11	Liverpool	42
12	Aston Villa	41
13	Leeds United	41
14	Manchester United	38
15	Blackpool	38
16	Sunderland	38
17	Portsmouth	37
18	Brentford	36
19	Huddersfield	35
20	Chelsea	33
21	Birmingham City	32
22	Leicester City	29

1939-40

1	Liverpool	57
2	Manchester United	56
3	Wolverhampton W.	56
4	Stoke	55
5	Blackpool	50
6	Sheffield United	49
7	Preston	47
8	Aston Villa	45
9	Sunderland	44
10	Everton	43
11	Middlesbrough	42
12	Portsmouth	41
13	Arsenal	41
14	Derby County	41
15	Chelsea	39
16	Grimsby	38
17	Blackburn Rovers	36
18	Bolton Wanderers	34
19	Charlton Athletic	34
20	Huddersfield	33
21	Brentford	25
22	Leeds United	18

Opposite: A player appeals to the linesman in 1936.

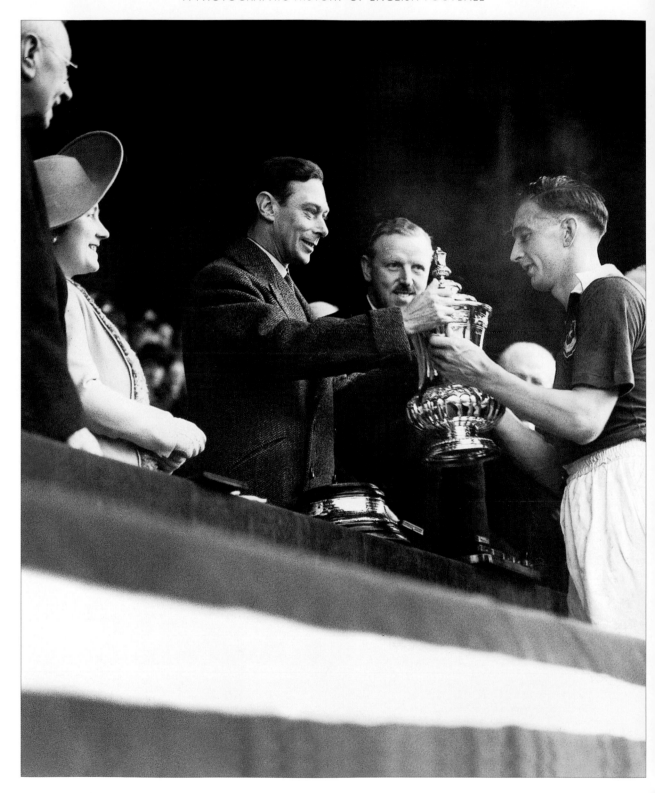

Arsenal buy Wolves star

In 1937-38 Arsenal became champions for the fifth time in eight seasons. Even so, the Gunners' air of invincibility was beginning to fade. The great Alex James retired at the end of the 1936-37 campaign, and in August 1938 Allison splashed out £14,000 on a replacement.

The man with the new British record price tag on his head was Bryn Jones. No doubt Wolves were reluctant to sell their Welsh international, not least because they had a burgeoning side and had just finished runners-up to Arsenal by a single point. The depth of the Highbury coffers proved decisive, however, and Arsenal got their man. Whether the weight of expectation rested heavily on his shoulders, Jones was not at his best in 1938-39, which would be the last full season for seven years. Arsenal slipped to 5th in the league, Everton taking top honours, with Wolves once again having to settle for the runners-up spot.

Pompey hold the cup for seven years

The season turned into a double agony for Wolves as they went down in the Cup Final too. They faced Portsmouth, a team languishing in the bottom half of the table, and were red-hot favourites to lift the trophy. Portsmouth used all manner of lucky omens and superstitions to aid their cause, as they had done in 1934. Bringing in comedian Bud Flanagan to relax the team hadn't worked back then, but manager Jack Tinn continued to put a lot of faith in his "lucky spats". There had been a lot of publicity surrounding Wolves' use of so-called "monkey gland" treatment to aid the performance of their players. It didn't help them on the big day. It is said that when the Pompey camp saw the spidery scrawl of their opponents in the official autograph book, they knew they had a golden opportunity. The hands that had signed the book had obviously been shaking, and those feelings of anxiety accompanied the Wolves players onto the pitch. Portsmouth ran out comfortable 4-1 winners and would remain Cup holders for seven years.

Arsenal become champions for the fifth time in eight seasons.

Pompey magic

Portsmouth beat the odds when they outplayed favourites Wolverhampton Wanderers to lift the F A Cup in 1939. Such was the quality of their play the 4-1 victory didn't flatter the victors.
Opposite: The greatest moment of Cup Final day: Guthrie followed by his victorious team receives the coveted trophy from the King in the royal box at Wembley while the Queen looks on.
Right: Jimmy Guthrie is chaired off the field carrying the Cup.

Billy Liddell

Billy Liddell was as modest a man as his shots were explosive, and won the adulation of the Kop – who dubbed their club Liddellpool – as one of their most talented outside-lefts (and later, central striker) ever. His career was interrupted by service in the RAF, and in the post-war years Liverpool fell into a decline that not even Liddell's individual flashes of brilliance could stem.

Signing for the Reds in 1938 from Dunfermline, the "Flying Scot" scored in his league debut in 1946, in an FA Cup game against Chester City, and then put away a hat-trick in his next, a 7-3 win against Manchester City, helping Liverpool to the league title in his first full season. He played a record 537 games for the club and scored 229 goals. Liverpool's 2-0 defeat to Arsenal in the FA Cup Final of 1950 marked a turning point, and the club was relegated in 1954. Liddell did, however, win 28 caps for Scotland, and shared with Stanley Matthews the honour of playing twice for Great Britain, in 1947 and 1955, against Rest of the World sides.

Liddell retired in 1960. Sadly, he won few medals in his 22 years wearing the red shirt, but had he played in his prime under Bill Shankly, he would surely have had a cabinetful.

Winterbottom becomes first England manager

It was during the war years that FA Secretary Stanley Rous proposed that the England side should have a full-time manager. His idea was accepted, and Walter Winterbottom, a teacher who had played centre-half for Manchester United, was given the job. Winterbottom's brief was purely team preparation; selection remained in the hands of the committee members.

Opposite: Now for the homecoming: Pompey captain, Guthrie, carries off the FA Cup under escort following his team's 4-1 victory over Wolves in 1939. With the outbreak of war just months away Portsmouth would remain Cup holders for seven years.
Right: Walter Winterbottom, England manager from 1946 until after the 1962 World Cup.

Wartime football boosts morale

The 1939-40 season was just three games old when it was aborted due to the outbreak of war. Initially all forms of football ceased, but Winston Churchill was among those who appreciated the morale-boosting role that the game could play. The Board of Trade even issued coupons to cover the purchase of football kit, effectively recognising that here was a commodity that had to be rationed, but not dispensed with entirely. Regional football was introduced, and although there were both league and cup competitions, the honours were hardly something to be coveted. Travel restrictions meant that clubs were allowed to field guest players, and those which had large numbers of soldiers stationed nearby reaped the benefit. Aldershot, for example, regularly fielded international players thanks to this highly flexible system.

Wartime internationals

After war was declared, in September of the following year, international football continued. But as with the revamped league competition, the matches were inevitably a victim of circumstance. In 1943, for example, Blackpool's young centre-forward Stan Mortensen made his debut - against England! Mortensen had been a substitute for the match against Wales and came on for the opposition after one of the Welsh players was injured.

30 games were played during the conflict, together with five "Victory" internationals between September 1945 and May 1946. These were not accorded official international status in the record books.

Football at war

Above: A scene at Upton Park where West Ham United played Leicester City showing the usual football fans watching the game - in Army uniform. This picture was taken the day before war was declared and emphasises the degree to which the war was becoming inevitable.

Opposite: Manchester United's stadium after a bomb had dropped through the roof of the main stand.

Left: All factories and institutions had their own roof spotters, usually members of staff who did an extra shift. The roof spotter's job was to act as an early warning to those inside the building of the approach of a raid. Here the roof spotter works on while West Ham play Chelsea in December 1940, at the height of the Blitz. The gate was less than 2000.

Fans flock back to the game

As had happened in 1918, the end of the global conflict brought the fans flocking back to football. The clubs had to assess the state of their stadiums and check on their players. Inevitably, war had claimed the lives of some, and those who did return for duty were seven years older. It was a chaotic period, with many clubs forced to try out players who might otherwise never have been given an opportunity. There was no time to restart a league programme in 1945-46, but the FA Cup made a welcome return to the sporting calendar. Football was back.

A break from hostilities

Above: Part of the vast crowd of 133,000 spectators at Hampden Park who watched England play Scotland on April 22 1944.
Opposite above: An England v Scotland game at Wembley in October 1941 gives fans some relief from the austerity and the trauma of the hostilities. Scotland's goalkeeper, Dawson, has a hard job to prevent England's forwards scoring from this clear-cut opportunity.
Opposite below: A dramatic moment in the league Cup Final at Blackburn. Gallimore, Preston's right back, was trying to stop the ball but instead kicked it into his own goal. Despite this, Preston beat Arsenal 2-1.

1945-1959
The Golden Era

The early postwar years were a golden era for English football. The global conflict might have been over but Britain faced years of austerity and rationing. Ex-servicemen had money burning a hole in the pockets of their demob suits and precious little to spend it on. When it came to mass entertainment and escapism, football had few rivals.

More than 35 million people crammed into football grounds all around the country when the league programme was relaunched in 1946-47. Within a couple of years the 40-million mark was surpassed.

League grows to 92 clubs

The huge wave of popularity led to many minor clubs seeking league status. In 1950 four applications were accepted. Colchester, Scunthorpe, Gillingham and Shrewsbury were added to the Division Three ranks, thereby increasing the league from 88 to 92 clubs.

The football that the fans flocked to see in those early postwar years was not always of the highest standard. The players that survived from the pre-war era were seven years older. Clubs were squeezed, since young talent could not be developed overnight. In an effort to steal a march on their rivals, many clubs tried out players on an unprecedented scale, giving opportunities to some who would scarcely have merited a look in days gone by. By the end of the 1946-47 campaign, a number of clubs had fielded more than thirty players in an effort to find a winning formula.

Above: The King presents the Cup to Harris, the Chelsea captain after they defeated their London rivals Millwall in the 1945 Southern League Cup Final. Public demand for the resumption of fixtures was high, encouraging the FA to alter the rules for the 1946 FA Cup so that teams played 2 legs at each round until reaching the semi-finals.

Right: A capacity crowd watches Chelsea play Moscow Dynamo when the Russian team toured Britain in the winter of 1945. The match ended in a draw with three goals scored by each side. Dynamo went on to defeat Cardiff, draw with Rangers and, in a match full of controversies, defeated an Arsenal side containing many guest players, by 4 goals to 3.

Opposite: Lawton scores the fourth goal for Britain when they faced the Rest of Europe at Hampden Park in May 1947. Britain defeated the Continental team comprising players from 9 countries by 6 goals to one; Mannion netting 3, Lawton 2 and Scotland's Billy Steel scoring one.

Left: Charlton face Bolton in the semi-final of the FA Cup at Villa Park in 1946.

Below: Clem Attlee shakes hands with Stanley Matthews as England line up to meet Belgium at Wembley in 1946. The postwar years brought greater interest in international football and England not only played abroad but entertained Continental teams more frequently. The national team travelled to Switzerland at the end of the 1946 season winning 1-0 but chalked up a remarkable victory in Portugal defeating their opponents by 10-0 with Lawton and Mortensen scoring 4 goals apiece.

Opposite: On a blisteringly hot day, Charlton's Duffy scores the winning goal in the 1947 Cup Final against Burnley. The goal, scored in the last minutes of extra time, averted the threat of a replay which had last been necessary in 1912 when Barnsley drew with West Brom.

Cullis and Busby turn to management

Of the 1930s stars, Tommy Lawton, Joe Mercer, Billy Liddell, Tom Finney and Bob Paisley were among those who successfully bridged the seven-year gap. And, of course, the incomparable Stanley Matthews, who had turned 30 but still had nearly twenty years of league football left in him. Wolves stalwart Stan Cullis managed just one more season before hanging up his boots. Former Manchester City and Liverpool half-back Matt Busby was 36 when the war ended and his thoughts had already turned to management. Cullis and Busby would become two of the dominant figures in the 1950s, locking horns as bosses of Wolves and Manchester United respectively, as they had done in their pomp as players. Each would lead his side to three championships, though their footballing philosophies could hardly have been more different.

Tragedy at Burnden Park
1945-46 saw all the clubs take stock of their playing staffs and facilities. Many grounds had been damaged during the war, and while repairs were carried out some ground-sharing went on. Old Trafford was one of those affected, and for some time Manchester United played their home matches at Maine Road. Arsenal and Spurs also put aside their traditional rivalry to share facilities in the early peacetime months.

There may have been no league fixtures that year but the Cup returned to provide the players and fans with some competitive football. As this was the only competition of the season the FA decided to increase the number of matches by making each tie up to the semi-final a two-legged affair. It was in the second leg of a sixth-round tie between Bolton and Stoke at Burnden Park that football saw one of its worst-ever tragedies. The gates were closed on this eagerly-awaited match, but thousands forced their way in by every conceivable means. In the resulting crush some of the steel barriers gave way and there were 33 fatalities. There was little appetite for the game to go ahead, but after some delay the teams played out a goalless draw, Bolton going through thanks to their 2-0 win in the first leg.

Traditional rivalries put aside as clubs share facilities

Charlton lose a Cup match but make it to Wembley

Bolton were beaten by Charlton in the semi-final, and the London club faced Derby at Wembley. For both sides it had been a marathon campaign. Derby needed a semi-final replay to beat Birmingham, and so played ten matches to reach the final. Charlton's run was unique. Having been beaten by Fulham in the away leg of their third-round tie, Charlton thus became the first club to reach the Cup Final having lost a match. Derby had just splashed out to sign Raich Carter from Sunderland and he helped the Rams to their first major honour. Charlton's Bert Turner scored at both ends to take the game into extra time, when the classier Derby side scored three times without reply.

Top: Some of the 90,000 spectators at the Burnley v Charlton Cup Final in 1947.
Left: Compton, the Manchester United goalkeeper, pressed by Blackpool's Mortensen makes a spectacular save in the 1948 Final. Mortensen and the newly-acquired Stanley Matthews presented a danger to the Manchester defence, but United were triumphant winning by 4 goals to 2 in a classic final.
Opposite: Manchester United captain Johnny Carey is carried on the shoulders of his enthusiastic team-mates after receiving the FA Cup from the King. Manchester had a difficult road to the Final, facing Division One teams in every round, the 6–4 defeat of Aston Villa in the third round being one of the highlights of the 1947-8 season.

Agonising wait for Liverpool

The first postwar FA Cup whetted the appetite for the return of league action. The 1946-47 fixture list replicated that of the aborted 1939-40 season, trying to give a semblance of continuity. Liverpool became the first postwar champions, inheriting the title Everton had won eight years earlier. At the beginning of the season the two clubs had both vied for the signature of Newcastle hotshot

Albert Stubbins. Both offered £12,500 and Stubbins is said to have opted for Anfield by tossing a coin. He proved his worth to the Reds, scoring 26 goals as Liverpool became involved in an exciting championship run-in.

The worst winter in living memory meant that the season ran into June. Liverpool went top after a 2-1 away win at Wolves, ending the latter's own title hopes. They then had an agonising two-week wait to see if Stoke could overhaul them by beating Sheffield United. The Potteries club lost and Liverpool were crowned champions for the fifth time.

Arsenal league champions

Opposite above left: Arsenal fans stream into Highbury. The Gunners topped the league in the 1947-48 season for the sixth time equalling the record set by Sunderland and Aston Villa.

Opposite above right: An enthusiastic Blackpool supporter gives vent to her feelings. Blackpool fans had much to be pleased about in the early 1950s having reached the FA Cup Final in 1948 and 1951 before winning in 1953. Both Mortensen and Matthews were stalwarts of the England team and Matthews was winner of the first Footballer of the Year award in 1948.

Opposite below: Middlesbrough gives Chelsea an anxious moment at Stamford Bridge in 1948.

Above: Players rush to the rescue as Arsenal team-mates Mercer and Leslie Compton collide during their match with Blackpool in 1949.

Left: Ben Fenton undergoes treatment by Charlton trainer Jimmy Trotter in 1949.

Third cup for Arsenal

Left: Fans queue overnight for tickets to the Arsenal v Spurs local derby in 1949. Although intense rivals the teams had shared Spurs' ground at White Hart Lane during the war when Highbury was used as a first-aid post and ARP centre.

Opposite above: Arsenal, the 1950 Cup winners, parade the trophy in Islington after defeating Liverpool 2-0, both goals scored by Reg Lewis. The Gunners were the first club to reach Wembley without playing outside their own city and the first to allow their players to spend the night before the Final at home.

Opposite below: Goring scores the first of Arsenal's goals against Manchester City in their 4-1 victory in April 1950.

Jackie Milburn

Few Newcastle United players are held in greater affection by the fans than Jackie Milburn, or "Wor Jackie" as he was known. A gifted centre-forward, Milburn had a winger's pace, having played out on the flanks in his early days. This talent, combined with his great shooting power and brilliance in the air made him the foremost central striker in the country in the 1950s.

Milburn achieved a scoring rate of a goal every other game with 178 goals in 11 years at the Tyneside club. He led the attack as Newcastle won the FA Cup three times in five seasons, in 1951, 1952 and 1955. He scored both goals in the team's 2-0 win over Blackpool in the 1951 FA Cup Final, and put away a classic header, rifled into the net just seconds into the game at Wembley to set up a 3-1 win over Manchester City four years later.

As the natural successor to Tommy Lawton in the England centre-forward position, Milburn scored 10 goals in his 13 international appearances. Part of a footballing family, with brothers who were also professionals; his nephews, Bobby and Jackie Charlton, were to follow him into the England team in the 1960s.

"Stop-gap" Mercer captains Arsenal to Cup glory

Arsenal won the league in 1947-48, and did so again five years later. The FA Cup also went to Highbury in 1950, but this was not a period of dominance to match the 1930s. The team included Joe Mercer and the Compton brothers, Denis and Leslie. Mercer had played in Everton's championship-winning side of 1939, and Arsenal regarded him as a short-term acquisition after the war. The irrepressible Mercer played on for eight seasons and was named Footballer of the Year in 1950, when he lifted the Cup as the Gunners' captain.

The Compton brothers could not have been more different. The flamboyant Denis played on the wing with a devil-may-care style. In that 1950 Wembley Final, against Liverpool, Compton was looking weary when someone handed him a tot of brandy. He perked up immediately and provided the cross which led to the second goal in Arsenal's 2-0 win.

Elder brother Leslie, a rugged centre-half, carved his name in the record books by winning his first cap for England at the age of 38 years 2 months, the oldest player to make his England debut.

Cup winners v League winners

Opposite: Arsenal pictured with the Cup before their match with Portsmouth in 1950. The south-coast team were league champions in two consecutive seasons finishing five points ahead of their nearest rivals Manchester United in the 1948-9 season. The margin was much tighter the following year when Portsmouth finished above Wolves on goal difference.

Right: An injured Nat Lofthouse is helped by nurses .

Nat Lofthouse

Nat Lofthouse remains a living legend at Bolton Wanderers, the club where he spent his entire playing career between 1946 and 1960. With 255 goals scored during that period, he is still the club's highest league scorer. A powerful centre-forward, he scored in every round of the FA Cup in the 1952-53 season, and although he finished on the losing side in the "Matthews Final", he had the consolation of picking up the Footballer of the Year award. Five years later he was on the winning side at Wembley, scoring both goals in Bolton's 2-1 win over a Manchester United side devastated by the Munich air disaster.

Lofthouse made 33 appearances in an England shirt, scoring an astonishing 30 goals, placing him joint third on the all-time list of England scorers. He is best remembered for his heroic contribution to England's victory away to Austria in the 1951-52 season. Having already scored one goal against the team ranked the best in Europe, he hit a second-half winner but was knocked unconscious in the process. His bravery and commitment earned him the tag the "Lion of Vienna".

Courageous Arsenal defeated
by Newcastle

Left: Arsenal keeper George Swindin stretches to reach the ball with Milburn and Robledo nearby in the 1952 Cup Final. Newcastle had high hopes of repeating the previous season's success when they defeated Blackpool by 2-0 in the Cup Final but eleven minutes before the whistle there was still no score. Arsenal struggled on valiantly, playing with 10 men from the 20th minute when Barnes was injured and despite the handicap had their chances to score. But the game was over when Newcastle's Robledo put the ball in the net with only minutes to go.
Above: Ernie Gregory, goalkeeper for West Ham, makes a save during the final training session before the start of the 1952-3 season.

Tom Finney

Dubbed the "Preston Plumber", Tom Finney was a brilliant ball-playing winger. A contemporary of Stanley Matthews, he shared many of Matthews' creative and skilful qualities. However, he was a much more versatile player; Matthews concentrated on being simply the best outside-right of his era. Finney was two-footed and could operate on either wing, and he also played as a central striker.

He played throughout his career for Preston North End and his 187 goals in 24 seasons for the club remains a record at Deepdale – testimony to his clinical finishing; but Finney was also a provider for other strikers. His loyalty to his home-town club probably cost him in terms of silverware, for he ended his illustrious career with no major honours.

Nevertheless, his talents did not go unnoticed and he earned 76 England caps. During his service for the national side he bagged 30 goals, setting a new record. Even now, on the list of all time record England scorers he lies at joint fifth, alongside Nat Lofthouse and Alan Shearer.

He received a rare footballing accolade in being twice named Footballer of the Year, in 1954 and 1957. And Bill Shankly, a former team-mate, once famously said that Finney would have been brilliant in any era, 'even if he'd been wearing an overcoat'. Rewarded for his loyalty to Preston and his services to football, Tom Finney became club president at Deepdale, and was knighted in 1998.

Left: 1953 Cup Winners Blackpool appear on the popular TV show What's My Line?
Opposite: Argentina score against England at Wembley when the teams meet for the first time in May 1951. Argentina's defence held on to their 1-0 lead until Mortensen equalised from a header and Milburn hit the back of the net 10 minutes before time.
Above: Tom Finney trains with the England team at Stamford Bridge.

England back in FIFA fold

This period was also notable for England's return to the international fold. The hatchet was finally buried on the row with FIFA over payments to amateurs, a dispute going back to 1928. The reconciliation was celebrated with a match between a Great Britain XI and a side representing Europe. Wilf Mannion was the star of the show, hitting a hat-trick, with Tommy Lawton grabbing a brace. Great Britain won the match 6-1.

In May 1947 England went to Lisbon and thrashed Portugal 10-0, debutant Stan Mortensen hitting four goals. In the next 12 months there were wins over Belgium and Sweden, and a dazzling 4-0 victory over Italy in Turin. Such results no doubt suggested to some that England were ready to reassume their position as world-beaters. The 1950s would disabuse the optimists of any such feelings.

England make their World Cup debut

Throughout the 1950s, when he was well into his 30s, Stanley Matthews remained a regular in the international side. In 1950 he got his chance to grace a World Cup, along with stars such as Mannion, Mortensen, Milburn, Wright and Finney. FIFA declared that the home international championship would constitute a qualifying group for the tournament, which was staged in Brazil. England won, and Scotland also earned a place as runners-up. The Scots declined, however, one of a number of withdrawals. Other notable absentees included Hungary, Austria, Germany, France and Russia. Just 13 teams took part in the competition, and England were installed as joint-favourites.

England are World Cup favourites.

Lawton signs for Third Division side

The shock of the 1947-48 season occurred off the pitch, when Chelsea and England centre-forward Tommy Lawton moved to Third Division Notts County in a record £20,000 deal. County quickly began recouping their huge investment with gates of 30,000, a three-fold increase on what they were used to. Lawton subsequently moved on to Brentford, and looked set for a career in management. But the man who had inherited Dixie Dean's mantle made a dramatic return to the top flight with Arsenal, and showed that even in his mid-30s he was still a fearsome competitor. His 231 league goals came in at well under a goal every other game, and he scored 23 goals for England in just 22 full internationals.

Lawton returns to the top flight

Busby's first trophy

In the first five postwar seasons Manchester United finished Division One runners-up four times, and fourth on the other occasion. The club finally got its hands on some silverware by winning the Cup in 1948. United twice came from behind against Blackpool to win 4-2, a match that was described as a classic for the purists. Blackpool's Stanley Matthews, who had been honoured with the inaugural Footballer of the Year award, was now 33 and all neutrals wanted to see him get a winners' medal. But two goals from Jack Rowley helped United to victory and ended the "Wizard of the Dribble" hopes for another year.

Matt Busby had inherited some good players when he took over as manager at Old Trafford in October 1945. He also bought wisely and moulded a side which was immediately challenging for top honours. The team was led by Johnny Carey, who played in every position except left-wing. Carey also had the unusual distinction of having played for both the Republic of Ireland and Northern Ireland, the latter thanks to his service in the British Army.

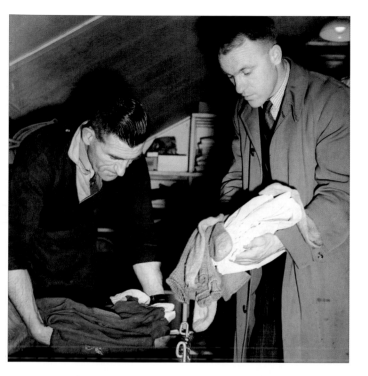

Opposite left: Tommy Lawton playing for Chelsea in 1946 before his departure for Third Division Notts County the following year. Lawton soon returned to top-flight football, signing for Arsenal at the start of the 1953-4 season. The Gunners had just won a record seventh league title but manager Tom Whittaker realised the need to bring new blood into the team.

Below: Stanley Matthews is presented to the Duke of Edinburgh before the 1953 Cup Final. It looked as though Matthews would be on the losing side for the third time when Blackpool was trailing 3-1 at the end of the first half. However, after the break Bolton faded and Blackpool's Mortensen scored 2 so that the teams were level at the start of injury time. In the final moments of the game Perry crashed the ball into the net and Blackpool won a thrilling 4-3 victory. A crowd of 200,000 lined the streets to welcome the team home.

Left: Tommy McBain (left) and Bill Shankly pack the Carlisle team kit before setting off for a Cup- tie.

"The Matthews Final"

If Manchester United and Wolves were the most consistent performers in the league during this period, Newcastle United were the most successful Cup side. Spearheaded by Jackie Milburn - "Wor Jackie" - and George Robledo, Newcastle won the Cup three times in five years. Blackpool were the first of their Wembley victims in 1951. Two goals from Milburn won the match, leaving Stanley Matthews to rue yet another missed opportunity.

Blackpool made it to Wembley again in 1953, their third appearance in six seasons. Trailing 3-1 to Bolton with 20 minutes left, it looked like a third agonising defeat. But in this most dramatic of all finals Blackpool drew level. Matthews crossed for Mortensen to score, and three minutes from time Mortensen crashed home a free-kick to level. With extra time looming, Matthews weaved yet another piece of magic on the right wing and crossed for Perry to rifle the ball into the net. The 38-year-old maestro finally got his hands on an FA Cup winners' medal, and the match would be forever known as the "Matthews Final".

The winning goal

Left: Lofthouse opens the scoring for Bolton after 90 seconds as the ball flies past Farm and into the net.
Opposite: The winning goal: while the tremendous crowd urges him on, the "Wizard of the Dribble", Stanley Matthews, streaks down the wing to beat Bolton's Wheeler (4), and puts the ball across to Bill Perry who scored the fourth and winning goal giving Blackpool the FA Cup and Matthews his first winners' medal.
Below: Matthews pictured in 1952, 22 years after his debut for Stoke.

Stanley Matthews

Stanley Matthews enjoyed a playing career spanning 32 years 10 months and was over 50 by the time he retired from top-class football. He is the oldest player ever to appear in English football's top flight. He is also the oldest England player, winning his last cap, at the age of 42, against Denmark in May 1957. He did not score in that match but his last goal in an international came against Northern Ireland in October 1956; he was 41 years 248 days, making him the oldest player to score for England. While it is conceivable that some of his records might be broken, it is inconceivable that Stanley Matthews' achievements will ever be eclipsed.

At the age of 15 Matthews joined his local side Stoke City and made his debut two years later. Matthews spent 17 years at the club, establishing himself as the best outside-right in world football and earning himself the tag "Wizard of the Dribble".

In his debut game for England in September 1934, he scored, helping the side to a 4-0 win over Wales. This was the start of a 20-year international career during which he won 84 caps, playing in the 1950 and 1954 World Cups. In the 1950 tournament in Brazil Matthews missed the humiliating 1-0 defeat at the hands of the USA; the selectors had decided to alternate Matthews and Tom Finney on the right wing and it was Finney who played that day in Belo Horizonte.

In 1947, Matthews joined Blackpool in a £11,500 transfer deal, but found himself on the losing side in the FA Cup Finals of 1948 and 1951. When Blackpool made it to Wembley again in 1953, all neutral supporters hoped he would finally get a winners' medal. Things looked bleak when opponents Bolton went 3-1 ahead, but 38-year-old Matthews inspired a terrific comeback, Blackpool triumphing as 4-3 winners. The match went down in footballing annals as "the Matthews Final".

Matthews was 46 when he left Blackpool, in October 1961, but incredibly he chose to return to Stoke as a player rather than retire. Four more years at the Potteries club saw Matthews play his last competitive match on 6 February 1965, five days after his 50th birthday. He had just received a knighthood in the New Year's Honours List and went out in style, with a 3-1 win over Fulham.

Matthews was twice Footballer of the Year, in 1948 and 1963, and was also the inaugural European Footballer of the Year in 1956. He died in February 2000, aged 85.

Shock defeat by USA

After a 2-0 win over Chile, England took on the USA in Belo Horizonte. The Americans rode their luck and scored the only goal of the game, a header by Larry Gaetjens. Matthews didn't play in the game that would go down as the blackest moment in England's 80 years of international football. The selectors decided that he and Finney should alternate on the right wing, an extraordinary decision given the fact that Finney was equally potent on the left or through the middle. Matthews returned for the last group match, but even his magic couldn't save the day. A 1-0 defeat by Spain wrapped up a miserable World Cup debut, and England didn't even stay to watch the remaining matches.

Magyars teach England a lesson

Any doubts that England were no longer guaranteed a place at football's top table were ended three years later, when a brilliant Hungary side came to Wembley. The Mighty Magyars, including Puskas, Hidegkuti and Kocsis, taught England a painful lesson in a match that ended 6-3. It was the country's first defeat on home soil. A return match in Budapest six months later showed it was no fluke; Hungary won that encounter 7-1. England full-back Alf Ramsey had witnessed this 13-goal fusillade at close quarters. It was an experience which left an indelible memory on him and would inform his views when he turned his thoughts to management.

First international defeat on home soil.

At the 1954 World Cup England went down 4-2 to reigning champions Uruguay at the quarter-final stage. In Sweden four years later, Walter Winterbottom was hampered by the loss of the Manchester United stars killed in the Munich disaster. England finished level on points with Russia and the two teams had to play off for the right to go through with Brazil. Russia won 1-0; England's third World Cup ended in disappointment once again.

Left: Billy Wright and Hungarian captain Puskas exchange flags before the start of their Wembley clash in November 1953. England's record of never having been beaten at home by a Continental team was shattered when the Magyars scored six goals with only three in reply.
Above: England's goalkeeper lies prostrate as Johnston retrieves the ball from the net after Hungary scored for the fourth time.

FA Cup Finals

1946	Derby County	v	Charlton Athletic	4-1
1947	Charlton Athletic	v	Burnley	1-0
1948	Manchester Utd	v	Blackpool	4-2
1949	Wolverhampton W	v	Leicester	3-1
1950	Arsenal	v	Liverpool	2-0
1951	Newcastle United	v	Blackpool	2-0
1952	Newcastle United	v	Arsenal	1-0
1953	Blackpool	v	Bolton W.	4-3
1954	West Bromwich A.	v	Preston N. E.	3-2
1955	Newcastle United	v	Manchester City	3-1
1956	Manchester City	v	Birmingham City	3-1
1957	Aston Villa	v	Manchester United	2-1
1958	Bolton Wanderers	v	Manchester United	2-0
1959	Nottingham Forest	v	Luton Town	2-1

The England International football team as they appeared in a friendly match against the Rest of Europe at Wembley on October 21 1953, when they drew 4-4. Alf Ramsey is second from the left in the back row, and Stanley Matthews is on the far left of the front row.

Opposite below: Captains peer into the pitch for the result of the toss prior to the kick-off of the match between Russian side Spartak and Arsenal. Contact between English and Continental clubs was growing but Chelsea, league champions in 1955, did not take part in the newly-established European Cup. Matt Busby's Manchester United was to enter the competition the following year.

Above: Manchester United's Taylor jumps to convert a corner but is beaten by the Birmingham keeper in 1955.

Left: The captains lead out their teams at Wembley in 1955. In a repeat of the 1952 final Newcastle's opponents, this time Manchester City, were forced to play a man short for most of the 90 minutes. Newcastle won 3-1 and collected the trophy for the sixth time.

Milestones 1945-1959

1945 With Old Trafford a bomb site, Matt Busby is appointed manager of Manchester United

1946 Walter Winterbottom becomes the first National Coach

33 spectators are killed when crowd barriers collapse at a Cup tie between Bolton and Stoke City

England rejoins FIFA after the dispute in 1928

England teams up with the other home nations to field a one-off postwar National side against the Rest of Europe resulting in a 6-1 victory for Great Britain

Derby County win the first FA Cup in the aftermath of the war by beating Charlton Athletic 4-1 in the Final

1947 First £20,000 transfer – Tommy Lawton from Chelsea to Notts County

Charlton beat Burnley 1-0 in the FA Cup Final

1948 Blackpool's Stanley Matthews wins the first Football Writers' Association Footballer of the Year award

1949 1,272,155 spectators make a record Football League attendance on 27th December

Fred Wall and Stanley Rous are knighted for their services to football

Sports Report is broadcast by BBC Radio for the first time

1950 The Football League increases the number of clubs from 88 to 92

England competes in the World Cup for the first time. The event is held in Brazil, but won by Uruguay and England fail to clear the group stages

Portsmouth wins the league championship for a second consecutive year, the unexpected postwar success of the club was because the team was joined by many ex-servicemen stationed in the town

1951 The increased use of floodlights, which were banned between 1930 and 1950, prompted the introduction of the white football

1953 Hungary beat England 6-3 at Wembley, England's first official defeat on home soil

1954 UEFA, Union of European Football Associations is formed

Fifth World Cup competition is held in Switzerland and won by West Germany - England compete but lose to Uruguay in the quarter finals

England suffers its biggest ever defeat when Hungary win 7-1 in Budapest

1955 First floodlit England international – England v Spain at Wembley

First floodlit FA Cup-tie between Brierley Hill and Kidderminster

Birmingham City becomes the first English club to participate in a European competition when it entered the Inter-City Fairs Cup (now UEFA Cup) reaching the semi finals but losing to Barcelona

1956 Portsmouth v Newcastle becomes the first league game to be played under floodlights

Real Madrid wins the first European Cup; there were no British teams in the 16 teams participating in the competition after Chelsea were instructed to decline the invitation to compete

ITV's first televised game is a Cup-tie between Bedford Town and Arsenal

1957 Juventus buy John Charles from Leeds for a record £67,000

Manchester United is the first British team to enter the European Cup competition

Chelsea become the first team to be transported to a league match by aeroplane when they travelled up to meet Newcastle

Jimmy Hill is elected as Chairman of the Professional Footballers' Association

1958 Sixth World Cup held in Sweden; the competition won by Brazil after England lost to the USSR in the play-offs between the group stage runners-up. This tournament became the first World Cup to be televised

Everton introduce under-soil heating to protect pitch from frost, the first club to do so

Manchester United lose 8 of their players as the team's plane crashes at Munich Airport on the return flight from a European Cup match against Red Star Belgrade

1959 Billy Wright, the England captain wins his 100th international cap and retires on 105

The Third Division North and South divide is scrapped in favour of one, national Third Division

The "Babes" make their bow

By 1950 the Manchester United side was ageing. There was also disquiet in the ranks as some of the players wanted the club to break the wage cap so that they could cash in during the twilight of their careers. Busby refused, and had already set his sights on a major rebuilding job. He was nurturing a crop of excellent youngsters at the Old Trafford academy, and these represented the future. The old guard had one last moment of glory, finally taking the title in 1951-52. The championship was secured with a 6-1 win over Arsenal, who themselves had a mathematical chance of winning the league. Afterwards, the transition process gathered pace. 18-year-old Jackie Blanchflower and 21-year-old Roger Byrne were the first to make the

Busby begins building process

breakthrough into the senior side, in November 1951. A local journalist commented that the "babes" had acquitted themselves well and, much to Busby's annoyance, this celebrated term soon became part of footballing folklore.

No stars proves no handicap for Pompey

While the Busby Babes were busy winning the FA Youth Cup five years in succession and slowly being incorporated into the first team, other sides were grabbing the headlines. Portsmouth peaked for two marvellous seasons, winning back-to-back championships in 1949 and 1950. The team had no real stars, not even an international in their line-up, showing that an outstanding unit could more than compensate for individual brilliance. The season in which they retained their crown, 1949-50, saw Pompey edge out Wolves on goal average. But as Portsmouth's bubble burst - they would be a Division Two side by the end of the decade - Wolves went on to rival Manchester United as the team of the era.

Above: Brazil's number 8, Valente, walks away with the ball followed by his team-mates and the referee after a penalty was awarded against the South Americans when they played England in May 1956. The Brazilians entertained the crowd with their ball skills but England won by 4 goals to 2, scoring two within the first few minutes of the game.
Opposite above: Luton play Leicester in particularly difficult conditions.

Long-ball game reaps dividends for Wolves

Unlike Busby, who encouraged his talented players to express themselves, Wolves boss Stan Cullis favoured a much more regimented approach. He regarded over-elaboration as a sin. The emphasis was was on getting the ball as quickly and as often as possible into the opposition's box. Some denigrated this tactic as simply "kick and rush", yet it reaped considerable dividends. Anchoring the side was the redoubtable Billy Wright, who would go on to make nearly 500 appearances in the famous Old Gold shirt. Wright set a new world record by making 70 consecutive international appearances, and he went on to become the first England player to win one hundred caps.

Wright makes 70 consecutive appearances for England

Apart from the championships of 1954, 1958 and 1959, Wolves also enjoyed some sparkling triumphs over top European opposition. In two memorable floodlit matches during the 1954-55 season Wolves came out on top against Moscow Spartak and a Honved side that boasted Puskas, Kocsis and several other members of Hungary's all-star team. As Honved were regarded as the supreme club side of the day, Cullis was quick to acclaim his men as world champions. This piece of self-publicity is said to have prompted Gabriel Hanot, a sports reporter with L'Equipe, to seek support for his idea to stage a cup competition for Europe's leading clubs. UEFA quickly took the idea on board and in September 1955 the first European Cup matches were held.

Drake makes history at Chelsea

Wolves could only finish runners-up in 1954-55, and it was Chelsea who earned the right to play in the first Champions Cup. Under pressure from the Football League, who were concerned that the new competition would undermine the domestic programme, Chelsea declined to enter. The only league success in the club's history did earn a special place in the record books, however. Ted Drake had won the championship with Arsenal in the 1930s and had now repeated that success as a manager, the first man to do that particular double.

Above: England and Russia line up at Wembley before the start of the international in October 1956, which the home team won by 5 goals to nil.
Below: John Charles trains with his brother Mel who also represented Wales.
Opposite: Jackie Henderson, signed twenty-four hours previously from Wolves for £18,000, paid dividends to his new club Arsenal when he scored a goal against West Bromwich Albion just ten minutes into the match.

John Charles

One of the first British players to ply his trade on the Continent, John Charles was dubbed "The Gentle Giant" by Juventus fans, the club he joined in 1957. It was an affectionate and appropriate nickname, for Charles, with a magnificent physique, was a strong and powerful footballer. Yet, despite his strength and the many physical battles he fought in a 16-year career, both as a centre-half and centre-forward, he was never once booked.

Charles began his career at Leeds United as a central defender. It was in the 1953-54 season that he showed his credentials as a striker, hitting 42 league goals for Leeds, a record to this day.

When he joined Juventus for a record £67,000, he made an immediate impact, hitting 28 goals in 34 games in his first season in Italy. He became Serie A's top marksman and his goals helped Juve to win the Italian championship. By the time he left Italy in 1962, he had a tally of 93 goals in 155 games. During Charles's five years at the club Juventus won the league title three times and the cup twice.

He became the youngest player ever to be capped for Wales. Even though he had played only a few games for Leeds, he was picked to join the line-up for what turned out to be a goalless draw against Northern Ireland at Wrexham on 8 March 1950; he was just 18 years 71 days old. Although he missed Wales's greatest moment in international football, Charles was a key figure in his country's achievement in reaching the quarter-finals of the 1958 World Cup. An injury sustained during a tough play-off battle with Hungary meant that Wales had to face the competition's eventual winners, Brazil, without Charles, going down 1-0.

After a spell back at Elland Road, Charles wound down his career with Roma and Cardiff City.

Duncan Edwards

Duncan Edwards was the jewel in the crown of the young and gifted Manchester United side that Matt Busby fashioned in the 1950s – the "Busby Babes" as they became known. Edwards came into the side as a half-back, but his athleticism and all-round ability meant that his influence spread all over the pitch. His tragic death from injuries sustained in the 1958 Munich air crash robbed football of what undoubtedly would have been one of the most outstanding players in the world game in the 1960s; he would probably have figured in the 1966 World Cup, when he would have been 29 years old.

Honours came early to Edwards. He made his debut for Manchester United at the age of 16, winning two championship medals, in 1956 and 1957 with Busby's talented team. When he won his first England cap in 1955 in a 7-2 victory over Scotland, he was just 18 years and 183 days old, a record which stood for more than 40 years until Michael Owen's England debut against Chile in February 1998. In his sadly short career, Edwards notched up 18 caps and scored five goals.

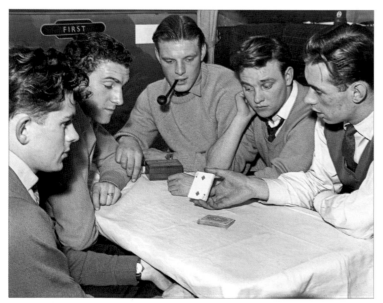

Above: Duncan Edwards, one of the central figures in Matt Busby's new team. United won the league in 1952 but Busby looked towards the future, devoting attention to finding a new crop of juniors who could be moulded to make formidable unit. By 1956 this new team was ready to compete on the world stage, and Busby had bought just three players: Taylor, Berry and Ray Wood.

Left: Members of the Manchester United team travel from Blackpool to London in 1957 (l-r: McGuinness, Foulkes, Jones, Colman and Wood).

Opposite left: The young Chelsea player, Jimmy Greaves, in training for his match against Wolverhampton in October 1957.

Opposite right: 1957: At Goodison Park engineers of the Merseyside and North Wales Electricity Board lay the first turf-warming system six inches below the surface of the pitch at a cost of £7000.

United romp to title by 11 points

Chelsea's decision to decline to enter the 1956 competition meant that Manchester United became the country's first champions to contest the European Cup. Busby's team earned the right by romping to the 1955-56 title by 11 points, equalling the biggest winning margin in the league's 68-year history. When Dennis Viollet scored the only goal of the match against Portsmouth on 21 April 1956, United were uncatchable.

By now the pieces of the jigsaw were all in place. Duncan Edwards had made his debut as a 16-year-old in 1953, with Tommy Taylor moving to Old Trafford from Barnsley in the same year for £29,999. Busby deliberately pitched the deal just short of £30,000 to try and ease the anxiety that might have accompanied a big-money move. Mark Jones, Eddie Colman, David Pegg and Bobby Charlton were others among the precociously talented crop of young players that Busby had assembled. In four years he had transformed a veteran side into one in which the average age was just 22.

Duncan Edwards makes his debut

"Push and run" brings success to Spurs

United retained their crown the following season, finishing eight points ahead of Tottenham. In style the Spurs side was closer to United than Wolves. Under Arthur Rowe the team had developed a marvellous "push and run" technique, which had brought the club the championship in 1951. Bill Nicholson and Alf Ramsey were members of that side, and the former joined the coaching staff at White Hart Lane when he finished playing. Spurs were also twice runners-up in the 1950s but their greatest moment, with Nicholson at the helm, still lay ahead.

United's European dream ended by Real Madrid

Meanwhile, United's first sortie into European competition ended at the semi-final stage, when they were beaten by holders Real Madrid. Tommy Taylor and Bobby Charlton earned United a 2-2 draw at Old Trafford, not enough to overturn a 3-1 defeat at the Bernebeu Stadium. Busby wasn't unduly worried. Earlier in the competition his team had beaten Anderlecht 12-0 on aggregate, and also put out Borussia Dortmund and Atletico Bilbao before going out to the best side in Europe. Youth was on United's side and they would be even stronger the following season.

"Villain" McParland makes it seven Cup wins

Before then there was the prospect of the coveted Double. Having wrapped up the league, United faced Aston Villa in the FA Cup Final. The key moment came after just six minutes, when Villa's Peter McParland clattered into United keeper Ray Wood, breaking the latter's cheekbone. Jackie Blanchflower took over in goal, badly disrupting United's rhythm. McParland rubbed salt into United's wounds by scoring both Villa goals in a 2-1 win. It was Villa's seventh victory, a record for the competition.

The incident involving Wood was one of a succession of injuries which cast a shadow over Wembley Finals in the 1950s. In 1956 Manchester City keeper Bert Trautmann suffered a broken neck in the 3-1 win over Birmingham City. In 1959 Nottingham Forest winger Roy Dwight was carried off with a broken leg, and Blackburn full-back Dave Whelan suffered the same injury a year later. Some dubbed it the "Wembley hoodoo", while others put the number of injuries down to the fact that the turf was too soft.

Right: Aston Villa goalkeeper Sims leaps but fails to stop Taylor's strike in the closing minutes of the 1957 Cup Final. A head-on charge by Villa's McParland on the Manchester goalkeeper left Wood unable to continue playing in goal. Despite the valiant efforts of Jackie Blanchflower who took his place, Manchester, playing with ten men, could not overcome the Villa defence.

Above: Villa captain Johnny Dixon holds the trophy aloft.

Opposite below: Manchester United's Cup finalists in 1957. Busby's team narrowly failed to win the trophy but had topped the league at the end of 1956 and 1957, qualifying for the embryonic European Cup. Playing against the wishes of the FA, United reached the semi-finals of the competition, eventually being knocked out by Real Madrid. (l-r, Inglis, Geoff Bent, Ray Wood, Mark Jones, Billy Foulkes, Dennis Viollet and Tom Curry. Front row: Jackie Blanchflower, Colin Webster, Wilf McGuinness, Tommy Taylor, Bill Whelan and David Pegg. With ball: Johnny Berry)

Eight United players killed in Munich tragedy

On 1 February 1958 United went to Highbury and won a sparkling match 5-4. The result kept them in second place in the league, looking ominously good to equal Huddersfield's and Arsenal's achievement of a hat-trick of championships. The team then headed to Belgrade to take on Red Star in the second leg of their European Cup-tie. Having won 2-1 at home, a 3-3 draw was enough to put United into the semis once again. On the return journey the plane stopped to refuel at Munich. In atrocious weather two attempted take-offs were aborted. The third attempt ended in disaster, the plane failing to get off the ground and slewing into the perimeter fence. There were 23 fatalities, including seven of the Babes. An eighth, Duncan Edwards, lost his battle for life two weeks later. Johnny Berry and Jackie Blanchflower survived but never played football again.

No sentiment as United go down fighting

The heart had been ripped out of United, yet amazingly, a side made up of reserve and youth team players, together with a couple of emergency signings, reached that year's FA Cup Final. There was no fairytale, however; two goals from Nat Lofthouse won the trophy for Bolton Wanderers.

Some suggested that the European Cup should be awarded to United as a mark of respect to the great players who had perished at Munich. But sentiment was not allowed to prevail and United's semi-final clash with AC Milan went ahead as scheduled. United lost 5-2 on aggregate. Having built two championship-winning sides, Busby immediately set about creating a third.

Having built two championship-winning sides, Busby immediately set about creating a third.

League Division One 1947-1959

1946-1947

1	Liverpool	57
2	Manchester United	56
3	Wolverhampton W.	56
4	Stoke	55
5	Blackpool	50
6	Sheffield United	49
7	Preston	47
8	Aston Villa	45
9	Sunderland	44
10	Everton	43
11	Middlesbrough	42
12	Portsmouth	41
13	Arsenal	41
14	Derby County	41
15	Chelsea	39
16	Grimsby	38
17	Blackburn Rovers	36
18	Bolton Wanderers	34
19	Charlton Athletic	34
20	Huddersfield	33
21	Brentford	25
22	Leeds United	18

1947-48

1	Arsenal	59
2	Manchester United	52
3	Burnley	52
4	Derby County	50
5	Wolverhampton W.	47
6	Aston Villa	47
7	Preston	47
8	Portsmouth	45
9	Blackpool	44
10	Manchester City	42
11	Liverpool	42
12	Sheffield United	42
13	Charlton Athletic	40
14	Everton	40
15	Stoke	38
16	Middlesbrough	37
17	Bolton Wanderers	37
18	Chelsea	37
19	Huddersfield	36
20	Sunderland	36
21	Blackburn Rovers	32
22	Grimsby	22

1948-49

1	Portsmouth	58
2	Manchester United	53
3	Derby County	53
4	Newcastle United	52
5	Arsenal	49
6	Wolverhampton W.	46
7	Manchester City	45
8	Sunderland	43
9	Charlton Athletic	42
10	Aston Villa	42
11	Stoke	41
12	Liverpool	40
13	Chelsea	38
14	Bolton Wanderers	38
15	Burnley	38
16	Blackpool	38
17	Birmingham City	37
18	Everton	37
19	Middlesbrough	34
20	Huddersfield	34
21	Preston	33
22	Sheffield United	33

1949-50

1	Portsmouth	53
2	Wolverhampton W.	53
3	Sunderland	52
4	Manchester United	50
5	Newcastle United	50
6	Arsenal	49
7	Blackpool	49
8	Liverpool	48
9	Middlesbrough	47
10	Burnley	45
11	Derby County	44
12	Aston Villa	42
13	Chelsea	40
14	West Bromwich Albion	40
15	Huddersfield	37
16	Bolton Wanderers	34
17	Fulham	34
18	Everton	34
19	Stoke	34
20	Charlton Athletic	32
21	Manchester City	29
22	Birmingham City	28

1950-51

1	Tottenham Hotspur	60
2	Manchester United	56
3	Blackpool	50
4	Newcastle United	49
5	Arsenal	47
6	Middlesbrough	47
7	Portsmouth	47
8	Bolton Wanderers	45
9	Liverpool	43
10	Burnley	42
11	Derby County	40
12	Sunderland	40
13	Stoke	40
14	Wolverhampton W.	38
15	Aston Villa	37
16	West Bromwich Albion	37
17	Charlton Athletic	37
18	Fulham	37
19	Huddersfield	36
20	Chelsea	32
21	Sheffield Wednesday	32
22	Everton	32

1951-52

1	Manchester United	57
2	Tottenham Hotspur	53
3	Arsenal	53
4	Portsmouth	48
5	Bolton Wanderers	48
6	Aston Villa	47
7	Preston	46
8	Newcastle United	45
9	Blackpool	45
10	Charlton Athletic	44
11	Liverpool	43
12	Sunderland	42
13	West Bromwich Albion	41
14	Burnley	40
15	Manchester City	39
16	Wolverhampton W.	38
17	Derby County	37
18	Middlesbrough	36
19	Chelsea	36
20	Stoke	31
21	Huddersfield	28
22	Fulham	27

1952-53

1	Arsenal	54
2	Preston	54
3	Wolverhampton W.	51
4	West Bromwich Albion	50
5	Charlton Athletic	49
6	Burnley	48
7	Blackpool	47
8	Manchester United	46
9	Sunderland	43
10	Tottenham Hotspur	41
11	Aston Villa	41
12	Cardiff	40
13	Middlesbrough	39
14	Bolton Wanderers	39
15	Portsmouth	38
16	Newcastle United	37
17	Liverpool	36
18	Sheffield Wednesday	35
19	Chelsea	35
20	Manchester City	35
21	Stoke	34
22	Derby County	32

1953-54

1	Wolverhampton W.	57
2	West Bromwich Albion	53
3	Huddersfield	51
4	Manchester United	48
5	Bolton Wanderers	48
6	Blackpool	48
7	Burnley	46
8	Chelsea	44
9	Charlton Athletic	44
10	Cardiff	44
11	Preston	43
12	Arsenal	43
13	Aston Villa	41
14	Portsmouth	39
15	Newcastle United	38
16	Tottenham Hotspur	37
17	Manchester City	37
18	Sunderland	36
19	Sheffield Wednesday	36
20	Sheffield United	33
21	Middlesbrough	30
22	Liverpool	28

1954-55

1	Chelsea	52
2	Wolverhampton W.	48
3	Portsmouth	48
4	Sunderland	48
5	Manchester United	47
6	Aston Villa	47
7	Manchester City	46
8	Newcastle United	43
9	Arsenal	43
10	Burnley	43
11	Everton	42
12	Huddersfield	41
13	Sheffield United	41
14	Preston	40
15	Charlton Athletic	40
16	Tottenham Hotspur	40
17	West Bromwich Albion	40
18	Bolton Wanderers	39
19	Blackpool	38
20	Cardiff	37
21	Leicester City	35
22	Sheffield Wednesday	26

1955-56

1	Manchester United	60
2	Blackpool	49
3	Wolverhampton W.	49
4	Manchester City	46
5	Arsenal	46
6	Birmingham City	45
7	Burnley	44
8	Bolton Wanderers	43
9	Sunderland	43
10	Luton	42
11	Newcastle United	41
12	Portsmouth	41
13	West Bromwich Albion	41
14	Charlton Athletic	40
15	Everton	40
16	Chelsea	39
17	Cardiff	39
18	Tottenham Hotspur	37
19	Preston	36
20	Aston Villa	35
21	Huddersfield	35
22	Sheffield United	33

1956-57

1	Manchester United	64
2	Tottenham Hotspur	56
3	Preston	56
4	Blackpool	53
5	Arsenal	50
6	Wolverhampton W.	48
7	Burnley	46
8	Leeds United	44
9	Bolton Wanderers	44
10	Aston Villa	43
11	West Bromwich Albion	42
12	Birmingham City	39
13	Chelsea	39
14	Sheffield Wednesday	38
15	Everton	38
16	Luton	37
17	Newcastle United	36
18	Manchester City	35
19	Portsmouth	33
20	Sunderland	32
21	Cardiff	29
22	Charlton Athletic	22

1957-58

1	Wolverhampton W.	64
2	Preston	59
3	Tottenham Hotspur	51
4	West Bromwich Albion	50
5	Manchester City	49
6	Burnley	47
7	Blackpool	44
8	Luton	44
9	Manchester United	43
10	Nottingham Forest	42
11	Chelsea	42
12	Arsenal	39
13	Birmingham City	39
14	Aston Villa	39
15	Bolton Wanderers	38
16	Everton	37
17	Leeds United	37
18	Leicester City	33
19	Newcastle United	32
20	Portsmouth	32
21	Sunderland	32
22	Sheffield Wednesday	31

1958-59

1	Wolverhampton W.	61
2	Manchester United	55
3	Arsenal	50
4	Bolton Wanderers	50
5	West Bromwich Albion	49
6	West Ham United	48
7	Burnley	48
8	Blackpool	47
9	Birmingham City	46
10	Blackburn Rovers	44
11	Newcastle United	41
12	Preston	41
13	Nottingham Forest	40
14	Chelsea	40
15	Leeds United	39
16	Everton	38
17	Luton	37
18	Tottenham Hotspur	36
19	Leicester City	32
20	Manchester City	31
21	Aston Villa	30
22	Portsmouth	21

1959-60

1	Burnley	55
2	Wolverhampton W.	54
3	Tottenham Hotspur	53
4	West Bromwich Albion	49
5	Sheffield Wednesday	49
6	Bolton Wanderers	48
7	Manchester United	45
8	Newcastle United	44
9	Preston	44
10	Fulham	44
11	Blackpool	40
12	Leicester City	39
13	Arsenal	39
14	West Ham United	38
15	Everton	37
16	Manchester City	37
17	Blackburn Rovers	37
18	Chelsea	37
19	Birmingham City	36
20	Nottingham Forest	35
21	Leeds United	34
22	Luton	30

Structural problems highlighted

The experience of the 1950s showed that England would have to work hard to match the skills of the top Continental and South American sides. There were also structural and organisational problems. In 1950 Stanley Matthews was with an FA touring side in Canada when his team-mates arrived in Brazil. And when the food was discovered to be unpalatable, Winterbottom found himself in charge of the catering! In 1958 the team arrived in Sweden to find there were no training facilities, and Winterbottom had to chase round looking for a suitable venue. There was a minor step forward in that senior players were given a voice on selection matters, but overall the running of the international side left a lot to be desired. Success at international level could no longer be achieved with a part-time manager who had responsibility without power. It was not until the next decade that things changed dramatically for the better. A man of vision was brought in, and freed from the shackles of the Selection Committee he was able to put his ideas into practice.

Billy Wright

Born in 1924, Billy Wright was one of Wolverhampton Wanderers' heroes in the 1950s. Short, tough, and a powerful header of the ball, he was the defensive backbone of the side. Having started out as a PT instructor, he made his debut for Wolves in 1941, took over the captaincy in 1947 and retained that role for 12 seasons. They were the glory days of the club, with Wright leading the team to F.A. Cup victory in 1949, followed in 1953/54 by the first of three League Championships in six years.

He began his international career in 1946, against Northern Ireland, and in 1959 he became the first player to reach 100 caps. Wright captained England in 90 of his 105 appearances, including three World Cups, in 1950, 1954 and 1958.

His last game for Wolves came in 1959, the year he married Joy Beverly of the Beverly Sisters and added a touch of glamour to what was already extraordinary popularity. After four years as manager of Arsenal, he became a sports journalist. He died in 1994.

Opposite above: Bobby Charlton on the training ground. Charlton, Viollet, Gregg and Foulkes were all fit to represent Manchester United in the 1958 FA Cup Final just months after the Munich disaster. Despite a spirited fight by United, Bolton won the match by 2 goals to nil.

Opposite below: Charlton scored the decisive goal from a header when England defeated Scotland by 1 goal to nil at Wembley on 11 April 1959. England captain Billy Wright celebrated receiving his 100th international cap, appearing as captain for the 85th time.

Above: Billy Wright waves to the crowd as he leads out the England team. Wright's contribution to international football was matched by his dedication to his club, Wolves, who finished top of the league in 1954, 1958 and 1959.

Left: An incident at Stamford Bridge. Spectators ran on to the pitch after Everton inside-left Collins had brought down Chelsea's Blunstone in a tackle.

A brilliant save by Springett, the Sheffield Wednesday goalkeeper, covered closely by Johnson, his right back, stops a shot by Clapton for Arsenal during the match at Highbury in August 1959. The new season got off to a bright start for the newly promoted Wednesday who defeated Arsenal by 1 goal to nil.

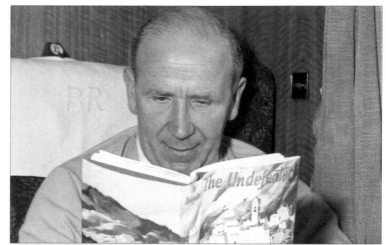

Sir Matt Busby

Matt Busby built three brilliant championship-winning sides in a glorious 26-year reign at Old Trafford. Busby spent his playing career at two of United's arch-rivals, neighbours Manchester City and Liverpool, winning an FA Cup winners medal with City in 1934.

He took over at Old Trafford after the Second World War and built a side which finished runners-up four times in five years. The title finally arrived in 1951-52, adding to an FA Cup victory over Blackpool in 1948.

As that ageing side was broken up, Busby scoured the country for the finest young players in the land. By the mid-1950s his outstanding young team, dubbed the "Busby Babes", looked as if it would dominate football for many years. There were successive league championships in 1956 and 1957. The team also twice made it to the sem-fiinals of the fledgling European Cup competition. It was on a return trip from a successful European quarter-final tie against Red Star Belgrade that the side was all but wiped out. Eight players lost their lives at Munich on 6 February 1958, and Busby himself was given last rites. He recovered to build yet another superb side in the 1960s. The likes of George Best and Denis Law were added to Munich survivors Bobby Charlton and Bill Foulkes. United lifted the FA Cup in 1963 and won the championship in 1965 and 1967. The latter success gave Busby yet another crack at the trophy he desperately wanted to win. The realisation of a long-held dream came at Wembley on 29 May 1968, when his side beat Benfica 4-1 in the European Cup Final. Busby became only the second British club manager to win the trophy. He was knighted for his achievements in the same year, retiring three years later. Busby died in 1994, an avid watcher of his beloved United right up to the end.

1960-1969
The World Stage

As the new decade got into its stride football faced a number of problems. Hooliganism, corruption and falling gates all gave cause for concern. On the pitch there was a marked increase in foul play, and fewer goals were scored as defences got on top. On a brighter note, Matt Busby built his third great side, English clubs made the breakthrough in European competition and the national side were crowned world champions.

Changing attitudes

By the 1960s people were enjoying greater affluence and had many more options when it came to spending their "leisure pound". The demand for cars and foreign holidays went up, while every form of entertainment had to compete with television. In the Swinging Sixties England was at the cutting edge of the pop music and fashion industries, and these were yet more diversions as the Baby Boomers came of age. There was also a distinct change in attitude, women no longer being content with playing a domestic role while the menfolk went off to the match.

Fears over televised matches

The effect of all these factors was reflected in declining attendances, particularly for struggling clubs or those perceived as unglamorous. As the footballing authorities sought ways to encourage more people through the turnstiles, the one avenue they naturally fought shy of was the televising of matches. In 1960 negotiations between the Football League and the Independent Television Authority fell through over fears that broadcasting a live game might have an adverse effect on attendances. Concerns were not allayed by the proposal to schedule the matches so that they didn't clash with any other football taking place. Within a couple of years, however, the broadcasting companies persuaded the Football League that a highlights package would not be detrimental to the game, and indeed could help to generate more interest and a wider fan base.

When Match of the Day took to the airwaves in 1964, it quickly became an institution.

When *Match of the Day* took to the airwaves in 1964, it quickly became an institution. Television turned the top players into celebrities as well as sportsmen. The authorities' fears that TV would lead to an army of armchair fans proved largely unfounded. However, seeing the likes of Greaves, Charlton and St John in action on the small screen did persuade a considerable number to switch their allegiance or to forge a new one. In short, the glamour clubs flourished at the expense of the rest.

Right: Forwards Johnny Haynes, Bobby Smith and Jimmy Greaves on England duty.

Above: The score changes but the outcome is not in doubt at an exhibition match in May 1961. Commentators attributed England's recent run of victories to Walter Winterbottom's newly adopted 4-2-4 formation introduced in the face of current tactics.

Opposite: Jimmy Greaves scores his first league goal for Chelsea against Tottenham Hotspur.

Hill leads campaign to end wage cap

The cult of celebrity had another important knock-on effect: the rise of player power. In the early 1960s players became aware of their worth, and realised that they were being sorely undervalued. Before 1960 even the sport's greatest names reaped little financial reward for the pleasure they brought to millions of fans. After hanging up their boots there was no life of luxury. The lucky ones found alternative employment. Tommy Lawton and Hughie Gallacher both ended up on the dole, the latter committing suicide by throwing himself under a train in 1957. In that same year the Players Union got a new chairman, Fulham's Jimmy Hill. Hill led the campaign to end the wage cap which stood at £20 a week, £17 during the close season.

Haynes becomes first £100-a-week footballer

It took Hill four years to garner the support he needed to act. This was because the Players Union had been emasculated by mass resignations over the same issue more than 30 years earlier. In the depression of the 1920s the Union had been unable to prevent clubs from reducing the maximum wage to £8 a week. In the intervening years the Football League hardly condescended to meet with players' representatives. But in January 1961 the threat of strike action made the authorities sit up and take notice. In June of that year the maximum wage was abolished. England captain Johnny Haynes became the first £100-a-week footballer, his chairman Tommy Trinder declaring that he was delighted at finally being able to properly reward his star performer, who was worth every penny to the club.

Opposite below left: Tottenham stars Jimmy Greaves and Danny Blanchflower leave to play Benfica in the semi-final of the European Cup in March 1962. After losing 3-1 in Lisbon, Spurs played in a thrilling second leg and were narrowly defeated by 4 goals to 3.

Opposite below right: Fulham's Jimmy Hill and Parker of Everton find themselves in the net while the ball sails past in January 1960.

Above: Blackburn goalkeeper fails to save and Deeley scores a second goal for Wolves in the 1960 Final. Blackburn fans were disappointed when left-back Wheelan broke his leg forcing their team to play more than half the match with only 10 men. The game ended in a 3-0 win for Wolves.

Opposite above: Johnny Haynes, who succeeded Billy Wright as England captain, leads his team out of the tunnel.

Johnny Haynes

Johnny Haynes was ardently loyal to Fulham, his only club, and that loyalty cost him dearly in terms of honours. At the time – Haynes was at Craven Cottage from 1952 to 1969 – the club was either in the Second Division or struggling in the lower reaches of the First.

England captain

Despite playing for an unfashionable and relatively unsuccessful club, Haynes established himself in the England side in the mid-1950s. An inside-forward who was noted for his wonderful passing, Haynes was a regular on the scoresheet. In his 56 England appearances he bagged 18 goals and in 1959, took over the captaincy of the national side after Billy Wright's retirement. He was an essential player in both the 1958 and 1962 World Cups, helping England to the quarter-final in the latter tournament.

Soon after the World Cup in Chile, in 1962, a serious car crash ended his international career. But loyal to the end, he turned out for Fulham for another seven years. A reward for that loyalty and an indication of how valued Haynes was can be seen in the fact that he became the first £100-a-week footballer after the maximum wage was abolished in 1961. He ended his footballing days as player-manager of Durban City after emigrating to South Africa.

England 9 Scotland 3

The early form of the international side in the 1960s was encouraging. After defeats in Spain and Hungary, England went on a fine run in the next six games. They rattled in 40 goals, including an 8-0 home win over Mexico and a 9-0 victory in Luxembourg. But the outstanding result was undoubtedly the 9-3 demolition of Scotland on 15 April 1961. It was a strong Scotland side - including Law, Mackay and St John - which came to Wembley for what was the decider in the home international championship. A Greaves hat-trick, together with two goals each from Johnny Haynes and Bobby Smith, contributed towards the Scots' worst-ever result in international football.

Above top: Prolific scorer Jimmy Greaves lashes the ball into the net when England met Spain in October 1960.
Above: Haffey, Scotland's goalkeeper, is beaten by Bobby Smith's shot, England's fifth goal.
Opposite below: Haffey falls to the ground in despair as England scores a seventh.
Opposite above: Despite a run of successes, England's lacklustre performance in the 1962 World Cup spelled the end of Winterbottom's tenure as manager. Mindful of the need to make a good showing in the next World Cup to be staged in England, the FA employed new manager Alf Ramsey and granted him autonomy in team selection.

Ramsey takes over from Winterbottom

Performances such as these boded well for the 1962 World Cup in Chile, but the tournament proved to be something of a disappointment. England did reach the last eight, squeezing through their group after a win, a draw and a defeat, but they were unconvincing. After a 3-1 defeat against holders Brazil they were on their way home.

The tournament marked the end of Walter Winterbottom's 16-year reign as England manager. In came Alf Ramsey, who had worked wonders at Ipswich, although he was said to be only third choice for the job.

Defeats against France and Scotland got the new regime off to an inauspicious start. Even so, Ramsey was soon predicting victory in the 1966 World Cup. Despite home advantage, England were not fancied to do well. The international side had lost just four times on home soil against overseas opposition, but as the optimists rested their hopes on fortress Wembley, the doom-mongers pointed to England's World Cup record since 1950.

Eastham takes Newcastle to court

Clubs might have had to pay their top players more but they still had the whip hand by dint of the "retain-and-transfer" system that was in place. Under this arrangement players were bound to their clubs even at the end of their contracts. In 1963 England international George Eastham was seeking a move away from Newcastle United and challenged this restriction of his freedom in the courts. The ruling went in his favour, with the prevailing system condemned as an "unreasonable restraint of trade".

Opposite: Blanchflower lifts the Cup. Following in the footsteps of Preston and Aston Villa, Spurs become the first side to complete the Double since 1897. Nicholson's team had secured the league title in mid-April but had to wait three weeks before meeting Leicester in the Cup Final. Spurs won 2-0. Left: Bill Nicholson and Danny Blanchflower. Nicholson celebrated a personal double having played in the 1951 Tottenham side that won the league before going on to manage the team that triumphed ten years later. Above: 23 November 1963: Arsenal players wear black armbands and stand in silent tribute to the late President Kennedy before the start of their match against Blackpool. (l-r) Eastham, Barnwell, McCullogh, Anderson, Clarke, MacLeod, Strong, Brown, Baker, Ure and Furnell.

Spurs become the century's first Double winners

On the pitch the decade got off to a sparkling start as Bill Nicholson's Spurs side became the first of the century to achieve the Double. The strength of the side was epitomised by the two wing-halves: granite-hard Dave Mackay and the cultured, cerebral Danny Blanchflower. Spurs began with a record run of 11 straight wins, and their 31 victories in all was another league best. 66 points equalled Arsenal's total of 1931. The team banged in 115 goals, a postwar record, and that was before the incomparable Jimmy Greaves had joined the club. Nicholson thus became only the second man to win the championship as both player and manager. The season took its toll in the latter stages of the Cup. Spurs needed a replay to beat Division Two side Sunderland in the 6th round, and they were below par when they took on Leicester City at Wembley. But top scorer Bobby Smith and Terry Dyson both beat City keeper Gordon Banks and history was made. Following the Cup successes of 1901 and 1921, and the championship in 1951, fans were already noting the club's peculiar affinity with the second year of the decade.

Bill Nicholson

Bill Nicholson spent his entire career at Tottenham, joining the club as a 16-year-old. When his playing days were over, Nicholson became a coach under Arthur Rowe, the architect of the "push and run" side that had won the title in 1951. He took over as manager in 1959, and assembled a team which took Rowe's ideas to dazzling new heights. His team combined superb ball skills with steely resolve, featuring players of the stature of Blanchflower and Mackay. In 1960-61 he guided Spurs through a glorious campaign which saw the team win 31 of their 42 league games, scoring 115 goals in the process. They secured the championship by an eight-point margin, then beat Leicester City 2-0 in the FA Cup Final, despite going into the game with an injury-ravaged squad. No twentieth-century team had won the Double, and many thought the demands of the modern game meant that it was unachievable. Nicholson proved the doubters wrong.

Spurs retained the Cup the following season, and in 1963 Nicholson became the first manager of a British club to win a European trophy. Spurs beat holders Atletico Madrid 5-1 in the Cup Winners' Cup Final in Rotterdam. Victory over Chelsea in the 1967 FA Cup Final meant that Nicholson had brought the trophy to White Hart Lane three times in seven years.

Nicholson stepped down during the 1974-75 season but remained associated with the club into his 80s.

Cup Winners Cup takes off

Spurs kept the Cup the following year, beating Burnley 3-1 in the final, but slipped to third in the league. Their European Cup campaign ended at the semi-final stage, when they went down 4-3 on aggregate to holders Benfica. Retaining the Cup in 1962 gave Spurs entry into the following season's Cup Winners' Cup competition. This had been launched in 1960, the brainchild of a group of European Football Federations. In just two seasons it had made more impact than the third European trophy up for grabs, the Inter-Cities Fairs Cup. Under the rules of the Fairs Cup, which had been launched in the mid-1950s, industrial towns and cities competed with each other, matches arranged to coincide with trade fairs. This meant that the first two tournaments took five years to complete! Moreover, a city could enter a club side or a representative XI. Between 1955 and 1958 Barcelona beat a London side including Kelsey (Arsenal), Blanchflower (Spurs), Greaves (Chelsea) and Haynes (Fulham). By the mid-1960s the competition had severed its connections with trade fairs and become a sought-after trophy for the top European clubs who failed to win their domestic league or cup.

Danny Blanchflower

Danny Blanchflower joined Tottenham Hotspur from Aston Villa for £30,000 in 1954. Over the next ten years Blanchflower, an intelligent wing-half with a sharp tactical brain, became a legend at White Hart Lane. He was the brains and the driving force of the side which, in the 1960-61 season, won the much sought-after Double; he was the first captain of the century to lift both trophies in one season. Following on from that unparalleled success it was fitting that Blanchflower won his second Footballer of the Year award — only Tom Finney had managed that achievement at the time.

Blanchflower steered Spurs to FA Cup victory the following season, even getting on the scoresheet himself in the team's 3-1 win over Burnley in the Final at Wembley. In what was to be his last but one season before retirement, Blanchflower inspired Tottenham to a 5-1 win over Atletico Madrid in the European Cup Winners' Cup Final, becoming the first captain of a British side to lift a European trophy.

Blanchflower was born in Belfast and played 56 times for Northern Ireland, where he also took on the captain's role. His most memorable moment with the national side was probably in the 1958 World Cup, when he led the side to the quarter-finals. He died in 1993, aged 67.

Opposite below left: Adamson of Burnley and Fulham's Cook and O'Donnell go for the ball as the teams fight for a place in the 1962 Cup Final. Burnley finishes as runners-up, losing in the Final to Spurs.
Opposite above: Leicester's Gordon Banks in training.
Opposite below right: When Bill Shankly arrived at Anfield in 1959 his first task was to help Liverpool regain its place in the First Division, and this was achieved by the beginning of the 1962-3 season.
Top right: After 10 years with Spurs, Danny Blanchflower retired in 1964. Alan Mullery, bought from Fulham, was Nicholson's choice to fill the gap left by Blanchflower.
Top left: Dave Mckay and his fellow Spurs can't hide their astonishment as White's corner swings in without anyone touching it.
Above: Fulham's Johnny Haynes in action.

First British side to win European trophy

In 1962-63 Spurs became the first British side to win a European trophy when they lifted the Cup Winners' Cup. They put out Rangers, Slovan Bratislava and OFK Belgrade en route to the final, where they faced holders Atletico Madrid. Despite missing Mackay through injury, Spurs ran out 5-1 winners. The key moment came in the second half when Spurs were 2-1 up. Terry Dyson floated a cross into the box and it swirled over keeper Madinabeytia into the net.

Nicholson ends Greaves' Italian nightmare

Jimmy Greaves scored two of the goals that night in Rotterdam. Greaves had been one of a number of high-profile players lured to the Continent by a bigger wage-packet and better lifestyle. His time at AC Milan following an £80,000 move from Chelsea had not been a happy one and he was only too pleased when Bill Nicholson paid £99,999 to bring him back to the First Division. It was a British transfer record, although Nicholson kept it below the six-figure mark so that Greaves wouldn't be burdened with the tag of the first £100,000 player. Denis Law had an equally unhappy time after leaving Manchester City to join Torino. The one outstanding success story in this regard was John Charles, the Leeds United and Wales star who was lionised by Turin fans after his move to Juventus in 1957.

Opposite left: Scenes of jubilation in Tottenham as Spurs rack up another first when they bring home Britain's first European trophy in May 1963.
Opposite right: Players parade the Cup Winners' Cup through the streets of Tottenham (l-r: Cliff Jones (rear), Bill Brown (front), Ron Henry, Jimmy Greaves (holding cup) and Terry Dyson).

Jimmy Greaves

Jimmy Greaves was a slightly built inside-forward with lightning-fast feet, a razor-sharp brain and a killer instinct in front of goal. Throughout the 1960s Greaves was the foremost goal-poacher in English football. Although closely associated with Tottenham Hotspur, he started his career at Chelsea where he became a teenage prodigy before joining AC Milan in 1961. His failure to settle in Italy, where he played just 15 games, enabled Spurs' boss Bill Nicholson to bring him to White Hart Lane for what was then the hefty price tag of £99,999.

Record goalscorer

During the following nine years Greaves hit 220 league goals for Spurs, including 37 in the 1962-63 season, both of which are still club records. He was the First Division's top scorer six times in that nine-year period. Despite a much-publicised, and ultimately victorious, battle with alcoholism, his goalscoring talents were evident throughout his career. By the time he retired, after playing for a number of seasons for another London club, West Ham, he had scored a total of 357 league goals, all in the First Division.

44 goals for England

Unfortunately for Greaves, in a decade which witnessed many of his most incredible achievements, he chose the worst possible moment to suffer a drop in form. He was Alf Ramsey's first-choice striker as the England team went into the 1966 World Cup, but was replaced by Geoff Hurst in the latter stages of the tournament. Despite missing several of the 1966 World Cup games, including the Final, he scored 44 times for England, putting him third behind Bobby Charlton and Gary Lineker in the all-time list of England strikers. But Greaves' haul came from just 57 international appearances, far fewer than either Lineker or Charlton, who won 80 and 106 caps respectively – testament to his magnificent goal-scoring talents.

Mackay suffers two broken legs in a year

After 1963 the great Spurs side broke up very quickly. It was a new-look team which brought the club its only other piece of silverware of the decade, a third FA Cup win in 1967. Of the eleven who had won the Cup Winners' Cup only Greaves was on the pitch when Spurs beat Chelsea 2-1. Most of the changes had been organic but one was the result of a tragedy: John White, the 27-year-old Scottish international inside-forward, was killed by lightning on a London golf course in July 1964. In the same year Dave Mackay broke his left leg twice within ten months, something which would have ended the career of a player with less resolve. But having missed out on that European glory night, Mackay battled back to play on for eight more years, including the Wembley Final of 1967.

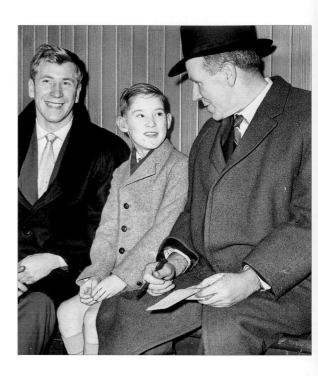

Dave Mackay

After starting his career with Heart of Midlothian, Dave Mackay joined Tottenham Hotspur in 1959. As a dynamic and inspirational half-back he provided the steel and drive in the great Spurs side of the early 1960s. Although he was already an established Scotland international before he joined Tottenham, it was at club level that Mackay enjoyed his greatest successes. Spurs celebrated Double was achieved in the 1960-61 season, and the team retained the FA Cup the following year. Injury forced him to miss the final of the European Cup Winners' Cup in 1963, when Spurs beat holders Atletico Madrid 5-1.

Footballer of the Year

His career looked in serious doubt as a result of two broken legs, sustained within a nine-month period in 1964, but the indomitable Mackay fought back to captain Spurs to another FA Cup triumph in 1967. The following season he transferred to Derby County where he led the team to the Division Two championship in 1968-69, an achievement which earned him the Footballer of the Year award, an honour he shared with Manchester City's Tony Book.

Ramsey's Ipswich take First Division by storm

The team that took the title from Spurs in 1962 was Alf Ramsey's unheralded Ipswich Town. The East Anglia club had risen from the Third Division (South) to English champions in just five years. Ramsey's men won the Division Two and Division One titles in successive seasons, the fourth club to record that particular achievement. Ramsey the player had been schooled in Spurs' great "push and run" side of the previous decade, and it was outstanding team play rather than brilliant individuals that carried Ipswich to the title. It would put Ramsey's name in the frame when the England job became vacant following the 1962 World Cup.

Exit Accrington Stanley

While Ipswich were riding high, one of the famous names in the English game was making a sad exit. Accrington Stanley, one of the League's founder members, had mounting debts and was forced to resign from the Fourth Division. This was yet another sign of the polarisation between the haves and have-nots, a trend that was set to continue.

Right: Accrington Stanley skipper Bob Wilson reads the bill for a match that was never to take place, the club being forced to resign from the league because of financial difficulties. Ironically, Exeter too was suffering from crippling debts.

Below: Spectators and staff show their feelings, as Ramsey's Ispwich are one goal away from winning the league title in 1962. Ramsey's side, recently languishing in the Third Division and with its absence of star players, were unlikely champions, tipped by pundits for relegation rather than triumph.

Opposite above: Bobby Charlton and his manager Matt Busby talk with a young fan.

Opposite below: Alan Mullery and captain Dave Mackay (right) hold the FA Cup after a 2-1 win over Chelsea in the 1967 Cup Final. Mackay and Greaves were the only representatives of the Tottenham side that won the Cup in 1962.

Everton champions in year of the big freeze

Accrington's demise was in sharp contrast to Everton, whose boss Harry Catterick had been on a spending spree in a bid to bring the glory days back to Goodison. The spine of the side was strong: keeper Gordon West, centre-half Brian Labone and centre-forward Alex Young. Everton didn't secure the title until 11 May 1963, when it became mathematically impossible for Spurs to catch them. The late finish to the season had been caused by a three-month winter freeze which had played havoc with the fixture lists. Over 400 games had to be postponed, disrupting the season even more than the big freeze of 1946-47. The Pools companies initially suffered like everyone else, before coming up with a novel solution to the problem. A Pools Panel made up of pundits decided the outcome of postponed matches. Punters were thus still able to have a flutter, although some of the experts' decisions were as controversial as any dubious offside.

Everton would remain top-six contenders for the remainder of the decade but would not clinch the title again until the start of the next. Meanwhile, there were two FA Cup appearances, against Sheffield Wednesday in 1966 and West Bromwich Albion two years later. Everton were favourites to win both. They had to come back from 2-0 down to beat Wednesday, Mike Trebilcock hitting two and Derek Temple grabbing the winner. In 1968 they went down to an extra-time goal from Albion's Jeff Astle.

Match-fixing scandal

By that time one of Catterick's early acquisitions had left the game in disgrace. Wing-half Tony Kay, who was capped once for England, was one of a number of players implicated in a match-rigging scandal, a story which broke in *The People* in April 1964. Kay, along with former Sheffield Wednesday team-mate Peter Swan was found guilty of conspiring to throw a match against Ipswich in 1962. Swan was also an England player, and went to Chile as part of the 1962 World Cup squad. Investigations revealed that the problem was even more widespread than at first thought, with an ex-player named Jimmy Gauld the chief orchestrator of the scam. Gauld received a four-year prison sentence and ten players were given life bans.

Bobby Charlton

Bobby Charlton won just about every honour in the game, at both club and international level. Football was in his blood; his brother Jack also became a professional footballer and his uncle was Jackie Milburn, a legend on Tyneside in the 1950s. A true gentleman of football, he was famed for playing the game in the spirit of genuine sportsmanship. Indeed in a sparkling 20-year career he was booked just once - for time-wasting when his side was losing!

Charlton was signed to Manchester United in 1955 as part of Matt Busby's grand scheme to comb the country for the best young talent in the land. In a wonderfully ironic turn, he scored twice against Charlton Athletic on his debut in 1956. He and the other "Busby Babes", as Busby's young team became known, looked set to dominate football for many years but on 6 February 1958 the team was all but wiped out in the Munich air crash. Charlton survived and recovered sufficiently to receive the first of his 106 England caps just a few weeks after the tragedy.

Deep-lying centre-forward

Originally a winger or inside-forward, Charlton developed into a deep-lying centre-forward and during the 1960s he was a key player in Busby's exciting new United side, and was equally influential for England. He distributed passes with pinpoint accuracy or burst forward to unleash thunderous shots with either foot. He helped England to World Cup glory in 1966; during the campaign, Mexico and Portugal both found themselves on the receiving end of his scoring power. His performances in that season won him the European Footballer of the Year award.

Triumph for Charlton

Two years later, in 1968, Charlton captained the United side which lifted the European Cup, scoring two goals in a 4-1 victory over Benfica at Wembley. It was an emotional and powerful triumph for Charlton, the team, and Busby, as it was during a campaign to win in Europe that so many of the "Busby Babes" had lost their lives in the Munich air crash, ten years earlier. Charlton played his 606th and final league game for United at Stamford Bridge in 1973.

During the 1970 World Cup in Mexico he played his final game for England in the quarter-final against West Germany. Many believe that England manager Alf Ramsey's decision to substitute Charlton in the second half, when England were 2-1 ahead, was a crucial factor in the team's defeat. His record 106 caps was subsequently overhauled, but his 49 goals has yet to be beaten. In 1994 he was honoured for his services to football – Sir Bobby Charlton.

Opposite: Manchester United 'keeper Gaskell goes to full stretch to snatch the ball from Leicester's Cross in the 1963 Cup Final. David Herd and later Denis Law, back from Turin, had reinforced Busby's side at the start of the '61-2 season. Both players paid dividends in the 1963 Final - Herd chalking up two goal and Law the third.

Bobby Moore

An Essex boy, Bobby Moore was West Ham's, and England's, gentleman-footballer. His modesty belied the inspirational leadership he showed when captaining club and country. Famed for his incisive tackling, timing and sureness in defence, he was also one of the most accurate passers of the ball the English game has ever seen.

Moore joined the Hammers in 1958 at the age of 17 and showed tenacious loyalty, playing 545 games for the club. He led them to their first-ever FA Cup Final win, over Preston North End in 1964, and the European Cup Winners' Cup the following year, in a 2-0 victory over Munich 1860.

England's youngest-ever captain

His international career was stellar. After a record 18 outings for England's youth team, Moore joined the senior side in 1962. He played in that year's World Cup in Chile, when England lost to Brazil in the quarter-finals. A year later, with Alf Ramsey in charge, Moore became England's youngest-ever captain, and in 1966 led his team out at Wembley to their historic 4-2 World Cup win against West Germany. Four years later, he captained the defending champions in Mexico, where in the group-stage game against Brazil he had one of his most memorable games. Moore and Pele's embrace at the end of the match, which Brazil won 1-0, was eloquent - full as it was of genuine mutual respect.

Classically skilful

In the 70s, after a series of disagreements with manager Ron Greenwood, Moore left West Ham to join Fulham and helped the team to reach the 1975 FA Cup Final – ironically, against 2-0 winners West Ham. He ended his playing days in the United States, then went into management, but with little success, first at Oxford City and then Southend.

Moore had seemed to have it all in the optimistic era of the 1960s – he was blond, handsome, gracious and classically skilful, with an uncanny ability to read the game. Tragically, he died at the age of 51, in 1993, from bowel cancer.

Alf Ramsey confers with England skipper, Bobby Moore. Ramsey's experience in building Ipswich was used to good effect as he worked to mould an England side that would play as a team, rather than give individual performances. In 1966 Ramsey called Moore 'my right-hand man, my lieutenant in the field'

The Shankly era

After Everton's 1963 championship, three clubs dominated the domestic game: Liverpool, Leeds and Manchester United. Liverpool had had a miserable time of things in the 1950s, much of it spent in the Second Division. Manager Phil Taylor was sacked in November 1959 and a month later a new messiah arrived. 46-year-old Bill Shankly was persuaded to leave Huddersfield and take over the reins at Anfield on a £2500 salary. Over the next three years he let some players go, revitalised the careers of others and made some key signings. These included Ron Yeats from Dundee United, Ian St John from Motherwell and Gordon Milne from Preston. The Reds stormed to the Second Division championship in 1961-62, and after just one year of consolidation in the top flight became champions in 1964. After a slow start that season, Liverpool took 47 points from 30 games to secure their 6th championship. Defensive football was on the way, yet Liverpool were in irresistible goalscoring form, particularly at Anfield. They banged in 60 goals in front of their home fans, an average of nearly three per game. Roger Hunt was again the goalscoring hero, hitting 31 of the team's 92 league goals.

First FA Cup win for Liverpool

The following season Liverpool suffered a reaction in their league form, slipping to 7th, but the club had two memorable Cup runs. They finally got their name on the FA Cup, thanks to a 2-1 win over a Leeds side which had just finished as runners-up in the league. After a cagey 90 minutes in which defences were on top, Liverpool scored through Hunt. Bremner hit an equaliser, then St John confirmed his status as an Anfield legend by heading in an Ian Callaghan cross. However, the hero of the hour was Gerry Byrne, who played for most of the match with a broken collarbone following an early clash with Bobby Collins. The use of substitutes was finally allowed the following season, initially just for injuries and then for tactical purposes too. After all the debilitating injuries that had dogged Wembley finals in recent years it was a decision that was long overdue.

Above: The Cup is held aloft by Liverpool skipper Ron Yeats and Gordon Milne, who had to stand down from the team because of injury, in the lap of honour at Wembley in 1965. Others are (l-r) Hunt who scored Liverpool's first goal, Smith and Stevenson. Shankly's team triumphed over Leeds by 2-1, all three goals being scored in extra-time.

Right: Ron Yeats and Ian St John at Euston Station, taking the Cup back to Anfield for the first time in Liverpool's 73-year history.

Opposite: Liverpool pose in 1965 with the FA Cup and the Charity Shield. However, having started the 1964-5 season as reigning champions, the club's performance in the league was less impressive. Liverpool finished in 7th place and Manchester United, the previous year's runners-up took the title, with Leeds hot on their heels.

Reds lose two finals

New Cup-holders Liverpool barely had time to draw breath before facing World Club champions Inter Milan in the semi-final of the European Cup. Liverpool pulled off a sensational 3-1 win over Helenio Herrera's much-vaunted side at home, but three controversial goals by the Italians at the San Siro turned the tie on its head. The ball was kicked out of keeper Tommy Lawrence's hands for one of Inter's goals, and the fact that such incidents went unpunished led Shankly and others to suspect that the officials had been bribed.

Liverpool recovered to lift the title again the following season. They also made it to the final of the Cup Winners Cup, following a titanic struggle with Celtic in the semis. They faced Borussia Dortmund at Hampden Park in the final, the German side winning 2-1 in extra-time.

Left: Denis Law signing autographs
Right: George Best and Manchester City's Mike Summerbee pose for photographers outside their boutique, Edwardia. Busby gave Best his first game for United on 14 September 1963 against West Bromwich Albion. It was not until December that Best was offered another opportunity to play and the famous line up of Charlton, Law and Best was born.

Denis Law

Playing alongside George Best and Bobby Charlton at Manchester United in the 1960s, Denis Law was the King of the Stretford End, an unstoppable firebrand, exciting and unpredictable going forward, a showman with one arm raised exultantly when he found the net, which he did so often – 236 goals in 399 appearances for the club. He scored the first, and created the other two, in United's 3-1 FA Cup Final victory over Leicester City in 1963, and his skill and infectious enthusiasm for winning helped the club to the league title in both 1964-65 and 1966-67. He was named European Footballer of the Year in 1964. In United's European campaigns, he scored four hat-tricks, but missed the 1968 European Cup-winning final with an injured knee.

30 goals for Scotland

Born in Aberdeen in 1940, he'd turned professional at Huddersfield Town in 1957, only to be poached by Manchester City in 1960, for a then record fee of £55,000. Another record fee, £100,000, took him to Torino the next year, but by 1962 he had joined United. On his international debut in 1958 aged 18, he was the youngest Scot to be capped since 1899, and his tally of 30 goals for Scotland (in 55 outings) was equalled only by Dalglish. The characteristic impish grin was broadly on display when he played in the Scottish side that beat England 3-2 at Wembley.

A passionate United man, Law found himself out of favour with manager Tommy Docherty in the declining side of the early 1970s, and in 1973 went back to rivals Manchester City, on a free transfer. There was to be no cockiness, pleasure or one-armed saluting when his backheeled goal against United sent his old club down to the Second Division in 1974. He called it a day at the end of that season, going out of the game he loved while he was still at the top of his form.

1966 World Cup

England's finest hour

England dispense with wingers

The ex-defender Ramsey brought a solid look to the England side. Nobby Stiles was the defensive anchor in front of a solid back four. Ramsey had wingers Ian Callaghan, John Connelly and Terry Paine in his squad but as the tournament progressed he decided to dispense with wide players altogether. That added to the defensive solidity of the team; the question now was whether they would be able to break the opposition down and score themselves.

Progress to the knockout stage was unspectacular. A dull, goalless draw against Uruguay was followed by 2-0 wins over Mexico and France. The quarter-final clash with Argentina was an explosive affair. The turning point came when Argentine captain Antonio Rattin was ordered off for verbally abusing the German referee after he had already been booked. There was a long delay as Rattin refused to leave the field. Geoff Hurst scored the game's only goal, a glancing header 13 minutes from time. The Hurst-Hunt strike partnership would continue for the rest of the tournament. Jimmy Greaves, the most prolific striker in the squad with 43 goals in just 51 appearances, had chosen the worst possible moment to suffer a loss of form.

Opposite: A clash of headgear as an England supporter reaches to shake hands with a Mexican supporter wearing a giant sombrero before the opening match of the World Cup tournament between England and Uruguay on 11 July 1966.
Above: Greaves runs towards goal pursued by Uruguay's Ubinas in an inglorious beginning to England's World Cup campaign. Despite winning 16 corners and making 15 shots on goal, England did not score and the match ended in a draw.

The sporting semi-final

Ramsey branded the Argentine players "animals" and refused to let his players swap shirts at the final whistle. This was just one of many ill-tempered encounters. Pelé had come in for very rough treatment as Brazil failed to make it beyond the group stages. By contrast, England's semi-final against Portugal was an oasis of sportsmanship. In a fast, free-flowing game Bobby Charlton scored twice, but England had to live on their nerves in the last few minutes as Eusebio pulled one back from the penalty spot.

Geoff Hurst

West Ham striker Geoff Hurst, knighted in 1998, has the proud distinction of being the only man ever to score a hat-trick in a World Cup Final – and the only first-class cricketer to win a World Cup medal at football. He batted for Essex against Lancashire in 1962, and, of course, played for England in their 1966 victory over West Germany.

Over 400 games for the Hammers

The 24-year-old Hurst had come into form at exactly the right time – even if many Germans still believe his second goal, which came off the underside of the bar, never crossed the line. He hadn't even played in England's opening game of the tournament, but having taken the place of the injured Jimmy Greaves and scored the winner against Argentina in the quarter-final, he kept his place.

Between 1959 and 1972, Hurst made over 400 League appearances for the Hammers, helping them to win the FA Cup in 1964 and the European Cup Winners' Cup the following year. In 1972 he moved to Stoke City, then after a period at West Bromwich Albion, went into management and helped with the national squad.

Above: Gordon Banks takes control in the World Cup Final. Banks did not concede a goal in the competition until the semi-final against Portugal.

Opposite: Jimmy Greaves puts an arm around the exhausted Alan Ball as the victorious England team leave the pitch. Greaves had played in the opening round of the competition but was replaced by Hurst when Greaves' form dipped.

Weber forces extra time

England's opponents in the final were West Germany. They had beaten a Uruguay side reduced to nine men in the quarter-finals, and in the semis Russia had also had a man sent off. Helmut Haller opened the scoring in the final, capitalising on a weak clearance from Ray Wilson after 13 minutes. Within minutes the teams were level as Bobby Moore flighted a free-kick onto the head of his West Ham team-mate Hurst, who powered the ball past Tilkowski. The third of the Hammers' contingent, Martin Peters, put England ahead with less than 15 minutes to go. The man whom Ramsey had described as "10 years ahead of his time" scored from close range after a Hurst shot was blocked. A West Germany free-kick in the last minute somehow found its way through a crowded box and Wolfgang Weber squeezed the ball in at the far post. It meant that extra time would be played for the first time since 1934, which was also the last occasion that the host nation had won the tournament.

Hurst's controversial goal

20-year-old Alan Ball was still full of running, and it was his right-wing cross 10 minutes into extra time that led to the most controversial moment in World Cup history. Hurst controlled the ball, turned and let fly, only to see his shot hit the underside of the bar. It bounced down and was cleared, but had the ball crossed the line? The referee consulted his Russian linesman who was in no doubt that it had. Hurst sealed victory by hammering in a fourth for England in the last minute. It also made him the only man to score a hat-trick in a World Cup final. Technology later suggested that he was fortunate not have his second goal ruled out, but that didn't detract from the jubilant scenes at Wembley on 30 July 1966. England were world champions. For Bobby Moore it was the completion of a memorable hat-trick of his own. He had captained the West Ham side which won the FA Cup in 1964 and the Cup Winners' Cup the following year. It was thus the third time in as many years that Moore had raised a trophy aloft at Wembley.

World Cup 1966 Results

GROUP 1

England	0	Uruguay	0
France	1	Mexico	1
Uruguay	2	France	1
England	2	Mexico	0
Uruguay	0	Mexico	0
England	2	France	0

	P	W	D	L	F	A	Pts
England	3	2	1	0	4	0	5
Uruguay	3	1	2	0	2	1	4
Mexico	3	0	2	1	1	3	2
France	3	0	1	2	2	5	1

GROUP 2

W.Germany	5	Switzerland	0
Argentina	2	Spain	1
Spain	2	Switzerland	1
Argentina	2	Switzerland	0
W.Germany	2	Spain	1
W.Germany	1	Argentina	1

	P	W	D	L	F	A	Pts
W.Germany	3	2	1	0	8	2	5
Argentina	3	2	1	0	4	1	5
Spain	3	1	1	1	2	3	3
Switzerland	3	0	1	2	1	7	1

GROUP 3

Brazil	2	Bulgaria	0
Portugal	3	Hungary	1
Hungary	3	Brazil	1
Portugal	3	Bulgaria	0
Portugal	3	Brazil	1
Hungary	3	Bulgaria	1

	P	W	D	L	F	A	Pts
Portugal	3	3	0	0	9	2	6
Hungary	3	2	0	1	7	5	4
Brazil	3	1	0	2	4	6	2
Bulgaria	3	0	0	3	1	8	0

GROUP 4

Sov.Union	3	N.Korea	0
Italy	2	Chile	0
Chile	1	N.Korea	1
Sov.Union	1	Italy	0
N.Korea	1	Italy	0
Sov.Union	2	Chile	1

	P	W	D	L	F	A	Pts
Sov.Union	3	3	0	0	6	1	6
N.Korea	3	1	1	1	2	4	3
Italy	3	1	0	2	2	2	2
Chile	3	0	1	2	2	5	1

QUARTER-FINALS

England	1	Argentina	0
W. Germany	4	Uruguay	0
Portugal	5	N.Korea	3
Sov. Union	2	Hungary	1

SEMI-FINALS

W. Germany	2	Sov. Union	1
England	2	Portugal	1

3RD PLACE PLAY-OFF

Portugal	2	Sov. Union	1

FINAL JULY 30 – WEMBLEY STADIUM

England	4	W. Germany	2
(Hurst 19, 100, 119,		(Haller 13, Weber 89)	
Peters 77)			
Aet ht: 1-1 90min 2-2.		Ref: Dienst (Swi)	
Att: 96,924.			

England: Banks, Cohen, Wilson, Stiles, J Charlton, Moore, Ball, Hunt, R Charlton, Hurst, Peters

West Germany: Tilkowski, Höttges, Schnellinger, Beckenbauer, Schülz, Weber, Haller, Overath, Seeler, Held, Emmerich.

Sir Alf Ramsey

Alf Ramsey was a cultured full-back in the famous Spurs "push and run" side which won the championship in 1951. He was capped 32 times for England between 1949 and 1954. After his playing days were over, Ramsey took over as manager of Ipswich Town. In seven years Ramsey took the unfashionable East Anglia club from the Third Division to the top flight, culminating in the league championship in 1961-62. It was on the strength of this achievement that he was offered the England manager's job in 1963. Ramsey was the first full-time incumbent and he insisted on being given sole responsibility for selection, a freedom that his predecessor had not enjoyed.

Early in his tenure as national team boss he predicted that England would win the 1966 World Cup. That looked a long way off when his side was hammered 5-2 by France in his first game in charge. Three years later, Ramsey fulfilled his promise as his "wingless wonders" triumphed, beating West Germany in the final.

After going out at the semi-final stage of the 1968 European Championship, England went to Mexico to defend their world crown. Many thought that Ramsey's squad in 1970 was even stronger than that which had won the tournament four years earlier. West Germany ended England's hopes at the quarter-final stage, coming back from 2-0 down to win 3-2. Some thought Ramsey's decision to take off both Charlton and Peters was instrumental in the defeat.

He survived that disappointment, and another quarter-final exit in the 1972 European Championship, when the Germans again proved to be the stumbling-block. He was finally dismissed after England drew with Poland at Wembley in 1973, a result which meant that England failed to qualify for the 1974 World Cup. Ramsey was knighted in the 1967 New Year's Honours list. He died in 1999.

Rise of Leeds

Don Revie's transformation of Leeds United was if anything even more dramatic than Shankly's at Liverpool. The Yorkshire club was flirting with relegation to the Third Division 1962, yet by the middle of the decade they were a formidable footballing machine. Revie had been a deep-lying centre-forward in the Manchester City side of the mid-1950s, and Footballer of the Year in 1955. Ten years later he was the architect behind a powerhouse Leeds side that was universally respected if not always admired. Players of the stature of Billy Bremner, Bobby Collins, Jack Charlton and Norman Hunter took Leeds to the top - or, more often, second place. 1964-65 was to prove all too typical: runners-up in the league and beaten finalists in the Cup.

New points record as defences get on top

After three more seasons of finishing in the top four, and defeat in 1966 Fairs Cup Final, Leeds finally won the title in 1968-69. And they did it in fine style, losing just twice in the League. 67 points set a new record, eclipsing Arsenal's 1931 tally by one. Leeds' goals column that season made interesting reading: 66 scored, just 26 conceded. At the beginning of the decade Spurs Double-winning side had scored 115 and let in 55. In that year even relegated Newcastle scored 86! English teams were now regularly coming up against Continental opposition, and in particular the miserly "catenaccio" system operated by Italian sides. Tight defence was seen as the key to success.

Opposite below left: Referee Ken Burns hears the views of the disgruntled Leeds players (l-r: Greenhoff, Bremner, Giles and Bell) after he disallows Leeds' equaliser in the semi-final of the 1967 FA Cup. Their opponents, Chelsea, reached the Final, defeating Leeds by 1 goal to nil. But Don Revie's team were to take the league in the following season, losing only twice. Revie's contribution was recognised: he was awarded Manager of the Year in both 1969 and 1970, the preceding recipients being Matt Busby and Jock Stein.

Opposite below right: Crowds at Craven Cottage cause officials to order the gates to be closed before the start of Fulham's derby with Chelsea.

Above: West Ham and England World Cup heroes Geoff Hurst, Bobby Moore and Martin Peters.

Left: North London rivalries are put aside for a moment when Spurs' Terry Venables (left) acts as best man for Arsenal centre-forward George Graham.

Faltering start for League Cup

Despite their reputation as "nearly men", Leeds did pick up two other trophies in the 1960s, a Fairs Cup and League Cup double in 1968. The latter competition had had a chequered history since Football League Secretary Alan Hardaker had championed it at the beginning of the decade. In the early years the top clubs boycotted the League Cup, feeling that it was an unwelcome addition to the fixture list. With three European trophies to aim for a second domestic cup competition hardly set the pulse racing. When Second Division Norwich City beat Fourth Division Rochdale over two legs in the 1962 final, the competition was in danger of withering on the vine.

Cup honours for Third Division sides

The turning point came in 1967, when the final became a one-legged affair at Wembley. The status was further enhanced with the award of a Fairs Cup place to the winners, provided they were in the First Division. That stipulation meant that Queen's Park Rangers and Swindon, winners in 1967 and 1969 respectively, weren't able to embark on a European adventure. Both were Third Division sides when they lifted the trophy and both came out on top against Division One opposition. Rodney Marsh inspired QPR to come back from a 2-0 deficit to win 3-2 against West Brom. In 1969 two extra-time goals from Swindon winger Don Rogers ended the hopes of an Arsenal side that had finished fourth in the championship. By the end of the decade, the League Cup had become firmly established, although critics pointed out that it remained a poor relation to the premier knockout competition. Certainly no Third Division side had come close to lifting the FA Cup in the 50 years that those leagues had been in existence.

Below: Spurs players celebrate their second goal, scored by Saul, in the 1967 Cup Final, an all-London affair. Tommy Docherty's Chelsea side were overwhelmed by Spurs' skill and tactics and even a late Chelsea goal, bringing the score to 2-1, didn't loosen Spurs' hold on the game.

Gordon Banks

Gordon Banks earned his first cap in 1963 and, following that debut, was a fixture in the England side for nearly a decade, including the glorious 1966 World Cup campaign. But perhaps his most memorable moment came on 7 June 1970 when, as the finest goalkeeper of his age, he thwarted the world's greatest player with probably the best save ever seen. Pele's crashing downward header was miraculously scooped off the line by Banks ten minutes into the England v Brazil World Cup group match at Guadalajara, Mexico. England lost that game but made it through to the quarter-final, where Banks' late withdrawal through illness was widely seen as a key factor in the team's defeat in the match against West Germany.

Career was cut short

Banks began his career at Chesterfield and established his reputation after a move to Leicester City, who he joined in 1959. In the 1961 FA Cup Final he was on the losing side when his team went down 0-2 to Tottenham Hotspur; he picked up another losers' medal two years later. Banks moved to another unfashionable club, Stoke City, in 1967. Five years later in 1972, soon after he had signed a long-term contract with the Potteries side, his career was cut short by a car accident in which he lost an eye.

Busby rebuilds again

Many would agree that the accolade of team of the decade belonged to Manchester United. Following the Munich disaster, Busby embarked on yet another rebuilding process. It proved to be a long journey. In the four seasons from 1959-60 United finished 7th twice, 15th and 19th. Ironically, it was in the season that they flirted with relegation that the new-look side won its first silverware. Opponents Leicester City had finished 4th that year, but two goals from David Herd and one from Denis Law made a mockery of the clubs' respective positions. Four months later 17-year-old George best made his debut for the club. Pat Crerand also joined United in 1963, while players such as David Sadler and John Aston were showing promise in the youth ranks. And of course, Busby also had Munich survivors Bobby Charlton and Bill Foulkes at his disposal.

European Cup goes to Old Trafford

After finishing runners-up to Liverpool in 1963-64,

United won the title twice in three seasons. In 1967-68 United had to be content with the runners-up spot again, this time to neighbours Manchester City. Yet this was to bring the club the proudest moment in its history. In the semi-final of the European Cup United took a slender 1-0 lead to the Bernebeu Stadium. Real Madrid went 3-1 ahead but two unlikely goals from Sadler and Foulkes put United into the final. Ten years on from Munich United went to Wembley to face a Benfica side which boasted the great Eusebio. He almost won the game for the Portuguese side with a thunderous shot in the dying minutes when the score stood at 1-1. But Alex Stepney made a great save and the game went into extra-time. United hit three in those 30 minutes. The first was a typical piece of virtuoso skill from Best; Brian Kidd, celebrating his 19th birthday, headed United into a 3-1 lead; and Bobby Charlton swept home his second of the match to make the final score 4-1. After the events of 1958 there was an element of natural justice as United became the first English club to win European football's premier trophy.

Above right: United team-mates Law and Kidd celebrate after Best scored in the first leg of the semi-final of the 1968 European Cup against Real Madrid.

Top: Players and staff of Manchester United on the pitch at Wembley on 29 May 1968, the day of the European Cup Final.

Above left: Pat Crerand (left) shares the moment of glory with Matt Busby. Ten years after the Munich disaster, Busby's dream is realised and a rebuilt Manchester United defeated Benfica by 4 goals to 1 to win the European Cup. Charlton and Foulkes, survivors of the crash, played at Wembley and Charlton had the satisfaction of scoring 2 of United's goals. In the following season, Busby announced his intention to step down as manager of the team to take on the role of general manager of the club.

Opposite: Best displays perfect balance and control.

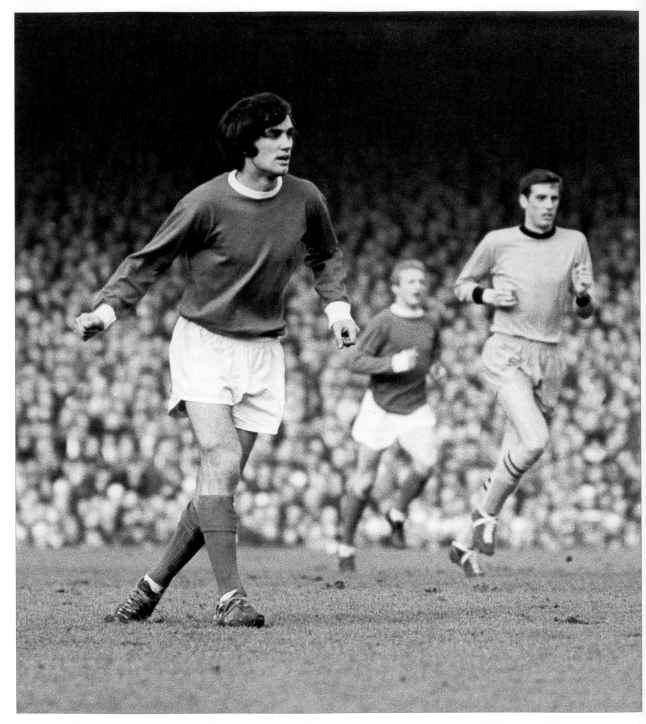

Above: George Best plays against Wolves at Molineux in 1966 and (opposite below) in action in the 1968-9 season. United were riding high on their European success and Best was at the peak of his form; top scorer for United in both 1967- 8 and the following season and voted European Footballer of the Year in 1968. But at the end of the 1968-9 season, Busby's team had slipped to 11th place in the league and Best was in conflict with the management.

George Best

George Best had everything: speed, strength, poise, creativity and incredible ball skills. A two-footed player, he was excellent in the air and fearless in the tackle and a lethal finisher. A team-mate in the Manchester United side of the 1960s once said that Best could have played in any outfield position - and outperformed the man who usually played there. By the time he was 22 he had won a European Footballer of the Year award and had a European Cup winners' medal. He looked set to win many more honours, yet the pressures of celebrity, combined with a tendency to press the self-destruct button all too often, meant that by his late 20s, his career in the top flight was virtually over.

Belfast Boy

Best was brought to Old Trafford from his home in Belfast in August 1961, when he was 15. Just two years later he made his debut for United and was soon a fixture in an exciting new side that Matt Busby was building. Busby recognised Best's natural talent and reasoned that it was best left alone. Consequently he had told the coaching staff not to try and teach the youngster anything. Later, despite all the headaches Best gave him, Busby never wavered in his view of the Irishman's ability on the field, claiming that he had never seen any other player who had so many different ways of beating an opponent.

After a stunning individual display in a 5-1 away victory over Benfica in the 1965-66 European Cup, he became the first pop star footballer and soon came under the most intense media scrutiny. Good-looking and fashionable, he was dubbed 'El Beatle' and for a time he managed to combine the life of a high-profile celebrity with outstanding performances on the pitch. But, inevitably, the revelling began to take its toll.

Best leaves United at 25

After United won the European Cup victory in 1968 it became necessary for Busby to reinforce the ageing team and Best felt that he should be more central to the make-up of the team. Unsurprisingly, this put pressure on relations between him, his team-mates and the club, which were already strained as a result of his high living and media profile. He walked out of Old Trafford in 1972, two days before his 26th birthday. The following decade saw him join a succession of clubs, both in Britain and America, but he would never reproduce the kind of dazzling displays which were a trademark of his younger days.

On the international front, Best was picked for Northern Ireland when he was 17, after just 15 appearances for United. Although he won 37 caps, he never really had the opportunity to show his skills on the world stage.

Long after he had hung up his boots, Best continued to find himself in demand as a football pundit and on the after-dinner circuit. However, his years of alcohol abuse finally caught up with him and in the summer of 2002 he underwent a liver transplant operation.

Left: Manchester United display the European Cup.

Opposite below: The 1968-9 Spurs team: back row Pearce, Beal, Collins, England, Jennings, Chivers, Knowles, Gilzean and Kinnear. Front Row: Bond, Robertson, Greaves, Mullery, Venables, Jones and Want. Martin Chivers had recently joined the side from Southampton commanding a record transfer fee of £125,000.

Opposite above: Allan Clarke shows his delight after scoring for Leicester in the semi-final of the Cup in 1969. Clarke's goal took Leicester to Wembley, going some way to justify the new record-breaking transfer fee of £150,000 paid to Fulham.

Below: Manchester City players train before the Final of the 1969 FA Cup in the red and black striped shirt they will wear on the day. City won the Cup, for the fourth time in their history, Young scoring the only goal of the match against Leicester. Mercer and Allison's new signings of Mike Summerbee (second from the left), Francis Lee (third from the left) and Colin Bell (fourth from the left) played a crucial role in City's league and Cup success in the late 1960s.

English clubs make their mark

The year after winning the World Cup England came back to earth with a bump as Scotland came to Wembley and won 3-2, a game in which Jim Baxter was at his mercurial best. The Scots lost little time in claiming to be unofficial world champions.

England went into the 1968 European Championship as favourites. After beating Spain in the quarter-final, it all went wrong against Yugoslavia. Alan Mullery was sent off for retaliation, the first England player to receive his marching orders, and the team went down 1-0.

At the end of a turbulent decade, English clubs had made their mark in Europe, winning five trophies in all. And the national side was once again on top of the world. The next decade would see continued success at club level, while the national side would find it hard to reach a World Cup, let alone win it.

League Division One 1960-1969

1959-1960

1	Burnley	55
2	Wolverhampton W.	54
3	Tottenham Hotspur	53
4	West Bromwich Albion	49
5	Sheffield Wednesday	49
6	Bolton Wanderers	48
7	Manchester United	45
8	Newcastle United	44
9	Preston	44
10	Fulham	44
11	Blackpool	40
12	Leicester City	39
13	Arsenal	39
14	West Ham United	38
15	Everton	37
16	Manchester City	37
17	Blackburn Rovers	37
18	Chelsea	37
19	Birmingham City	36
20	Nottingham Forest	35
21	Leeds United	34
22	Luton	30

1960-61

1	Tottenham Hotspur	66
2	Sheffield Wednesday	58
3	Wolverhampton W.	57
4	Burnley	51
5	Everton	50
6	Leicester City	45
7	Manchester United	45
8	Blackburn Rovers	43
9	Aston Villa	43
10	West Bromwich Albion	41
11	Arsenal	41
12	Chelsea	37
13	Manchester City	37
14	Nottingham Forest	37
15	Cardiff	37
16	West Ham United	36
17	Fulham	36
18	Bolton Wanderers	35
19	Birmingham City	34
20	Blackpool	33
21	Newcastle United	32
22	Preston	30

1961-62

1	Ipswich	56
2	Burnley	53
3	Tottenham Hotspur	52
4	Everton	51
5	Sheffield United	47
6	Sheffield Wednesday	46
7	Aston Villa	44
8	West Ham United	44
9	West Bromwich Albion	43
10	Arsenal	43
11	Bolton Wanderers	42
12	Manchester City	41
13	Blackpool	41
14	Leicester City	40
15	Manchester United	39
16	Blackburn Rovers	39
17	Birmingham City	38
18	Wolverhampton W.	36
19	Nottingham Forest	36
20	Fulham	33
21	Cardiff	32
22	Chelsea	28

1962-63

1	Everton	61
2	Tottenham Hotspur	55
3	Burnley	54
4	Leicester City	52
5	Wolverhampton W.	50
6	Sheffield Wednesday	48
7	Arsenal	46
8	Liverpool	44
9	Nottingham Forest	44
10	Sheffield United	44
11	Blackburn Rovers	42
12	West Ham United	40
13	Blackpool	40
14	West Bromwich Albion	39
15	Aston Villa	38
16	Fulham	38
17	Ipswich	35
18	Bolton Wanderers	35
19	Manchester United	34
20	Birmingham City	33
21	Manchester City	31
22	Leyton Orient	21

1963-64

1	Liverpool	57
2	Manchester United	53
3	Everton	52
4	Tottenham Hotspur	51
5	Chelsea	50
6	Sheffield Wednesday	49
7	Blackburn Rovers	46
8	Arsenal	45
9	Burnley	44
10	West Bromwich Albion	43
11	Leicester City	43
12	Sheffield United	43
13	Nottingham Forest	41
14	West Ham United	40
15	Fulham	39
16	Wolverhampton W.	39
17	Stoke	38
18	Blackpool	35
19	Aston Villa	34
20	Birmingham City	29
21	Bolton Wanderers	28
22	Ipswich	25

1964-65

1	Manchester United	61
2	Leeds United	61
3	Chelsea	56
4	Everton	49
5	Nottingham Forest	47
6	Tottenham Hotspur	45
7	Liverpool	44
8	Sheffield Wednesday	43
9	West Ham United	42
10	Blackburn Rovers	42
11	Stoke	42
12	Burnley	42
13	Arsenal	41
14	West Bromwich Albion	39
15	Sunderland	37
16	Aston Villa	37
17	Blackpool	35
18	Leicester City	35
19	Sheffield United	35
20	Fulham	34
21	Wolverhampton W.	30
22	Birmingham City	27

1965-66

1	Liverpool	61
2	Leeds United	55
3	Burnley	55
4	Manchester United	51
5	Chelsea	51
6	West Bromwich Albion	50
7	Leicester City	49
8	Tottenham Hotspur	44
9	Sheffield United	43
10	Stoke	42
11	Everton	41
12	West Ham United	39
13	Blackpool	37
14	Arsenal	37
15	Newcastle United	37
16	Aston Villa	36
17	Sheffield Wednesday	36
18	Nottingham Forest	36
19	Sunderland	36
20	Fulham	35
21	Northampton	33
22	Blackburn Rovers	20

1966-67

1	Manchester United	60
2	Nottingham Forest	56
3	Tottenham Hotspur	56
4	Leeds United	55
5	Liverpool	51
6	Everton	48
7	Arsenal	46
8	Leicester City	44
9	Chelsea	44
10	Sheffield United	42
11	Sheffield Wednesday	41
12	Stoke	41
13	West Bromwich Albion	39
14	Burnley	39
15	Manchester City	39
16	West Ham United	36
17	Sunderland	36
18	Fulham	34
19	Southampton	34
20	Newcastle United	33
21	Aston Villa	29
22	Blackpool	21

1967-68

1	Manchester City	58
2	Manchester United	56
3	Liverpool	55
4	Leeds United	53
5	Everton	52
6	Chelsea	48
7	Tottenham Hotspur	47
8	West Bromwich Albion	46
9	Arsenal	44
10	Newcastle United	41
11	Nottingham Forest	39
12	West Ham United	38
13	Leicester City	38
14	Burnley	38
15	Sunderland	37
16	Southampton	37
17	Wolverhampton W.	36
18	Stoke	35
19	Sheffield Wednesday	34
20	Coventry	33
21	Sheffield United	32
22	Fulham	27

1968-69

1	Leeds United	67
2	Liverpool	61
3	Everton	57
4	Arsenal	56
5	Chelsea	50
6	Tottenham Hotspur	45
7	Southampton	45
8	West Ham United	44
9	Newcastle United	44
10	West Bromwich Albion	43
11	Manchester United	42
12	Ipswich	41
13	Manchester City	40
14	Burnley	39
15	Sheffield Wednesday	36
16	Wolverhampton W.	35
17	Sunderland	34
18	Nottingham Forest	33
19	Stoke	33
20	Coventry	31
21	Leicester City	30
22	Queen's Park Rangers	18

FA Cup Finals

1960	Wolverhampton W.	v	Blackburn Rovers	3-0
1961	Tottenham H.	v	Leicester City	2-0
1962	Tottenham H.	v	Burnley	3-1
1963	Manchester Utd	v	Leicester City	3-1
1964	West Ham Utd	v	Preston N.E.	3-2
1965	Liverpool	v	Leeds United	2-1
1966	Everton	v	Sheffield W.	3-2
1967	Tottenham H.	v	Chelsea	2-1
1968	West Bromwich A.	v	Everton	1-0
1969	Manchester City	v	Leicester City	1-0

Matt Busby never wavered in his view of George Best's ability on the field, claiming that he had never seen any other player who had so many different ways of beating an opponent.

1970-1979
Triumph in Europe

English clubs had won five European trophies in the 1960s. In the next decade Liverpool alone almost managed that. The Reds embarked on a period of domination the like of which the game had never seen. As their traditional rivals found it hard to maintain the pace, two new contenders emerged. Derby County and Nottingham Forest won the title three times between them, a remarkable achievement by the controversial manager who took both clubs from the Second Division to the top of the pile: Brian Clough.

Division Two teams get to Wembley

If Derby County and Nottingham Forest were the surprise packages in the league, there were several in the cup competitions. Between 1970 and 1980 seven Division Two sides made it to Wembley, while Division One strugglers Stoke and Ipswich also struck a blow for the underdog.

Ironically, as English sides prospered in Europe, the fortunes of the national team declined. After going to Mexico as holders in 1970, England suffered successive failures in the next two World Cup qualification campaigns.

Opposite: Leeds celebrate Mick Jones' goal in the 1970 FA Cup Final, believing that the Cup was theirs. But the celebrations were short-lived. Two minutes later Hutchinson scored to make it 2-2. Extra time at Wembley was followed by extra time in the replay at Old Trafford, where Chelsea ended victorious against a Leeds side recognised as one of the English league's greatest teams.
Below right: Harris and Hollins parade the FA Cup after Chelsea's 2-1 win in the replay against Leeds United.
Below left: New Year, 1971, the terraces at Ibrox Park where 66 fans died as a result of a crush when departing spectators tried to make their way back to the stand after Rangers scored a late goal in the derby match against Celtic. It raised questions about ground safety in British football stadiums which were not fully addressed until the end of the next decade.

Fences go up to counter hooligan threat

The 1970s also saw the introduction of a three-up, three-down system, and red and yellow cards for onfield misdemeanours. From 1974 the players also got to choose their own Player of the Year. It wasn't until the seventh vote took place, in 1980, that their choice, Terry McDermott, coincided with that of the Football Writers Association. On a more worrying note, the twin problems of indebtedness and hooliganism continued to cast a shadow over the game. Fences started to go up to try and counter the threat of pitch invasions, which became an increasingly common occurrence. The fact that few clubs were operating in the black didn't stop transfers from continuing their upward spiral, and before the end of the decade the English game had seen its first million-pound transfer.

Mexico 1970

Wonder save by Banks denies Pelé

The decade began with a footballing jamboree in Mexico. Many thought the squad Sir Alf Ramsey took to defend England's world crown was stronger than that which had won the Jules Rimet trophy four years earlier. Things got off to a bad start in Bogota, where England were acclimatising to the kind of temperatures they would face in Mexico. Bobby Moore was accused of stealing a bracelet and taken into custody. Although the charge was soon dropped, the incident overshadowed the squad's pre-tournament preparations.

England are joint favourites

England and Brazil were the joint favourites, and they were drawn in the same group. After each side had recorded a victory, the two teams met in Guadalajara. After a bright start by England, Jairzinho beat Cooper on the right wing and picked out Pelé with his cross. Pelé powered a downward header just inside the far post, but somehow Banks managed to scoop it up and over the bar. It was hailed as one of the greatest saves of all time. Pelé set up Jairzinho for the only goal of the match 14 minutes into the second half, but England had reason to be optimistic. Peters and Lee had missed chances, and Astle missed a golden opportunity when he came on as substitute. There was every indication that the two teams would meet again in the final.

England throw away 2-0 lead

That hope disappeared in Leon, where England faced West Germany in the quarter-final. 2-0 up through goals from Mullery and Peters, England looked odds-on to go through. In the second half Beckenbauer beat Peter Bonetti to pull one back for the Germans. The Chelsea keeper had been a late replacement for Banks, who had gone down with stomach cramps before the game. Suddenly it was the German side which had the momentum. Ramsey took off Bobby Charlton and Peters, replacing them with Colin Bell and Norman Hunter. A back header from Uwe Seeler looped agonisingly over Bonetti's head, forcing extra time. England's misery was complete when Gerd Muller, who would go on to be the tournament's top scorer, volleyed the winner from close range.

Two years later, West Germany again proved to be the stumbling-block in the quarter-final of the European Championship. Helmut Schoen's side was at its peak, and England had no answer as the Germans cruised to a 3-1 victory at Wembley. Ramsey's men earned a goalless draw in Berlin a fortnight later, but the damage had been done. Worse was to come the following year, and it would be a disappointment too many for the England manager.

Left: Members of the England team training at the Atlas Club in Guadalajara as they prepare for their match against Brazil in the 1970 World Cup in Mexico.

Opposite above: As they receive cars and membership of the RAC, some of the England World Cup squad pose for photographs. The 1970s saw the beginnings of sponsorship which was to develop as a major feature in the 1980s.

Opposite below left: Martin Chivers scores for Tottenham Hotspur. Spurs had paid £125,000 for Chivers in 1968 and throughout the early 1970s continued to pay big money in transfer deals. However, the decade was not particularly successful for the London club and they spent the 1977-78 season in Division Two.

Opposite below right: Footballers on fashion parade – Bob McNab, Geoff Hurst and Peter Marinello show that they can impress off the pitch as much as on it!

Double for Arsenal

Domestic football in the new decade got off to a dramatic start, Arsenal coming through with a late burst to record a famous Double in 1970-71. It was ten years on from Spurs' achievement, and fate decreed that the Gunners had to win their last match at White Hart Lane to secure the title. A Ray Kennedy goal settled the issue. Arsenal had been six points off the pace with six weeks to go, but 27 points from the last 16 games was unstoppable championship form. Almost inevitably it was Leeds who missed out, pipped by a single point.

Arsenal also left it late in the Cup. They needed a last-minute penalty to salvage a draw against Stoke in the semi-final before winning the replay 2-0. Five days after the Spurs match Arsenal went to Wembley for the 64th and final match of the campaign.

They were up against a Liverpool side that was in a state of flux. The likes of Tommy Lawrence, Ron Yeats, Peter Thompson, Roger Hunt and Ian St John had all disappeared as Shankly overhauled the squad completely. Teenager Emlyn Hughes had arrived from Blackpool in 1967. He had been joined by John Toshack, Larry Lloyd, Steve Heighway and Brian Hall in a new-look side. There were also two *Shankly's new look Liverpool* youngsters who would enjoy very different fortunes at the club. Shankly paid Wolves £100,000 for striker Alun Evans. He would show flashes of what he could do at Anfield but overall the verdict was one of disappointment. The same could hardly be said of Shankly's £35,000 buy from Scunthorpe, who sat in the stands to watch his new team-mates take on Arsenal. His name was Kevin Keegan.

Above: In extra time, Charlie George slams the ball into the net past Liverpool's keeper Ray Clemence to provide the goal that won Arsenal the FA Cup and the Double in the 1970-71 season; they had won the league with just one point to spare over Leeds United.

Left: The Double-winning Arsenal team arrive aboard an open-top bus at Islington Town Hall for a civic reception.

Opposite above: Members of the Arsenal team that had won the 1970 Fairs Cup (from 1972, the UEFA Cup), set off for the airport for a flight to Rome where they were to play Lazio at the start of their defence of the title.

Opposite below: Goal-scorer Martin Peters is lifted in celebration by Martin Chivers as Geoff Hurst rushes to congratulate and Scotland's Frank McLintock shouts in dismay in England's 3-1 win at Wembley in the Home Championships of 1971.

George hits Wembley winner

When Steve Heighway opened the scoring in extra time, it seemed that Keegan was about to take his place in a Cup-winning team. But Eddie Kelly poked in a scrappy equaliser, and Charlie George rifled in a 25-yard winner. It was a special day for Frank McClintock, who had suffered a string of Wembley disappointments. He was named Footballer of the Year for leading Arsenal to the fourth Double in history. Gunners' boss Bertie Mee received many plaudits, although credit was also due to the groundwork laid down by his predecessor, Billy Wright.

Derby take title in sunny Spain

Derby County finished a respectable 9th that year. Brian Clough had been at the Baseball Ground for four years, taking the club up as Division Two champions in 1968-69. 4th place in their first year back in the top flight was an excellent effort by the Rams. 9th this time round was

Clough's team beat Liverpool and Leeds for their first championship

still respectable. But to a perfectionist such as Clough that was never good enough. In 1972 his side won the title, albeit by the narrowest of margins and in the most dramatic circumstances. Derby beat Liverpool in their last game of the season to go one point clear at the top. Clough and his men then promptly decamped to Majorca, leaving Liverpool and Leeds - who both had one remaining fixture - to do their worst. Leeds needed just a point at mid-table Wolves. If they failed, Liverpool could go top with a win at Arsenal.

In the event neither club could meet its target. Leeds went down 2-1, while Liverpool were held to a goalless draw. Liverpool thought they'd won it with a last-minute goal from Toshack, but it was disallowed. Derby were champions for the first time in their history.

Hereford humble Newcastle

Leeds had the consolation of winning the centenary FA Cup Final, Allan Clarke scoring the only goal of the match against holders Arsenal. The highlight of the 1972 FA Cup came in the third round, when Hereford took on Newcastle United. The Southern League side seemed to have had their moment of glory with a 2-2 draw at St James's Park. In the replay at Edgar Street Hereford rode their luck until ten minutes from the end, when Malcolm Macdonald finally found the back of the net. Ronnie Radford sent the 15,000 crowd delirious with a 30-yard screamer, and Ricky George slotted home the winner in extra time. Hereford went on to draw 0-0 with West Ham before going down 3-1 at Upton Park in a replay. The club's Cup heroics helped to earn them election to the Football League the following season.

Opposite: The Leeds squad at the beginning of the 1972-73 season. The early 1970s were a part of the golden age for the club. They won the league in 1974 and were runners-up three years in succession between 1970 and 1972, and also had a series of good Cup runs.

Above top left: George Best in happier days. By the early 1970s, his career in the top flight was almost over. In December 1972 he was transfer-listed by the club after a series of failures to turn up for training and matches, as well as disagreements with United's new manager, Frank O'Farrell, who was sacked by the board at the same time as Best was given his marching orders. Ironically on the same day as United told him they no longer wanted him as a player, Best had written to the club saying he no longer wished to play for them.

Above top right: Liverpool's Kevin Keegan races for the ball in his team's match against Birmingham City in 1973. Keegan won European Footballer of the Year twice in the 1970s.

Above: Smiles on the faces of Leeds manager Don Revie and club captain, Billy Bremner as they hold the FA Cup which the club won in 1972, the competition's centenary year when they beat Arsenal 1-0.

Billy Bremner

Despite beginning his career as a winger, it was at the heart of the brilliant Leeds United side of the late 1960s and early 1970s that Billy Bremner made his name and where he enjoyed a phenomenal run of success. He forged a formidable midfield partnership with Johnny Giles and, although Giles was regarded as the skilful artist and canny ball-player, Bremner's superb passing and incisive forward runs made him a vital cog in the Elland Road machine.

54 caps for Scotland

As captain, Bremner led the side to two league championships, in 1968-69 and 1973-74, and to FA Cup victory over Arsenal in 1972. Leeds United also had two successful Inter-Cities Fairs Cup campaigns, in 1968 and 1971. Regrettably, Bremner's haul of runners-up medals was even bigger: Leeds finished runners-up in the league on five occasions during Bremner's era, and were beaten FA Cup finalists three times. After the team's defeat at the hands of Bayern Munich in the 1975 European Cup Final, Bremner moved to Hull City, and then finished his playing career at Doncaster.

Capped 54 times for Scotland, Bremner's appearances for his national side fell one short of Dennis Law's all-time record. His greatest triumph on the international stage was when he led the Scots in the 1974 World Cup Finals in West Germany, where they were unbeaten and unlucky to be eliminated on goal difference.

No stranger to controversy, he and Liverpool's Kevin Keegan became the first British players to be sent off at Wembley when they exchanged blows during the 1974-75 Charity Shield match. This was followed shortly afterwards by the decision to award a life ban from the Scottish FA following a misconduct charge during a trip to Copenhagen for a European Championship match. He died in 1997.

Stoke win League Cup after 7-hour marathon

The 1971-72 League Cup matched the FA Cup for drama. Entry to the League Cup was now compulsory and competition was fierce. Stoke and West Ham fought out a seven-hour semi-final marathon, a Terry Conroy goal settling the tie after two legs and two replays. Stoke beat Chelsea 2-1 in the final, and had thus played twelve games to get their hands on their first piece of silverware in their 109-year history. 35-year-old George Eastham hit the winner, his first goal for nearly two years. It was also a first medal at club level for 34-year-old Gordon Banks.

Clough quits Derby

Clough and his assistant, Peter Taylor, were the toast of Derby after winning the championship in 1972, yet barely a year later they and the club had parted company. The outspoken and abrasive Clough had not always endeared himself to the directors at the Baseball Ground, who feared that his controversial outbursts might land the club in hot water. In the autumn of 1973 relations worsened and Clough and Taylor resigned. Derby initially fared better than Clough. Former player Dave Mackay took over and he would lead the Rams to another championship in 1975. But by the end of the decade Derby would be back in Division Two, while Clough and Taylor would be managing the European champions.

Above: 'The Charlton Brothers'. During the 1970s Jackie (left) and Bobby Charlton continued to be successful at both club and national level. Jackie was an important member of the great Leeds team of the early years of the decade while Bobby remained loyal to Manchester United, despite the club's struggle to remain mid-table. At the end of the 1972-73 season Bobby retired, having played 751 games and scored 247 goals for the club.
Opposite: The 1971 Liverpool squad, pictured with manager Bill Shankly. The seventies was a decade of success for Liverpool with wins in the premier competitions at home and in Europe.

First European trophy for Liverpool

By the 1972-73 season Shankly had completed his rebuilding process. Liverpool stormed to a record 8th championship, using just 16 players all season. They made it a domestic and European double by winning the UEFA Cup, which had replaced the Fairs Cup the previous year. The fact that UEFA wanted to take the competition under its umbrella, as it had the Cup Winners' Cup a decade earlier, made no difference to English clubs' domination. Arsenal, Leeds and Spurs had won the last three finals, adding to Leeds' and Newcastle's victories at the end of the 1960s. Liverpool were thus bidding to bring the trophy back to England for the sixth successive year.

They faced holders Spurs in the semi-final and took a narrow 1-0 lead to White Hart Lane for the second leg. Martin Peters, who had moved to Spurs for a record £200,000 after the 1970 World Cup, scored twice in a 2-1 win, but Heighway's away goal put Liverpool through.

In the final they faced a highly rated Borussia Moenchengladbach side that included Netzer, Bonhof, Heynckes and Vogts. The first leg at Anfield showed Shankly at his cunning best. He played Brian Hall instead of John Toshack, feeling that the smaller, quicker man might get more joy against the German defence. Torrential rain forced an abandonment after 30 minutes, but in that time the Liverpool boss had seen that Moenchengladbach were susceptible to the high ball. 24 hours later Toshack was in the side champing at the bit after being left out of the original line-up. His flicks created two goals for Keegan and the Reds won 3-0. The German side nearly turned it round, winning the return leg 2-0, but Liverpool had their hands on their first European trophy.

Toshack and Keegan bring Liverpool first Euro success

Manchester United relegated

In 1973-74 Southampton finished 20th in the league and became the first Division One side to suffer from the new three-up, three-down system. Manchester United, European champions just six years earlier, finished one place below the Saints and found themselves in Division Two for the first time since 1938. The Manchester derby at Old Trafford has gone down in folklore as the game in which Denis Law, who had returned to his former club, backheeled the goal which put United down. Law, playing his last game before hanging up his boots, did put City one up, and after a pitch invasion that was the score when the game was halted four minutes from time. Several days later, the Football League decided to allow the result to stand. However, in the final table United finished four points behind Southampton and five adrift of Birmingham, the team which just avoided the drop. Manager Tommy Docherty would bring a new young side back to the top flight as Division Two champions the following year.

Ramsey sacked after "clown" denies England

The 1973-74 season saw a number of managerial bombshells. Hard on the heels of Clough's acrimonious departure from the Baseball Ground, Sir Alf Ramsey finally paid the price for failure. On 17 October 1973 a 1-1 draw against Poland ended England's hopes of qualifying for the 1974 World Cup. Poland keeper Jan Tomaszewski had been dubbed a "clown" but he was in inspired form on that night at Wembley. England peppered his goal for 90 minutes, but it took an Allan Clarke penalty to beat him. By then Poland were one up, Domarski's shot squeezing under Shilton's body. The fact that Poland went on to be one of the teams of the tournament in Germany, playing some delightful football on their way to finishing third, was of little consolation. Nor could it save Ramsey, who had been sacked a month earlier.

Revie takes England job

Joe Mercer was given temporary charge of the England team, and in July the FA announced that Don Revie would take over. Leeds had just won the title, five points ahead of arch-rivals Liverpool. Revie's men had been under threat from the FA following their appalling disciplinary record in previous seasons. In this campaign it was their footballing qualities which took the eye. Leeds went on a 29-match unbeaten run to win their second championship in style. Revie's decision to take the England job may have had something to do with the *Poland end England's 1974 World Cup dream* fact that he now had an ageing side that would need a major overhaul sooner rather than later. The man who stepped into Revie's shoes was Brian Clough, but he was barely there long enough to claim a car-parking space, let alone put his stamp on the team. Amid rumours of a dressing-room bust-ups between manager and players, Clough departed after just 44 days in charge.

Opposite below: Ian Porterfield's (right) shot flies over Leeds goalkeeper, Harvey, to score the goal that gave Second Division Sunderland a miraculous FA Cup victory against the favourites.

Opposite above: A delighted Sunderland manager, Bob Stokoe, hugs Porterfield after the team's stunning win.

Above: Allan Clarke scores from a penalty to put England level at one goal apiece with Poland. The draw in this game was not sufficient to take England through to the 1974 World Cup Finals in West Germany.

Johnny Giles

When Johnny Giles joined Leeds United from Manchester United in 1963 they were a Division Two side. Even in those days, at a cost of £35,000, Leeds got a bargain, for over the next 12 years Giles was a major influence in helping turn Don Revie's side into a force to rival Manchester United and Liverpool.

Leeds playmaker

Giles was originally a winger but at Leeds he became a superbly skilled and creative midfield playmaker, forming an almost telepathic partnership with the fiery Billy Bremner. In his first season at the club, 1963-64, Leeds won promotion to the First Division. During the following 10 years Leeds were never out of the top flight – never finishing lower than fourth in the table and twice taking the championship. Giles went on to win the FA Cup with Leeds in 1972, adding to the winners' medal he gained when he was part of Manchester United's victory over Leicester City nine years earlier. He also won two winners' medals in the Fairs Cup, but missed out on a European Cup victory when Leeds lost 2-0 to Bayern Munich in Paris in 1975. Soon after that defeat Giles left Elland Road for West Bromwich Albion.

As a Republic of Ireland international for nearly two decades, playing his 59th and last game in 1979, it was fitting that he ended his playing career with Shamrock Rovers.

Leeds fans riot as Bayern are crowned European champions

Jimmy Armfield took up the reins and although Leeds slipped to 9th in the league, they did make it to the 1975 European Cup Final. Leeds dominated in the early stages against holders Bayern Munich. They were unlucky not to be awarded a penalty and also had a Lorimer strike ruled out. Bayern weathered the storm and won the match with late goals from Roth and Muller. Leeds fans went on the rampage after the game and the club received a three-year ban from European competition. It hardly mattered as it was the end of a glorious era. Leeds were more commonly to be found in mid-table for the rest of the decade and were relegated early in the next.

Above: QPR's Stan Bowles strides confidently away from the goalmouth after scoring against Manchester United; Martin Buchan looks on disconsolately. That season, 1973-74, saw Manchester United relegated to Division Two when they scored only 32 points from 42 games.
Opposite above left: Hero – Kevin Keegan soars in the air to score England's second goal in their 2-0 win over Wales at Cardiff in 1974.
Opposite above right: Villain – Keegan lands a right to the jaw of Leeds captain Billy Bremner when the pair got into a brawl during the 1974 Charity Shield match.
Opposite below: The 1974 FA Cup Final saw Liverpool win 3-0 against Newcastle United. Here Keegan powers home the opening goal; he would later score the third.

Another World Cup exit for England

If Revie had timed his Elland Road exit well, his decision to take on the England job was to prove no great boost to his managerial career. He failed to establish a settled side, and although the usual club versus country wrangle didn't help matters, Revie himself contributed to the problem with constant changes in personnel. England failed to reach the last eight of the 1976 European Championship, and in July the following year he handed in his resignation. England were on the brink of yet another World Cup exit and Revie headed off to the Middle East with comments that he jumped before he was pushed ringing in his ears.

Ron Greenwood stepped into the breach and that autumn guided England to victories in their last two World Cup qualifying matches. A 2-0 win over Italy merely reversed the result in Rome. It was the victory over Luxembourg by the same score that settled England's fate, the Italians going through on goal difference. As in 1974, England lost out to a side that went on to do well in the tournament - Italy would finish fourth - but after the heady days of 1966, and to a lesser extent 1970, it was a bitter pill to swallow.

Fixtures postponed to increase England's chances

The gruelling nature of the domestic season was highlighted as a contributory factor in the national team's fortunes. Grudgingly, the Football League finally accepted the postponement of fixtures prior to key international matches.

League Division One 1970-1979

1969-1970

1	Everton	66
2	Leeds United	57
3	Chelsea	55
4	Derby County	53
5	Liverpool	51
6	Coventry	49
7	Newcastle United	47
8	Manchester United	45
9	Stoke	45
10	Manchester City	43
11	Tottenham Hotspur	43
12	Arsenal	42
13	Wolverhampton W.	40
14	Burnley	39
15	Nottingham Forest	38
16	West Bromwich Albion	37
17	West Ham United	36
18	Ipswich	31
19	Southampton	29
20	Crystal Palace	27
21	Sunderland	26
22	Sheffield Wednesday	25

1970-71

1	Arsenal	65
2	Leeds United	64
3	Tottenham Hotspur	52
4	Wolverhampton W.	52
5	Liverpool	51
6	Chelsea	51
7	Southampton	46
8	Manchester United	43
9	Derby County	42
10	Coventry	42
11	Manchester City	41
12	Newcastle United	41
13	Stoke	37
14	Everton	37
15	Huddersfield	36
16	Nottingham Forest	36
17	West Bromwich Albion	35
18	Crystal Palace	35
19	Ipswich	34
20	West Ham United	34
21	Burnley	27
22	Blackpool	23

1971-72

1	Derby County	58
2	Leeds United	57
3	Liverpool	57
4	Manchester City	57
5	Arsenal	52
6	Tottenham Hotspur	51
7	Chelsea	48
8	Manchester United	48
9	Wolverhampton W.	47
10	Sheffield United	46
11	Newcastle United	41
12	Leicester City	39
13	Ipswich	38
14	West Ham United	36
15	Everton	36
16	West Bromwich Albion	35
17	Stoke	35
18	Coventry	33
19	Southampton	31
20	Crystal Palace	29
21	Nottingham Forest	25
22	Huddersfield	25

1972-73

1	Liverpool	60
2	Arsenal	57
3	Leeds United	53
4	Ipswich	48
5	Wolverhampton W.	47
6	West Ham United	46
7	Derby County	46
8	Tottenham Hotspur	45
9	Newcastle United	45
10	Birmingham City	42
11	Manchester City	41
12	Chelsea	40
13	Southampton	40
14	Sheffield United	40
15	Stoke	38
16	Leicester City	37
17	Everton	37
18	Manchester United	37
19	Coventry	35
20	Norwich City	32
21	Crystal Palace	30
22	West Bromwich Albion	28

1973-74

1	Leeds United	62
2	Liverpool	57
3	Derby County	48
4	Ipswich	47
5	Stoke	46
6	Burnley	46
7	Everton	44
8	Queen's Park Rangers	43
9	Leicester City	42
10	Arsenal	42
11	Tottenham Hotspur	42
12	Wolverhampton W.	41
13	Sheffield United	40
14	Manchester City	40
15	Newcastle United	38
16	Coventry	38
17	Chelsea	37
18	West Ham United	37
19	Birmingham City	37
20	Southampton	36
21	Manchester United	32
22	Norwich City	29

1974-75

1	Derby County	53
2	Liverpool	51
3	Ipswich	51
4	Everton	50
5	Stoke	49
6	Sheffield United	49
7	Middlesbrough	48
8	Manchester City	46
9	Leeds United	45
10	Burnley	45
11	Queen's Park Rangers	42
12	Wolverhampton W.	39
13	West Ham United	39
14	Coventry	39
15	Newcastle United	39
16	Arsenal	37
17	Birmingham City	37
18	Leicester City	36
19	Tottenham Hotspur	34
20	Luton	33
21	Chelsea	33
22	Carlisle	29

1975-76

1	Liverpool	60
2	Queen's Park Rangers	59
3	Manchester United	56
4	Derby County	53
5	Leeds United	51
6	Ipswich	46
7	Leicester City	45
8	Manchester City	43
9	Tottenham Hotspur	43
10	Norwich City	42
11	Everton	42
12	Stoke	41
13	Middlesbrough	40
14	Coventry	40
15	Newcastle United	39
16	Aston Villa	39
17	Arsenal	36
18	West Ham United	36
19	Birmingham City	33
20	Wolverhampton W.	30
21	Burnley	28
22	Sheffield United	22

1976-77

1	Liverpool	57
2	Manchester City	56
3	Ipswich	56
4	Aston Villa	51
5	Newcastle United	49
6	Manchester United	47
7	West Bromwich Albion	45
8	Arsenal	43
9	Everton	42
10	Leeds United	42
11	Leicester City	42
12	Middlesbrough	41
13	Birmingham City	38
14	Queen's Park Rangers	38
15	Derby County	37
16	Norwich City	37
17	West Ham United	36
18	Bristol City	35
19	Coventry	35
20	Sunderland	34
21	Stoke	34
22	Tottenham Hotspur	33

1977-78

1	Nottingham Forest	64
2	Liverpool	57
3	Everton	55
4	Manchester City	52
5	Arsenal	52
6	West Bromwich Albion	50
7	Coventry	48
8	Aston Villa	46
9	Leeds United	46
10	Manchester United	42
11	Birmingham City	41
12	Derby County	41
13	Norwich City	40
14	Middlesbrough	39
15	Wolverhampton W.	36
16	Chelsea	36
17	Bristol City	35
18	Ipswich	35
19	Queen's Park Rangers	33
20	West Ham United	32
21	Newcastle United	22
22	Leicester City	22

1978-79

1	Liverpool	68
2	Nottingham Forest	60
3	West Bromwich Albion	59
4	Everton	51
5	Leeds United	50
6	Ipswich	49
7	Arsenal	48
8	Aston Villa	46
9	Manchester United	45
10	Coventry	44
11	Tottenham Hotspur	41
12	Middlesbrough	40
13	Bristol City	40
14	Southampton	40
15	Manchester City	39
16	Norwich City	37
17	Bolton Wanderers	35
18	Wolverhampton W.	34
19	Derby County	31
20	Queen's Park Rangers	25
21	Birmingham City	22
22	Chelsea	20

Opposite: Bill Shankly offers a prayer of thanks as Liverpool win the league championship by three points from rivals Arsenal in the 1972-73 season. The following season, Shankly's last at the helm, Liverpool were beaten into second place by Leeds.

FA Cup Finals

1970	Chelsea	v	Leeds United	2-1
1971	Arsenal	v	Liverpool	2-1
1972	Leeds United	v	Arsenal	1-0
1973	Sunderland	v	Leeds United	1-0
1974	Liverpool	v	Newcastle United	3-0
1975	West Ham United	v	Fulham	2-0
1976	Southampton	v	Manchester United	1-0
1977	Manchester United	v	Liverpool	2-1
1978	Ipswich Town	v	Arsenal	1-0
1979	Arsenal	v	Manchester United	3-2

End of an era as Shanks steps down

When Ron Greenwood picked his first England side, he named seven Liverpool players. By the middle of the decade they were the team everyone had to beat. In 1973-74, having finished runners-up to Leeds and beaten Newcastle Utd in the FA Cup Final, Liverpool were the latest club to experience a shock managerial resignation. Bill Shankly announced his retirement, ending his 15-year reign at Anfield. After Liverpool's 3-0 demolition of Newcastle at Wembley, Liverpool fans had prostrated themselves at Shankly's feet on the pitch. Two months later he was gone. His final act was a typically shrewd move. The Liverpool way was to strengthen well before it was necessary. Competition was so fierce that players dreaded being sidelined through injury for fear that they might not get back in the team. It was after Shankly unveiled his last signing, Arsenal's Ray Kennedy, that he shuffled off the stage. The Liverpool board may have been worried that the Shankly aura might continue to pervade Anfield in the way that Busby's had at Old Trafford. In the event the break was swift and final, something Shankly was said to have found surprising and hurtful.

Bill Shankly

When Bill Shankly left Anfield for the last time after winning the 1974 FA Cup, it brought down the curtain on a glorious 15-year reign. In that time Shankly had turned Liverpool from a struggling, unambitious club into one of the most formidable sides in world football.

Waking the sleeping giant

Shankly had had success with the other clubs he had managed - Carlisle, Grimsby, Workington and Huddersfield - but was hampered by their lack of vision and unwillingness to invest. Liverpool, on the other hand, was a true sleeping giant, and it was Shankly who woke it up and unleashed it on the world. Promotion to the top flight came in 1961-62, his second full season at the club. After just one season of consolidation Liverpool won the championship. Over the next 10 years he steered the club to two more league titles and two FA Cup victories. He also lifted the UEFA Cup in 1973, Liverpool beating Borussia Moenchengladbach in the final. The man from Glenbuck, Ayrshire was revered by fans and players alike, who loved his dry wit. He certainly laid the foundations for the side which dominated the English game in the 1970s and 1980s. Shankly died in 1981. His name adorns a pair of gates at the entrance to his beloved Anfield and his spirit pervades the club to this day.

Another League and European double for the Reds

Opposite top: A fan adorns Bill Shankly with a scarf as he bids farewell to Anfield after fifteen years as Liverpool's manager.
Opposite below: The Aston Villa team, with manager Ron Saunders (pointing), inspect the Wembley pitch before their League Cup Final match against Norwich in 1975. Villa won the tie 1-0.
Above: Alan Taylor scores the second of his two goals which clinched the FA Cup for West Ham against London rivals Fulham in the 1975 Final.
Above top: West Ham's Trevor Brooking is mobbed by fans after the team's defeat of their Second Division rivals.

In 1975-76 Queen's Park Rangers were the surprise package. Led by England captain Gerry Francis, QPR were top of the league when they'd completed their fixtures. But Liverpool could pip them by winning their last game, at Molineux. Wolves had to win to have any chance of avoiding relegation and they scored first. The Reds came back to win 3-1, however. Wolves were down and Paisley had his first championship under his belt. He also matched Shankly's feat of three years earlier by capturing the UEFA Cup in the same season. Liverpool put out a Barcelona side that boasted Johan Cruyff in the semis, then faced FC Bruges in the final. The Belgians rocked Liverpool by taking a 2-0 lead at Anfield, but the Reds staged a magnificent fightback to win 3-2. Bruges also scored first in the second leg, but a Keegan strike won the trophy for Liverpool.

Strikes bring Sunday football

1974 saw Sunday football played for the first time. This was a tentative move and by no means uncontroversial. A combination of rail and power strikes persuaded the authorities to sanction these matches. Sunday trading laws meant that grounds could not simply open for business as they would on any other day. There were legal restrictions on charging at the gate and clubs circumvented these by selling programmes at the turnstiles for the normal entrance price. These games proved to be very popular with the fans and Sunday soccer would eventually become a way of life.

Paisley emerges from "boot room" to take over at Anfield

The famous Anfield "boot room" had been established during the Shankly years. Bob Paisley, Joe Fagan, Ronnie Moran and Reuben Bennett were the key men in the backroom team. Paisley was given the top job, everyone took a step up in the pecking order and a seamless transition was effected.

In Paisley's first season in charge Liverpool finished runners-up to Derby. It was notable for two inspired purchases as Paisley showed he had Shankly's golden touch in the transfer market. Northampton's Phil Neal joined the Reds in a £60,000 deal in October 1974. A month later Terry McDermott, who had played against Liverpool in that year's Cup Final, arrived from Newcastle for £170,000.

Above: The Manchester United squad, with manager, Tommy 'The Doc' Docherty (far right), at the end of the 1975-76 season. Although the club lost the 1976 FA Cup Final to Southampton, they won the following year and were back on track after their spell in Division Two during 1974-75.

Opposite bottom: United's Alex Stepney watches the ball go into the net as Bobby Stokes' goal, the only goal of the match, secures the 1976 FA Cup for Southampton.

Opposite middle: West Ham's Frank Lampard and Manchester City's Rodney Marsh race for the ball during a league game at the beginning of the 1975-76 season. Despite West Ham's Cup win in 1975, they struggled to avoid relegation at he end of the 1975-76 season.

Opposite top: The 'Saints come rolling home' – the Southampton players who won the 1976 FA Cup travel through the streets of their home city, lined by 175,000 people, to attend a civic reception.

United reach successive Cup Finals

1975-76 marked Manchester United's return to the First Division, and Tommy Docherty's young side was immediately chasing the double. They eventually finished third in the league, but in the FA Cup Final they were hot favourites to beat Lawrie McMenemy's Southampton, who had finished only sixth in the Second Division. Mick Channon and Peter Osgood led the line for Southampton but it was a solitary goal from Bobby Stokes seven minutes from time that brought the club its first major honour.

McMenemy's Southampton lift the Cup

United returned to Wembley the following year and this time they faced a Liverpool side which was seeking an unprecedented treble. Having secured a 10th league title, Liverpool had to play two Cup Finals in quick succession. The dream was ended at Wembley, where Docherty's burgeoning young side came out on top. Only Alex Stepney remained from the glory team of the 1960s. Stepney saw a Jimmy Case thunderbolt fly past him, cancelling out a Stuart Pearson shot which had squeezed under Clemence's body. A Lou Macari effort deflected off Jimmy Greenhoff for United's winner. It was an outrageous fluke but after the previous year's disappointment neither United nor the Doc were worried about that.

Keegan bows out as Liverpool become champions of Europe

Five days later Liverpool had to pick themselves up as they made their bid to become only the second English side to win the European Cup. Their quarter-final clash with St Etienne had been the key match in their run to the final. St Etienne, the previous year's beaten finalists, had scored a 1-0 win at home, and were outstanding at Anfield. The French side scored to cancel out a Keegan goal, and even after Ray Kennedy restored Liverpool's lead on the night, the Reds still trailed on away goals. Enter David Fairclough, who came on with 20 minutes to go and scored the winner after a breathtaking solo run. "Supersub" had done it again.

Liverpool eased into the final with a win over FC Zurich. They travelled to Rome to face a Borussia Moenchengladbach side for the second time in a major final. The players shrugged off their FA Cup disappointment with an excellent 3-1 victory. It was a great day for two veterans. Tommy Smith, who had made his debut in 1963, headed in a Heighway corner to make it 2-1. Smith was a relative newcomer compared to Ian Callaghan, who had been at Anfield when the club was fighting for promotion to the top flight in the late 1950s.

It was also a special day for Kevin Keegan, playing his last game in the famous No. 7 shirt. His £500,000 move to SV Hamburg had already been agreed. Keegan didn't manage to get on the scoresheet in his final appearance but he gave Berti Vogts a torrid time. The ace German marker finally made a rash challenge, bringing Keegan down inside the box. Penalty king Phil Neal fired in the team's third goal, and Liverpool had equalled Manchester United's achievement of 1968.

Left: After Liverpool's European Cup victory in 1977, Kevin Keegan signed for SV Hamburg. Above: Emlyn Hughes, Liverpool captain, holds the European Cup aloft, after the club's 3-1 win over Borussia Moenchengladbach.

Kevin Keegan

For a player who knew he wasn't the most naturally gifted in the game, Kevin Keegan demonstrated that a football career can be built as much on hard work, commitment and self-belief as on virtuoso skills. Surprisingly powerful in the air for a small man, he had a rocketing shot that made him a notable goal-scorer, and was always looking to create opportunities for others during six glorious years at Liverpool FC, after Bill Shankly brought him to Merseyside in 1971 from Scunthorpe United, paying just £35,000.

European Footballer of the Year

Keegan scored in his very first game, and he soon made himself vital at the heart of the team. The very next season he netted 22 goals, helping Liverpool to win both the League Championship and the UEFA Cup. He scored twice in Liverpool's 3-0 victory over Newcastle in the 1974 FA Cup Final, and was named the Footballer of the Year in 1976 after the Reds again took the league title and he scored in both legs of the final of the UEFA Cup when they beat Bruges.

The Anfield faithful paid handsome tribute when Keegan was lured to Hamburg in a record £500,000 deal, for he had played 230 games and scored 68 goals in the famous red shirt. Playing in the Bundesliga, he twice won European Footballer of the Year, in 1978 and 1979, the only British player ever to do so.

63 England caps

First appearing for England (against Wales) in 1972, his international career spanned 10 years, during which he won 63 caps (31 of them as captain) and scored 21 goals. The end came when he missed a vital chance in a second-round match against Spain in the 1982 World Cup, and was then dropped for a European Championship qualifying game by Bobby Robson. Keegan soon quit international football.

But his return to the English league provided a happier swansong. At Southampton and finally at Newcastle, he came right back into form and helped the Geordie side to win promotion to the First Division at the end of the 1983-84 season.

Returning to Tyneside as manager in 1992, he took the Magpies back to the top flight in short order, then made a surprise move to Fulham. Though he confessed to feelings of inadequacy at the end of his tenure as England manager, he showed he could still work his magic at club level, establishing Manchester City as a Premiership force once again before stepping down during the 2004-05 season.

Above top: Arsenal's Liam Brady leaps over a tackle from David Geddis of Ipswich in the 1978 FA Cup Final. Despite Brady's athleticism, he was on the losing side as Ipswich won with a single goal from Roger Osborne.
Above: Arsenal's Malcolm MacDonald leaves the pitch at Wembley after his team's defeat in the FA Cup Final. His dejection can be understood – he had been on the losing side in a Wembley Final twice before, with Newcastle United, in the FA Cup in 1974 and the League Cup in 1976.

Dalglish the new No. 7 hero

Keegan went on to win the European Footballer of the Year award twice while at Hamburg. The blow of losing a player who had become a legend in his six years at Anfield was softened as Paisley went north of the border for a big-name replacement. 26-year-old Kenny Dalglish arrived in Liverpool a month after Keegan's departure. He had scored over a hundred goals for Celtic, the club he had joined at the age of 16. By the end of his first season at Liverpool he had notched 30, putting him well on the way to becoming a double centurion. The Kop had a new idol in the famous number 7 shirt.

Kenny Dalglish

Already established as a legend at Celtic after a decade of service to the club he joined straight from school, Kenny Dalglish transferred to Liverpool in 1977. A month after Kevin Keegan had left Anfield for SV Hamburg, Liverpool boss Bob Paisley swooped to buy the most feared striker in the Scottish League.

Hundred league goals for Liverpool

Dalglish proved his worth to the club over the next 14 years, both as a player and as a manager; he became the idol of the Kop. In November 1983, he scored his hundredth league goal for Liverpool, the first player to reach that landmark both north and south of the border. He won five championship medals and three European Cups before taking over the reins from Joe Fagan in May 1985, in the wake of the Heysel Stadium disaster. With Dalglish as player-manager, Liverpool won the coveted Double in the 1985-86 season.

On the international stage, the player widely considered to be the greatest ever to wear the red of Liverpool also won a record 102 caps for Scotland, scoring 30 goals at international level to match Denis Law's record.

Forest storm to the championship

Kenny Dalglish had arrived at Anfield in a blaze of publicity. There had been less of a fanfare when Paisley signed centre-back Alan Hansen from Partick Thistle for £100,000 a couple of months earlier. The 1977-78 season also saw the arrival of a third Scot who would become an Anfield legend. Paisley paid Middlesbrough £350,000 for midfielder Graeme Souness, who provided skill and steel in the heart of the midfield.

Three quality additions to a European Cup-winning side wasn't enough for Liverpool to retain the title in 1977-78. The Reds trailed in seven points behind Brian Clough's newly-promoted Nottingham Forest. Following the Leeds debacle, Clough had been reunited with Peter Taylor and taken over at Forest. The team only went up in third place behind Wolves and Chelsea and were tipped to make a rapid return to Division Two. Instead, Forest made it a Championship and League Cup double, with mighty Liverpool having to settle for second-best in both cases.

Opposite above: Kenny Dalglish moves in to score the goal that put the holders of the title, Ipswich, out of the 1978-79 FA Cup competition. It was Dalglish's second season at Liverpool and he had proved worthy of the record £440,000 paid to bring the Celtic striker to Anfield as a replacement for Kevin Keegan. In his first season, Dalglish scored 31 goals in 62 appearances for the club.
Opposite below: A Dalglish diving header beats Chelsea's Micky Droy but hits the woodwork in a league game in March during the 1977-78 season when Liverpool turned out runners-up to Nottingham Forest in the championship.
Above left: Ipswich's Mick Mills holds up the Cup for the fans after the team's 1-0 win over Arsenal in the 1978 FA Cup Final.
Above right: Just one year later and Arsenal reverse their fortunes to take the Cup to Highbury in a 3-2 win over Manchester United.

Clough matches Chapman's record

Clough's side included ex-Derby players John McGovern, John O'Hare and Archie Gemmill, together with former Liverpool stopper Larry Lloyd. Clough added Kenny Burns, turning the former Birmingham City bad boy into the Footballer of the Year. There was also Viv Anderson, a young attacking full-back who became England's first black player when he took the field against Czechoslovakia on 29 November 1978. But the key acquisition was probably Peter Shilton, bought from Stoke for £270,000, the highest amount ever paid for a goalkeeper. Forest lost just three games all season, conceding only 24 league goals, and took the title with four games to spare. Clough followed in the illustrious footsteps of Herbert Chapman in taking two clubs to the championship.

Forest lose only three games all season

Liverpool retain European Cup

Forest also got the better of Liverpool in the 1978 League Cup Final, a John Robertson penalty settling the issue at Old Trafford after a goalless draw at Wembley. Having been pipped for domestic honours twice, Liverpool made sure they didn't finish the season empty-handed by retaining their European crown. FC Bruges were their Wembley opponents. The Belgians set their stall out defensively, inviting Liverpool to try and break them down. The Reds managed to do so just once, Dalglish chipping the keeper delightfully for his 30th goal of the season.

Osborne overcome as Ipswich lift FA Cup

Between 19 November 1977 and 9 December 1978 Forest were unbeaten in the league. Their only defeat in any competition was an FA Cup quarter-final tie with West Bromwich Albion, who won 2-0. Having beaten the country's form team, West Brom went down to Ipswich in the semis, and it was the East Anglian club who were the surprise winners of the trophy. That game will be remembered for the Roger Osborne goal which beat favourites Arsenal in the final. Osborne was so overwrought with the occasion that he was substituted, apparently through sheer nervous exhaustion. His goal took the Cup to Portman Road for the only time in the club's history.

Above: Arsenal's goalkeeper tries to thwart a Liverpool attack as Graeme Souness looks on during a league match in the 1978-79 season when honours were shared - Liverpool won the league and Arsenal the FA Cup.
Opposite: Nottingham Forest goalkeeper, Peter Shilton, and team-mate, Tony Woodcock, hold the League Cup after the team's 3-2 win against Southampton in 1979. The late 1970s were a golden time for Nottingham Forest. Under manager Brian Clough, they won the league in 1978, the European Cup in 1979 and the League Cup in 1978 and 1979.

Milestones 1970-1979

1970 Manchester City wins the European Cup Winners' Cup and the League Cup

Ninth World Cup is held in Mexico; Brazil wins the competition for the third time and wins the Jules Rimet trophy outright. England lost to West Germany 3-2 in the quarter finals

First football song to reach No. 1 in the charts – 'Back Home' by the England World Cup squad

Chelsea and Leeds meet in the FA Cup Final and draw; the first draw in a Final at Wembley caused a rematch which Chelsea won

1971 Chelsea wins European Cup Winners' Cup

1972 UEFA Cup, formally the Fairs Cup, won by Tottenham Hotspur

1973 Liverpool become the first club to win the league title and a European Cup when they win the UEFA Cup

1974 Last FA Amateur Cup Final

League football played on Sunday for the first time

England did not qualify for the tenth World Cup held in West Germany, which was won by the host nation

Football Hooliganism fast becoming known as the 'English Disease' after 100 Chelsea fans were arrested for rioting at Luton Town and 50 Manchester United fans were arrested in Stoke on the same day at the beginning of the season

1976 Yellow card introduced

1977 Liverpool win the European Cup for the first time

1978 Liverpool win the European Cup for the second year running

English FA lifts its ban on overseas players

Eleventh World Cup competition held in Argentina and England failed to qualify again – the host team won

Viv Anderson becomes the first player of Afro-Caribbean origin in the England squad in a match against Czechoslovakia

1979 First £1,000,000 transfer sees Trevor Francis move from Birmingham City to Nottingham Forest

Nottingham Forest wins the European Cup

Liverpool becomes the first league side to wear their sponsors' name, Hitachi, on their shirts

Reds set new defensive record

1978-79 saw Liverpool and Forest dominant once again, although this time their roles were reversed. On 9 December 1978 Liverpool ended Forest's year-long unbeaten run in the league. The Forest bubble didn't burst, however, and they again lost just three times in the league. Incredibly, that was only good enough to earn them second place behind a Liverpool side that was in record-breaking mood. Forest's 60 points would have won the championship on numerous postwar occasions. Liverpool themselves had won with that same points tally in 1973 and 1976, and Derby's two titles had been won with a lesser total. Liverpool lost one more game than Forest but 30 wins and eight draws gave them 68 points, one better than the record set by Leeds in 1968-69. The Reds' defence was phenomenal conceding just 16 goals all season.

Million-pound Francis wins European Cup for Forest

If Liverpool had reclaimed their domestic crown from Forest, it was Clough's men who took Liverpool's mantle as champions of Europe. The two sides were unlucky to be drawn together in the first round of the European Cup, a game that would have graced the final. New young striking sensation Garry Birtles scored one of the goals as Forest took a 2-0 lead to Anfield. There they fought out a goalless draw and it was Forest who went forward to try and bring Europe's premier cup back to England for the third successive year. They did so, but not without a scare or two. In their semi-final against Cologne Forest could only draw 3-3 at home. But Clough masterminded a 1-0 win in Germany, Ian Bowyer scoring the goal which put Forest into the final.

They faced Swedish champions Malmo in the Olympic Stadium, Munich. The hero of the hour was Trevor Francis, who headed the only goal of the game just before the break. Francis had become Britain's first million-pound footballer earlier in the season, Birmingham City finally being forced to part with their prize asset. Francis had not been eligible to play in the earlier European ties. His first taste of European football had won the premier trophy and paid off a large chunk of that record fee.

Above: Trevor Francis and Nottingham Forest captain, John McGovern hold up the European Cup as the victorious team are driven through the streets of Nottingham in celebration of their superb achievement.
Left: The joy on Arsenal's Alan Sunderland's face says it all, after he snatches a last-gasp winner in the 1979 FA Cup Final to beat Manchester United 3-2.

Brian Clough

Brian Clough was the fans' choice to be given the England manager's job in the 1970s and early 1980s. The accepted wisdom was that it was his outspoken, abrasive style that cost him a chance of getting the top job rather than his footballing credentials, which were of the highest order.

Clough had been a prolific goalscorer with Middlesbrough and Sunderland, and was capped for England before his playing career was cut short through injury. In 1965 30-year-old Clough became the youngest manager in the league when he took over at Hartlepool, but it was when he moved to Derby County that he established his reputation. He led the Rams to the Division Two championship in 1969, and after two years of consolidation in the top flight, his side won the league title in 1972. The team reached the semi-final of the European Cup the following year, losing 3-1 on aggregate to Juventus. Derby fans were up in arms when Clough left the Baseball Ground following a disagreement with the board. After an infamous 44-day reign at Leeds United at the beginning of the 1974-75 season, Clough embarked on a glorious 18-year association with another unfashionable club, Nottingham Forest. He won the championship in 1977-78, relegating Liverpool to second place for once. In doing so he became only the third manager in history to win the title with two different clubs. In 1979 he won the European Cup with a 1-0 win over Malmo. The goal was scored by Trevor Francis, whom Clough had made the first £1 million player. Forest retained the trophy the following year, a John Robertson penalty giving the team victory over Hamburg. Clough also won the League Cup four times during his reign at the City Ground. He retired after the team was relegated in 1993. Brian Clough died on 20 September 2004.

Brady stars in five-goal Wembley thriller

The last FA Cup Final of the decade provided a goal flurry in the dying minutes. Arsenal, with Liam Brady in imperious form, took a 2-0 lead over Manchester United and seemed to be coasting to victory. Some United fans were already making their way to the exits when goals from McQueen and McIlroy, in the 86th and 88th minutes, levelled the match. Man-of-the-match Brady had the final word, setting up the move which ended with Alan Sunderland scoring from a Graham Rix cross.

Liverpool domination set to continue

The 1979 FA Cup Final was refreshing in that it was untypical of the trend, which was for scoring fewer goals and conceding fewer. The decade's champions had, on average, scored 69.9 goals and let in 32.2. In the 1960s the average had been 87.3 and 45.7; in the 1950s it was 92.4 and 51.2. In 1961-62 Ipswich conceded 67 goals on their way to the title, which compared favourably with the number of goals scored by championship-winning sides of the 1970s. The new orthodoxy was getting men behind the ball, denying the opposition space and protecting leads.

15 of the 60 teams that had made it to the finals of the three European competitions over the decade were English, and ten of those had been successful. Liverpool had led the charge, and the Anfield juggernaut showed every sign of rolling on into the 1980s.

Above: Argentinian international, Osvaldo 'Ossie' Ardiles pictured in his Tottenham shirt soon after he, and international team-mate, Ricky Villa, joined Spurs. The signing of the two stars of the 1978 World Cup was a coup for Spurs manager, Keith Burkinshaw.

1980-1989
Glory and Tragedy

In the 1980s Liverpool continued their stranglehold on the English game, their level of performance and trophy haul enduring a number of personnel changes, including two at managerial level. By the middle of the decade it was Everton who posed the greatest threat, and their two championships meant that only twice in the decade did the title leave Merseyside.

Above: Joe Jordan of Scotland and England's Dave Watson battle for the ball at Wembley.
Opposite:Goalkeeper Peter Shilton of Nottingham Forest punches the ball clear of the goal as Arsenal attack. Arsenal won the match 1-0, but Forest were in fine form in 1980 and were to beat SV Hamburg in the European Cup Final.

Heysel, Hillsborough and Bradford

If the city of Liverpool basked in the glory of being footballing top dogs, it also suffered two horrific tragedies. A total of 135 people lost their lives in the Heysel and Hillsborough disasters. On 11 May 1985, less than three weeks before the Heysel tragedy, Bradford entertained Lincoln City in their last match of the season. It should have been a joyous occasion, Bradford celebrating promotion to Division Two as champions. A discarded cigarette set the wooden stand ablaze and 56 died in the inferno. These three events put the game into its proper perspective. Liverpool boss Kenny Dalglish declared that football was "irrelevant" as the city struggled to come to terms with the tragic events at Hillsborough. These disasters also led the game's administrators to realise that fencing in spectators may have prevented pitch invasions, but it also prevented fans from escaping life-threatening situations.

European victory for Forest

The decade began much as the last one had ended, with Liverpool and Nottingham Forest vying for supremacy at home and in Europe. In 1980 the Reds took the championship but crashed out of the European Cup at the first hurdle to Dinamo Tbilisi. Forest came through some tough matches, even surviving a home defeat against Dynamo Berlin. A Trevor Francis double helped Forest turn that tie around and they marched on to meet Kevin Keegan's SV Hamburg in the Final. The showcase events were becoming worryingly sterile affairs and this was no great advertisement for the game. John Robertson scored the only goal, cutting in from the left and firing home from 20 yards. Francis had been sidelined through injury and the team was content to sit back and play on the break. When Hamburg did manage to carve an opening, they found Shilton in prime form.

Brooking sets up Hammers

Forest also made it to the League Cup Final, for the third year running. There was no hat-trick of wins, though. A catastrophic mix-up between Shilton and Dave Needham allowed Wolves' Andy Gray to score the game's only goal.

Also playing in the famous Old Gold shirt that day was Emlyn Hughes, recently arrived from Liverpool. In his 13 years at Anfield he had won just about every honour in the game - except the League Cup.

The 1980 FA Cup Final was also settled by a solitary goal. Arsenal must have thought their name was on the Cup after coming through a mammoth semi-final against Liverpool which went to three replays, seven hours of football in total. A Brian Talbot goal finally broke the deadlock and put the Gunners into the Final for the third year running. They faced a West Ham side that had finished 7th in Division Two but a rare header from midfield maestro Trevor Brooking was enough to give the Hammers victory. It was a red-letter day for 17-year-old Paul Allen, the youngest player ever to appear in an FA Cup Final.

Arsenal miss out in Cup Winners Cup

Arsenal's dramatic win over Manchester United the previous year had put them through to the Cup Winners' Cup competition and the Gunners made it through to the Final. Valencia provided the glamorous opposition, but 120 minutes of football produced no goals and this became the first major Final to be decided on penalties. Argentine World Cup hero Mario Kempes missed, but parity was restored when Liam Brady also failed with his spot-kick. Graham Rix was the unlucky man to miss the vital kick and the trophy went to Spain. Arsenal were left with the unique distinction of returning to Highbury empty-handed despite having gone through the tournament unbeaten.

England's Euro failure

In the European Championship England dropped just one point in their eight qualifying matches to reach the finals, which were staged in Italy. A revised format saw the eight countries split into two groups with the winners of each contesting the Final. Tear gas had to be used to quell disturbances as England opened with a goalless draw against Belgium. Marco Tardelli scored the only goal of the game when England met the hosts in the second game. England were out without registering a single goal, although they did manage a 2-1 win against Spain in a meaningless final group match.

Three points for a win

By 1981 concern over the state of the game was being expressed in high places. A lot of the fare on offer was of indifferent quality; hooliganism was a cancer that was proving difficult to excise; and with the country in the grip of recession a match-day ticket became a luxury some fans could ill afford. Liverpool's dominance didn't help matters. Gates were barely above the 20 million mark, half what they had been in the golden postwar years. Several clubs were teetering on the edge of bankruptcy, Wolves among them.

The Football League announce plans to make the game more attacking.

The Football League announced that from 1981-82, there would be three points for a win. The message was clear: football was entertainment as well as sport, and the carrot of three points would surely make teams think twice about putting up the defensive drawbridge.

Villa take the championship

The intervening season brought plenty of drama, not least of which was the sight of Liverpool languishing in 5th place in the league. The Reds lost just eight games, which was as good as anyone, but had drawn as many as they'd won. It was Ron Saunders' Aston Villa who took the title, for the first time in 71 years. Villa used just 14 players all season and seven of them were ever-present. Ex-Coventry player Dennis Mortimer captained the side, forming an impressive midfield axis with Gordon Cowans and Des Bremner, who provided skill and steel respectively. Up front Peter Withe and Gary Shaw made up a potent little-and-large strike force. Flying winger Tony Morley was responsible for many assists and was also a regular on the scoresheet himself.

Ardiles and Villa in Cup classic

1981 saw Spurs continue their love affair with years ending in one. In the FA Cup Final Manchester City's Tommy Hutchinson scored twice, the second of which he would rather not have claimed. A Glenn Hoddle free-kick deflected off him and earned Spurs a replay. Keith Burkinshaw had pulled off the transfer coup of the year when he brought Ricardo Villa and Osvaldo Ardiles to White Hart Lane after Argentina's World Cup victory in 1978. In 1981 the two shared in a spectacular triumph. The teams put on a terrific display when they returned to Wembley for the replay. With minutes to go and the score 2-2, Villa danced his way through the City defence to score what many regard as the best individual goal ever in a Cup final.

Opposite right: Ricky Villa holds aloft the FA Cup for the crowds of admiring fans gathered in the streets outside Tottenham Town Hall in 1981. Following a 1-1 draw against Manchester City, Tottenham went on to win the replay at Wembley 3-2.
Above: Aston Villa's Peter Withe scores against Stoke in a 1-1 draw, gaining an important point for the team which ended the 1980-81 season at the top of the First Division for the first time in 71 years.
Opposite left: Referee Clive Thomas is mobbed by West Ham players as he overrules the linesman's offside flag in the 1981 League Cup Final.
Right: Ipswich Town manager Bobby Robson brings back the UEFA Cup having defeated Dutch side AZ 67 Alkmaar 5-4 on aggregate.

Rush signs from Chester

Although the two major domestic honours had escaped them, Liverpool did add two more trophies to the cabinet. The Reds finally added the League Cup to their tally, though they needed a replay to beat West Ham. An Alan Hansen header gave Liverpool a 2-1 victory. Making only his second full appearance that night at Villa Park was young striker Ian Rush, who had signed from Chester City for £300,000 having played just 33 games in Division Four.

Having broken their League Cup duck, Liverpool proceeded to form a firm attachment to it. Victories over Spurs, Manchester United and Everton in the next three Finals set a new record and gave the club outright ownership of the trophy.

Liverpool's third Euro success

1981 also brought Liverpool a third European Cup success. Alex Ferguson's Aberdeen and Bayern Munich were among their scalps en route to the final. There they met six-time winners Real Madrid, whose side included ex-West Brom star winger Laurie Cunningham. It was a cagey contest, Alan Kennedy breaking the deadlock with a shot from an acute angle nine minutes from time. The victory meant that Liverpool joined Bayern and Ajax as three-time winners of European club football's most prestigious trophy.

Bob Paisley

Although people often speak of Shankly and Ferguson as the greatest managers to grace the English game, in terms of honours won nobody can match the achievements of Bob Paisley. He took over from Shankly after the FA Cup victory over Newcastle in 1974, 35 years after joining the club. Paisley had been a member of Liverpool's title-winning side of 1947, joining the coaching staff on his retirement seven years later. But it was for his nine years at the helm that he will be best remembered. He led the club to six championships and three League Cups, but it was his four European trophies that set him apart from his peers. His team lifted the UEFA Cup in 1976 with a victory over FC Bruges. The following year he made Liverpool the third British side to win the European Cup when Liverpool beat Borussia Moenchengladbach 3-1 at the Olympic Stadium in Rome. Liverpool retained the trophy the following year, beating Bruges once again in a major Final. The hat-trick was completed in 1981, Alan Kennedy scoring the goal which beat Real Madrid. The affable Geordie stepped down in 1983, signing off with a championship and League Cup double. On the latter occasion, Graeme Souness took the unprecedented step of ushering the manager up the 39 Wembley steps to collect the trophy. Paisley died in February 1996.

Muhren and Butcher lift Robson's Ipswich

Bobby Robson's Ipswich Town made it a European double by lifting the UEFA Cup. Ipswich had finished runners-up in the league, their formidable line-up including Terry Butcher, Paul Mariner, Alan Brazil and John Wark. Like Spurs, the team had two outstanding overseas players, the Dutch midfield duo Frans Thijssen and Arnold Muhren. Ipswich overcame Dutch champions AZ 67 Alkmaar 5-4 on aggregate in the Final. Wark scored a record-equalling 14 goals during the campaign. Wark, Thijssen and Mariner made it an Ipswich clean sweep in the PFA awards, with Thijssen topping the Football Writers poll.

Robson's careful housekeeping at Ipswich showed that success could be had for a modest outlay. Many clubs wielded the chequebook all too readily and huge amounts were changing hands. Some players would prove to be worth every penny. In October 1981 Ron Atkinson paid his former club West Bromwich Albion £1.5 million to bring Bryan Robson to Old Trafford. A decade later that would look a knockdown price. Steve Daley, Kevin Reeves, Justin Fashanu and Gary Birtles were among those whose form - and value - slumped dramatically after high-profile moves.

In one remarkable move Clive Allen joined Arsenal from Queen's Park Rangers, and was sold on to Crystal Palace two months later without having kicked a ball. Allen's cut of the two million-pound deals was around £100,000, players receiving 5% of the fee provided they didn't seek a move.

Bryan Robson moves from The Hawthorns to Old Trafford.

Swansea's rollercoaster

While Robson was signing for United, an unfamiliar name sat on top of Division One. John Toshack's Swansea had leapt from the Fourth Division to the top flight in just four seasons. They won seven and drew one of their first 10 games and went on to finish 6th in the championship. Relegation came the following year, however, and by 1986 they were back in the basement, a repeat of the rollercoaster ride Northampton Town had taken in the 1960s.

Above: Steve Perryman and John Gregory clash during the 1982 FA Cup Final between Spurs and QPR.
Right: England's Trevor Francis in action against Scotland at Wembley.
Opposite bottom: The 1981 Charity Shield is shared by Aston Villa and Spurs, following a 2-2 draw. Goalscorers Peter Withe of Villa (left) and Mark Falco of Tottenham pose with the trophy.
Opposite top: Bob Paisley with Graeme Souness.

Spurs bounce back

Spurs were battling on four fronts in 1981-82. They went down to Barcelona in the Cup Winners' Cup Final and lost to Liverpool in the Final of the League Cup, renamed the Milk Cup after its new sponsor. A late equaliser by Ronnie Whelan took the game into extra time. The Spurs players were visibly deflated. Paisley told his men to look raring to go for another 30 minutes. Whelan and Rush scored to make the final score 3-1 to the holders.

In goal for Spurs that day was Ray Clemence, who had moved to White Hart Lane the previous summer for £300,000. His old team had come back to haunt him, and his new club had tasted Wembley defeat for the first time.

Hoddle's decisive penalty

Spurs finished 4th in the league, 16 points behind champions Liverpool. A possible "quadruple" had been reduced to a single battlefront: the FA Cup. Glenn Hoddle scored the two goals which salvaged Spurs' season. It was his deflected shot which earned Spurs a 1-1 draw against Second Division QPR. He then struck a 6th-minute penalty in the replay to bring the Cup back to White Hart Lane for the second year running.

It was a day of mixed emotions for Ardiles and Villa. Since their semi-final victory over Leicester, Britain had gone to war with Argentina over the Falkland Islands. Under the circumstances it would have been impossible for the two to play in the Final. Both were diplomatically moved on, though Ardiles would return to White Hart Lane when hostilities ended.

Above: Watford's John Barnes, and Arsenal's Kenny Sansom struggle for a high-ball in a match that Watford went on to win 2-1.
Below right: Hoddle scores the penalty in the replay that would win Tottenham the FA Cup in 1982.
Opposite: The Tottenham squad included two Argentinian players, Ossie Ardiles (third from right) and Ricardo Villa (far right) who were unable to play in the FA Cup Final as Britain was at war with Argentina.

FA Cup Finals

1980	West Ham United	v	Arsenal	1-0
1981	Tottenham Hotspur	v	Manchester City	1-1 (3-2)
1982	Tottenham Hotspur	v	Queen's Park Rangers	1-1 (1-0)
1983	Manchester United	v	Brighton H.A.	2-2 (4-0)
1984	Everton	v	Watford	2-0
1985	Manchester United	v	Everton	1-0
1986	Liverpool	v	Everton	3-1
1987	Coventry City	v	Tottenham Hotspur	3-2
1988	Wimbledon	v	Liverpool	1-0
1989	Liverpool	v	Everton	3-2

Milestones 1980-1989

1980 Nottingham Forest wins the European Cup for the second year running

1981 Queen's Park Rangers install an artificial playing surface at their home ground, Loftus Road, the first club to do so; however the pitch was re-turfed in 1987

Liverpool wins the European Cup for a third time

Football League introduces three points for a win

1982 The League Cup becomes the Milk Cup under a sponsorship deal with the Milk Marketing Board

Aston Villa wins the European Cup after beating Bayern Munich in the Final, meaning six consecutive successes for English clubs in the competition

Twelfth World Cup held in Spain sees Italy winning the competition after England lost in the second group stages to West Germany

England record their greatest victory at Wembley by beating Luxembourg 9-0

1983 The Football League is sponsored by Canon

Tottenham Hotspur becomes the first football club to be floated on the Stock Exchange

1984 Liverpool's fourth win in the European Cup Final

1985 Everton win the European Cup Winners' Cup

A fire in a wooden stand at Bradford City's ground kills 56 spectators

39 fans die as a result of rioting during the European Cup Final at the Heysel Stadium in Brussels. As a result UEFA place an indefinite ban on English football clubs entering European competitions; ending a winning streak by British clubs which saw them winning seven out of eight European Cup titles since 1977

1986 Thirteenth World Cup, held in Mexico and won by Argentina but famous for Maradona's 'Hand of God' goal against England in the quarter-finals

Two substitutes allowed in FA and League Cup matches

Aberdeen manager Alex Ferguson becomes the new Manchester United manager

The First Division is reduced to twenty teams

1987 Re-election to the Football League abolished and automatic promotion for the winners of the Conference established

To celebrate its centenary the Football League played a Football League vs. Rest of the World one-off fixture at Wembley, which saw the Football League win 3-0

1988 Transfer of Ian Rush from Juventus to Liverpool for £2.8m establishes a new record transfer fee

1989 95 football fans crushed to death at the beginning of an FA Cup semi-final match between Liverpool and Nottingham Forest at Sheffield Wednesday's Hillsborough ground (the total number of deaths became 96 when Tony Bland died four years later). Lord Justice Taylor is commissioned to investigate the tragedy

Aston Villa make it six in a row

The domestic season ended with Aston Villa bringing the European Cup back to England for the 6th year running. Ron Saunders had departed and it was coach Tony Barton who found himself in the hot seat as Villa battled through to play Bayern Munich in the Final. Villa, with just two modest UEFA Cup campaigns in the 1970s behind them,

Teenager stand-in keeper Nigel Spink is Villa hero.

had put out Dynamo Berlin, Dynamo Kiev and Anderlecht along the way. Bayern was the last club to hold the trophy before English sides took over and they were favourites to end that period of domination. It looked even more likely when Villa lost keeper Jimmy Rimmer 10 minutes into the game. 19-year-old rookie Nigel Spink took over and proceeded to have a storming match. A mishit shot by Peter Withe from a Tony Morley cross won the game. It meant that Rimmer - on United's bench for their 1968 triumph - now had two European Cup winners' medals having played a total of 10 minutes in the two finals.

Ron Greenwood's England

30-year-old Peter Withe was the new European champions' only representative in Ron Greenwood's squad that went to Spain for the World Cup. The team's qualification had not been the smoothest. Defeats in Basel,

Oslo and Bucharest left England needing Switzerland to win in Romania. They did, and Greenwood showed his appreciation by donning a Swiss FA tie at the World Cup draw.

England were seeded, somewhat surprisingly, and got off to a dream start. Bryan Robson made World Cup history by scoring after just 27 seconds against France. That set up a 3-1 win over a team that would go on to reach the semi-final. But while France got stronger, England fell away. Victories over Czechoslovakia and Kuwait had put England into the second phase with maximum points, a record matched only by Brazil. In the second round mini-league England found themselves up against West Germany and hosts Spain. They created the better chances against the Germans but also survived a scare when Rummenigge hit the bar from 25 yards. After Germany beat Spain 2-1, England took on the hosts needing to win by two goals to go through. Once again they failed to take their chances, against a team that had nothing to play for. The performance was summed up by a glaring miss from substitute Kevin Keegan. The game ended goalless and England were out.

Robson becomes new England boss

It marked the end of Greenwood's reign as national team boss. It was shades of 1962 as the FA named Bobby Robson as his successor. Ramsey had peaked at the right time, taking an unheralded side to the top of the league. Robson had spent relatively little in guiding his team to the runners-up spot in the past two seasons, together with a UEFA Cup victory.

Graham Taylor's Watford finish second

Luton and Watford were promoted to Division One in 1981-82, and the following season were a breath of fresh air in the top flight. They decided that attack was the best form of defence. Only four teams scored more than David Pleat's Luton. Unfortunately, the worst defensive record in the division meant that they finished 18th, surviving with a win over Manchester City on the last day of the season.

Graham Taylor's Watford ended the season second to Liverpool, both in goals scored and league position. Watford had taken five years to get from the basement to Division One, but made a better fist of it than Swansea once they got there. Elton John had taken over as chairman

in 1976, when the team was a mid-table Division Four outfit. But it was the appointment of Taylor that was undoubtedly the key to Watford's meteoric rise. The team was always dangerous going forward, Luther Blissett and Ross Jenkins spearheading the attack. Blissett's performances earned him an England call-up, and he scored a hat-trick in his first full appearance, against Luxembourg in December 1982.

Refereeing inconsistencies

The resurgence of attacking football was partly down to the new three-points-for-a-win system. This term the authorities showed their determination to stamp out cynical play by making professional fouls a sending-off offence. This remained a grey area, however, with the seriousness of the misdemeanour left to the referee's discretion. The season was peppered with controversial incidents, some of which resulted in dismissal while others merely earned a caution.

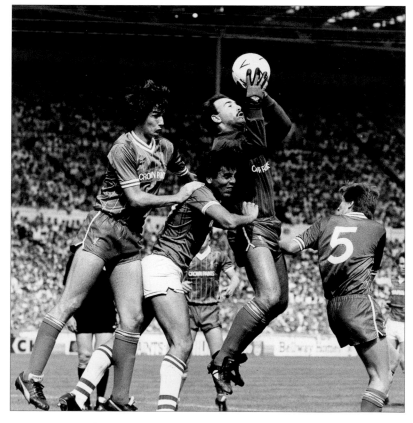

Opposite left: Peter Withe and Nigel Spink of Aston Villa with the European Cup.
Opposite right: Gary Lineker is among Leicester City players celebrating when Ian Wilson scores against Fulham, helping Leicester pursue promotion to the First Division.
Above: A scene at the opening ceremony of the 1982 World Cup held in Spain. England were to perform well in the initial stages but could not maintain the momentum.
Right: Liverpool goalkeeper Bruce Grobbelaar holds on to this Everton cross during the 1984 Charity Shield, but a later mistake would see Everton win the match 1-0.

Paisley leaves Anfield

1982-83 saw Bob Paisley end his 43-year association with Anfield. Paisley had won 13 major trophies in nine years, plus a string of Charity Shield successes. The FA Cup was missing from his haul, but he was still comfortably the most successful manager in history. He bowed out with two more trophies. By April Liverpool were 16 points clear and had the championship sewn up. After Ronnie Whelan's extra-time winner against Manchester United in the Milk Cup Graeme Souness pushed his manager up the Wembley steps to accept the trophy, something which had never happened before.

Brighton test United

In the 1983 FA Cup Final Brighton took on Manchester United. Brighton were propping up the league and on their way to Division Two. They had the chance of easing the pain of relegation by beating Ron Atkinson's attractive United side which had finished a point behind Watford in third place. They very nearly pulled it off. Gordon Smith headed Brighton into a first-half lead, but Stapleton and Wilkins put United in front after the break. A dramatic late equaliser took the game into extra-time, and in the dying seconds Smith fluffed his lines with only Gary Bailey to beat. Brighton's chance evaporated in that moment; United cruised to a 4-0 win in the replay.

Above: Liverpool, who topped the league in 1982, display the League Cup which they won in the same year.
Opposite top left: Liverpool celebrate their win the 1984 Milk Cup Final against Everton at Maine Road.
Opposite bottom left: Watford players salute their fans after defeating Birmingham to enter the FA Cup semi-finals.
Opposite top right: Everton manager Howard Kendall leaves the pitch after his team's FA Cup Final win over Watford in 1984.
Opposite bottom right: The Everton scorers Andy Gray (left) and Graeme Sharp celebrate their Cup win.

Fagan sets up three in a row

Striker Michael Robinson had set up Smith for that golden chance to win the Cup Final for Brighton. He was soon a Liverpool player, one of the first pieces of business concluded by the new Anfield boss, 62-year-old Joe Fagan. Fagan, who had been at the club since the late 1950s, won three trophies in his first season, something that not even Paisley had achieved. Liverpool's 15th championship was also their third in a row, which meant that the club equalled the achievement of Huddersfield in the 1920s and Arsenal a decade later.

The Milk Cup Final pitted the Reds against Everton in the first ever Merseyside Final. It was scoreless after 120 minutes, and in the replay at Maine Road Graeme Souness scored the goal which gave Liverpool their fourth successive victory and won the trophy outright.

Fagan's hat-trick was completed at the Olympic Stadium in Rome, where Liverpool overcame a Roma side that enjoyed home advantage. Liverpool took the lead on the quarter-hour, Phil Neal pouncing on a defensive error. Roma equalised on the stroke of half-time and that's the way the scores stood after extra time. Steve Nicol's penalty miss was wiped out by Bruno Conti. Bruce Grobbelaar looked to be the calmest man in the stadium, causing much mirth as he pretended that his knees had turned to jelly. If his clowning was designed to put Graziani off, it worked. He blazed over, leaving Alan Kennedy to calmly slot home the crucial penalty. It was the second time that Kennedy had scored the decisive goal in a European Cup Final.

Kendall's Everton beat Watford

Everton made up for their unlucky defeat in the Milk Cup by beating Watford in the FA Cup Final. After a long time in the doldrums, former Goodison hero Howard Kendall was building a side capable of competing with their neighbours. Kendall had been a key member of the championship-winning side of 1970, the last major honour that the club had won. Graham Sharpe and Andy Gray scored the goals which left Watford fans in tears - quite literally in the chairman's case.

Forest robbed of UEFA final place

Spurs made it another English double in Europe by beating holders Anderlecht in the UEFA Cup Final. Both legs ended 1-1 and Spurs came out on top in the first Final to be decided on penalties. This victory was to take a surprising twist 13 years later, when it was revealed that Anderlecht had bribed the referee who took charge of the second leg of their semi-final against Nottingham Forest. In that game Anderlecht overturned a 2-0 deficit to win the tie 3-2. The Belgian side was awarded a dubious penalty, and Forest also had a goal disallowed. These decisions led some in the Forest camp to believe they had been cheated but it was not until 1997 that their suspicions were confirmed. The referee in question had been killed in a car crash by then, but that didn't stop Forest instituting legal proceedings in pursuit of compensation. They came up against UEFA's 10-year statute of limitations regarding retrospective disciplinary action. Financial reparation would hardly have made up for a night of European glory, and to Forest fans 1984 will be remembered as the year they were robbed.

England fail again

The familiar pattern of success in Europe and failure at international level continued as England missed out on the 1984 European Championship. A penalty by former European Footballer of the Year Allan Simonsen gave Denmark a crucial 1-0 win at Wembley, and that country's first-ever victory over England. This result, together with a goalless home draw against Greece, put paid to England's chances and it was the Danes who went to France for the finals.

Barnes dazzles against Brazil

While that tournament was being played out, England went on a three-match tour of South America. There was a defeat by Uruguay and and a draw against Chile, but it was the 2-0 win over Brazil which grabbed the headlines. The first goal, a towering header from Mark Hateley, was typically English. The second, a dazzling solo effort by Watford's John Barnes, bore comparison with any Brazil had ever scored.

Ian Rush

The Welsh predator Ian Rush was a goal machine while he played for Liverpool FC, with a first touch and pace that gave him a phenomenal strike-rate. Born in 1961, he began his playing career at Chester, moving to Anfield in 1980 and acquiring legendary status with the Kop. In 658 games for Liverpool, he scored an incredible 346 goals.

Apart from the 1987-88 season when he made a brief, ill-fated move to Juventus, he remained at Liverpool for 16 years. With them he won the championship five times and the FA Cup on three occasions. He scored in each of those three Wembley finals, and his aggregate tally of five goals remains a Cup Final record. Rush won the European Cup with Liverpool in 1984, his 32 goals during that campaign earning him the golden boot award. That year was the highpoint of his career, as he was also named double Footballer of the Year.

He also captained Wales, for whom he scored a record 28 goals in 73 games. He joined Leeds in 1996 and later played for Newcastle, Wrexham and Sydney Olympic.

Heysel tragedy rocks English football

1984-85 saw Liverpool fail to win a trophy for the first time in nine years. They lost the European Cup Final to a Michel Platini penalty but that was an irrelevance after it was clear that there had been fatalities at the Heysel Stadium. There had been fighting between Liverpool and Juventus fans before the match, and the collapse of a wall precipitated the tragedy. 39 supporters, mostly Italian, were killed. Liverpool fans were deemed to be primarily responsible and an indefinite ban was imposed on all English clubs competing in European competition.

Everton romp

The Heysel disaster and the Bradford fire, which occurred only weeks earlier, rocked football to the core. The season had also witnessed some of the worst acts of hooliganism ever seen, prompting the government to set up a task force to address the issue.

These events overshadowed the achievements of an Everton side which won two trophies playing champagne football. Howard Kendall's men romped to the title with a record 90 points, 13 clear of their Liverpool rivals. Kendall joined the select group to have won the championship as both player and manager.

It was the first leg in a treble, Everton having reached both the Cup Winners' Cup and FA Cup Finals. Having taken the scalp of Bayern Munich 3-1 on aggregate in the semis, Everton faced Rapid Vienna in the Cup Winners' Cup Final. Austria's legendary striker Hans Krankl scored Rapid's consolation goal in a 3-1 defeat and was quick to sing Everton's praises for the quality of their performance. Andy Gray, Trevor Steven and Kevin Sheedy had all been on target.

Opposite: Liverpool's Ian Rush holds the Charity Shield in 1986.
Above left: The pairing of John Barnes and David Bardsley was to prove too much for the Arsenal defence as Watford defeated them 3-1.
Above right: Chris Waddle of Tottenham rescues his side by scoring against up-and-coming Oxford United to send the game into extra time.
Left: Wimbledon, perhaps the most unconventional and unlikely team in the First Division at the time, celebrate a 3-0 win over Sheffield Wednesday. John Fashanu and Wally Downes embrace Vinny Jones (with his back to the camera), who only three weeks prior to this game had been employed as a hod-carrier.

First Cup Final dismissal halts Liverpool

The FA Cup proved to be a trophy too far. Everton went down 1-0 to Manchester United, Norman Whiteside curling in a beautiful winner in extra time. The first 90 minutes had been largely uneventful, until with 12 minutes to go Peter Reid pounced onto a loose ball and was upended by Kevin Moran. The referee deemed it a professional foul and sent the Irishman off, the first Cup Final dismissal. The incident served to galvanise the United side, and they carved out other scoring opportunities apart from the one delightfully taken by Whiteside. Two years earlier he had become the youngest-ever player to score in a Wembley Final - 17 years 324 days - when United lost to Liverpool in the Milk Cup. No doubt this strike gave the Irishman more satisfaction.

Norman Whiteside strike sinks Everton.

Dalglish steps up as player-manager

Joe Fagan had already announced that the 1985 European Cup Final would be his last game in charge. Liverpool made yet another internal appointment, but surprised many by opting for a player-manager: Kenny Dalglish. With the Paul Walsh-Ian Rush strike partnership flourishing, Dalglish was content to spend time in the dugout. His team didn't have things all their own way, and at one point they trailed champions Everton by 11 points. The Reds needed to win their last seven games, five of them away, and hope that others would slip up. On the last day of the season they needed to win at Stamford Bridge and it was Dalglish who scored the game's only goal.

A week later Everton again had to settle for second best in the first Merseyside FA Cup Final. Lineker escaped Hansen's clutches to open the scoring. When Rush equalised, the omens looked bad for Everton, as Liverpool had never lost a game when their Welsh striker was on target. So it proved again. Craig Johnston put the Reds into the lead and Rush rifled in a third six minutes from time. Liverpool thus joined the Spurs and Arsenal as the century's only Double winners.

Future stars

Two future Liverpool stars lined up in the Oxford United side which beat QPR in the Milk Cup Final. Ray Houghton and John Aldridge were in the side which had climbed from Division Three to Division One in successive seasons. It was an outstanding achievement for a club that had been on the verge of bankruptcy in 1982.

Lineker fires England in Mexico

England were unbeaten in qualifying for the World Cup finals, although they had been held to a draw by Romania, Finland and Northern Ireland. Defeat by Portugal and a goalless draw against Morocco left Bobby Robson's men facing an early exit. He was hampered by a shoulder injury to his inspirational captain, Bryan Robson, whose tournament was over. Vice-captain Ray Wilkins was sent off against Morocco, the first England player to be given his marching orders in a major tournament. Star striker Gary Lineker, who had topped the scoring chart with 30 goals for Everton, was playing with his arm in plaster. England needed to beat Poland in the final group match and did so in style. Hodge, Reid, Steven and Beardsley came in for Robson, Waddle, Wilkins and Hateley, and the team put on a show guaranteed to wake up the supporters who had dubbed this "the group of sleep". Lineker grabbed the headlines with a hat-trick in a 3-0 win.

Maradona's "Hand of God"

Another brace by Lineker helped England to a 3-0 victory over Paraguay, setting up a quarter-final clash with Argentina. The best and worst of Diego Maradona caused England's downfall. He picked up the ball on the halfway line and beat half the team to score the goal of the tournament and one of the greatest of all time. But before then he had punched the ball into the net when challenging for a high ball with Peter Shilton. Lineker made it 2-1, heading in his sixth goal of the tournament. He would be the tournament's hotshot, but the "hand of God" along with the genius of Maradona had put paid to England's hopes.

Opposite left: Glenn Hoddle of Spurs on the ball in an England World Cup qualifying game.
Opposite right: Goal-scorer Norman Whiteside holds aloft the FA Cup after Manchester United defeat Everton by a goal to nil in extra time in the 1985 Cup Final.
Above: Gary Lineker, by now Everton's star striker, celebrates scoring for England against Northern Ireland in 1986.

Kenny Dalglish

When Joe Fagan stepped down as Liverpool manager at the end of the 1984-85 season, the club surprised many by naming Kenny Dalglish as his successor. The Anfield trend of appointing from within was thus continued, but instead of a member of the backroom team it was someone who was still performing at the height of his powers. Fittingly, it was Dalglish who scored the goal at Stamford Bridge which secured the championship the following May. Victory over Everton in the FA Cup Final meant that Dalglish had achieved the Double in his debut season as a manager. He added two further championships before resigning in February 1991, citing the pressures of the job as the reason for his decision to stand down. He returned to the managerial fray with Blackburn Rovers. He had Jack Walker's millions at his disposal and used the money wisely. He steered Rovers to the Premiership title in 1995, the club's first championship since 1914. He thus became only the fourth manager in history to win the title with two different clubs. After another brief spell out of the game he took over at Newcastle. He led the club to the FA Cup Final in 1998 but couldn't prevent Arsenal from completing the Double.

Division One 1980-1989

1979-1980

1	Liverpool	60
2	Manchester United	58
3	Ipswich	53
4	Arsenal	52
5	Nottingham Forest	48
6	Wolverhampton W.	47
7	Aston Villa	46
8	Southampton	45
9	Middlesbrough	44
10	West Bromwich Albion	41
11	Leeds United	40
12	Norwich City	40
13	Crystal Palace	40
14	Tottenham Hotspur	40
15	Coventry	39
16	Brighton	37
17	Manchester City	37
18	Stoke	36
19	Everton	35
20	Bristol City	31
21	Derby County	30
22	Bolton Wanderers	25

1980-81

1	Aston Villa	60
2	Ipswich	56
3	Arsenal	53
4	West Bromwich Albion	52
5	Liverpool	51
6	Southampton	50
7	Nottingham Forest	50
8	Manchester United	48
9	Leeds United	44
10	Tottenham Hotspur	43
11	Stoke	42
12	Manchester City	39
13	Birmingham City	38
14	Middlesbrough	37
15	Everton	36
16	Coventry	36
17	Sunderland	35
18	Wolverhampton W.	35
19	Brighton	35
20	Norwich City	33
21	Leicester City	32
22	Crystal Palace	19

1981-82

1	Liverpool	87
2	Ipswich	83
3	Manchester United	78
4	Tottenham Hotspur	71
5	Arsenal	71
6	Swansea	69
7	Southampton	66
8	Everton	64
9	West Ham United	58
10	Manchester City	58
11	Aston Villa	57
12	Nottingham Forest	57
13	Brighton	52
14	Coventry	50
15	Notts County	47
16	Birmingham City	44
17	West Bromwich Albion	44
18	Stoke	44
19	Sunderland	44
20	Leeds United	42
21	Wolves	40
22	Middlesbrough	39

1982-83

1	Liverpool	82
2	Watford	71
3	Manchester United	70
4	Tottenham Hotspur	69
5	Nottingham Forest	69
6	Aston Villa	68
7	Everton	64
8	West Ham United	64
9	Ipswich	58
10	Arsenal	58
11	West Bromwich Albion	57
12	Southampton	57
13	Stoke	57
14	Norwich City	54
15	Notts County	52
16	Sunderland	50
17	Birmingham City	50
18	Luton	49
19	Coventry	48
20	Manchester City	47
21	Swansea	41
22	Brighton	40

1983-84

1	Liverpool	80
2	Southampton	77
3	Nottingham Forest	74
4	Manchester United	74
5	Queen's Park Rangers	73
6	Arsenal	63
7	Everton	62
8	Tottenham Hotspur	61
9	West Ham United	60
10	Aston Villa	60
11	Watford	57
12	Ipswich	53
13	Sunderland	52
14	Norwich City	51
15	Leicester City	51
16	Luton	51
17	West Bromwich Albion	51
18	Stoke	50
19	Coventry	50
20	Birmingham City	48
21	Notts County	41
22	Wolverhampton W.	29

1984-85

1	Everton	90
2	Liverpool	77
3	Tottenham Hotspur	77
4	Manchester United	76
5	Southampton	68
6	Chelsea	66
7	Arsenal	66
8	Sheffield Wednesday	65
9	Nottingham Forest	64
10	Aston Villa	56
11	Watford	55
12	West Bromwich Albion	55
13	Luton	54
14	Newcastle	52
15	Leicester City	51
16	West Ham United	51
17	Ipswich	50
18	Coventry City	50
19	Queen's Park Rangers	50
20	Norwich City	49
21	Sunderland	40
22	Stoke	17

1985-86

1	Liverpool	88
2	Everton	86
3	West Ham United	84
4	Manchester United	76
5	Sheffield Wednesday	73
6	Chelsea	71
7	Arsenal	69
8	Nottingham Forest	68
9	Luton Town	66
10	Tottenham Hotspur	65
11	Newcastle United	63
12	Watford	59
13	Queen's Park Rangers	52
14	Southampton	46
15	Manchester City	45
16	Aston Villa	44
17	Coventry City	43
18	Oxford United	42
19	Leicester City	42
20	Ipswich Town	41
21	Birmingham City	29
22	West Bromwich Albion	24

1986 87

1	Everton	86
2	Liverpool	77
3	Tottenham Hotspur	71
4	Arsenal	70
5	Norwich City	68
6	Wimbledon	66
7	Luton Town	66
8	Nottingham Forest	65
9	Watford	63
10	Coventry City	63
11	Manchester United	56
12	Southampton	52
13	Sheffield Wednesday	52
14	Chelsea	52
15	West Ham United	52
16	Queen's Park Rangers	50
17	Newcastle United	47
18	Oxford United	46
19	Charlton Athletic	44
20	Leicester City	42
21	Manchester City	39
22	Aston Villa	36

1987-88

1	Liverpool	90
2	Manchester United	81
3	Nottingham Forest	73
4	Everton	70
5	Queen's Park Rangers	67
6	Arsenal	66
7	Wimbledon	57
8	Newcastle United	56
9	Luton Town	53
10	Coventry City	53
11	Sheffield Wednesday	53
12	Southampton	50
13	Tottenham Hotspur	47
14	Norwich City	45
15	Derby County	43
16	West Ham United	42
17	Charlton Athletic	42
18	Chelsea	42
19	Portsmouth	35
20	Watford	32
21	Oxford United	31

1988-89

1	Arsenal	76
2	Liverpool	76
3	Nottingham Forest	64
4	Norwich City	62
5	Derby County	58
6	Tottenham Hotspur	57
7	Coventry City	55
8	Everton	54
9	Queen's Park Rangers	53
10	Millwall	53
11	Manchester United	51
12	Wimbledon	51
13	Southampton	45
14	Charlton Athletic	42
15	Sheffield Wednesday	42
16	Luton Town	41
17	Aston Villa	40
18	Middlesbrough	39
19	West Ham United	38
20	Newcastle United	31

Opposite: A jubilant Alan Hansen raises the FA Cup. In Dalglish's first season as player-manager, Liverpool defeated Everton 3-1 in the 1986 Final to achieve the rare feat of winning the Double. Rush, netting two, and Johnston a third, were responsible for the Reds' Cup glory but Dalglish himself scored the goal against Chelsea that secured the 1985-6 league title for Liverpool.

Moves abroad

Lineker's World Cup form caught the eye of many big Continental sides, and in the summer of 1986 Barcelona coach Terry Venables paid £4.25 million to see if he could reproduce his scoring form in La Liga. Although Everton no doubt would have preferred to keep Lineker, the fee represented a healthy profit on the £800,000 they had paid Leicester in July 1985.

Venables had already added Mark Hughes to his squad, and Juventus had agreed a £3.2 million deal to take Ian Rush to Turin, although the latter move would not take place until the end of the 1986-87 season.

According to the established principle, Rush should have signed off from Liverpool with a victory in the Littlewoods Cup, which was the League Cup's latest incarnation. Rush put the Reds in front against Arsenal at Wembley in the knowledge that in the previous 143 matches in which he'd got on the scoresheet the team had never lost. The run came to an end in the 144th match. Charlie Nicholas had never recaptured his Celtic form since moving to Highbury but he hit two goals to bring Arsenal their first silverware for eight years.

Ferguson replaces Atkinson at Old Trafford

Liverpool were also knocked off top spot in the league. Everton took their second title in three years, this time by a nine-point margin. The big managerial story of the season came in November, when Ron Atkinson's five-year reign at Old Trafford came to an end. United had won the FA Cup twice and never finished lower than 4th in the league. But with the championship going to Merseyside with monotonous regularity and a Cup Winners' Cup semi-final their best effort in Europe, it simply wasn't good enough. Aberdeen boss Alex Ferguson was appointed. Ferguson had broken the Celtic-Rangers duopoly, winning the Scottish title on three occasions. He had also led the Dons to Cup Winners' Cup glory in 1983 when they overcame Real Madrid.

Aberdeen boss Alex Ferguson had broken the Celtic-Rangers duopoly, winning the Scottish title on three occasions.

Ferguson's first major signings were Viv Anderson and Brian McClair, in the summer of 1987. United had just ended the season in 11th place, their worst finish since returning to the top flight in 1975.

Wimbledon's meteoric rise

Five places above United at the end of the 1986-87 season was Wimbledon. Dave Bassett's side had gone from non-league to Division One in nine years, and 6th place in their first season represented a phenomenal achievement. Swansea had done exactly the same five years earlier, but the Dons would prove to have much more resilience as a top-division side.

For Coventry and Scarborough 1986-87 was a memorable season, albeit at different ends of the footballing scale. Coventry met Spurs in the FA Cup Final. Spurs had never finished on the losing side in their seven previous appearances. Coventry ended that run and in the process picked up the club's first major honour. Coventry twice came from behind, their second equaliser a spectacular flying header from Keith Houchen. The winner came in extra-time, when Gary Mabbutt deflected a McGrath cross into his net. Coventry coach John Sillett did a Wembley jig to rival Nobby Stiles' effort in 1966.

Play-offs introduced

Neil Warnock's Scarborough became the first club to win automatic promotion to the Football League. The system of applying for re-election was scrapped; the 4th Division's bottom club would change places with the winners of the Vauxhall Conference.

Play-off matches were also introduced in all divisions. The team which finished just above the automatic relegation spot entered into a play-off with the three clubs that had just missed promotion from the division below. Charlton finished in that precarious position in Division One but survived the two-match ordeal.

The play-offs were introduced to make the run-in more exciting, with fewer "dead" matches. It was also designed over two seasons to decrease the size of Division One from 22 clubs to 20.

In the second year Chelsea finished fourth from bottom and lost their Division One status at the expense of Middlesbrough.

Liverpool back on top

Liverpool, meanwhile, were back on top. After three seasons in which the Merseyside clubs had taken the top two spots, in 1987-88 Everton slipped to 4th and Manchester United were the closest challengers. Even then, Ferguson's men finished nine points behind a team that looked stronger than ever. John Barnes, Ray Houghton and Peter Beardsley - bought from Newcastle for a record £1.9 million - all added even more flair to the Anfield machine.

Liverpool went 29 matches unbeaten, equalling Leeds' 1974 record. Everton's Wayne Clark scored the goal which prevented Liverpool from taking the record outright, but the Reds lost just once more in the campaign to match Everton's record points tally. Both finished on 90, although Liverpool had played two games fewer. Their 17th championship was secured with four matches to spare.

Opposite: Arsenal captain Kenny Sansom holds aloft the Littlewoods Cup after two goals from Charlie Nicholas saw Liverpool defeated 2-1.
Above: Arsenal's Niall Quinn lines up a volley that narrowly misses its target and is just tipped wide by Spurs and former England keeper Ray Clemence.
Below: Everton's Gary Stevens and Manchester United's Arthur Albiston bear down on the ball in a Charity Shield match.

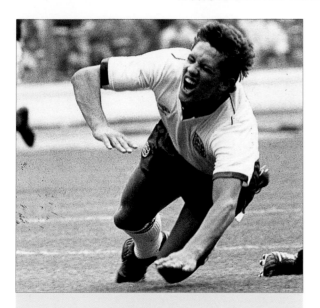

Gary Lineker

Sports broadcaster Gary Lineker's role in the consortium that rescued Leicester City was fitting, for it was where, in 1978, his playing career began. Known for lightning acceleration, he scored 26 goals in 1983, helping Leicester back into the First Division. Two years later, he signed for Everton and scored 30 goals in his first season, winning him the PFA and Football Writers' Player of the Year.

He did well initially at Barcelona under Terry Venables, but was later less consistent. Though he contributed to Barca's Cup Winners' Cup victory in 1989, he came back to England that summer to join Venables at White Hart Lane. In 1991 Spurs won the F.A. Cup, beating Nottingham Forest, and in his final season at the club put away a relegation-saving 28 League goals.

It is as a marksman for England, however, that he's most celebrated, with 80 caps and 48 goals – only one fewer than Bobby Charlton. Six of those, including a hat-trick against Poland, came in the 1986 World Cup in Mexico, winning him the Golden Boot. Four years later at Italia 90, it was Lineker's 80th-minute equaliser that kept England in the semi-final against West Germany, though the side went out on penalties. The 1992 European Championships made a frustrating end to Lineker's England career, as he was substituted by Graham Taylor in the final game, against Sweden. He ended his playing days with two seasons in the Japanese League, at Grampus Eight.

Wimbledon's FA Cup glory

A second double looked a foregone conclusion as Liverpool faced Wimbledon in the FA Cup Final. The Dons had finished a commendable 7th this term but surely they couldn't overturn the mighty Reds. The bookies didn't think so, making Liverpool 1-4 favourites. Wimbledon were fearless, committed and no respecters of reputations. They had already gone to Anfield and won.

Peter Beardsley had the ball in the net, only for the referee to disallow it - for a foul on Beardsley! Laurie Sanchez's glancing header from a Dennis Wise free-kick gave the Dons a 36th-minute lead. After 61 minutes John Aldridge was brought down in the box. Aldridge had a perfect record from his previous 11 spot-kicks that season. The 12th was saved by Dave Beasant. It was the first penalty save in an FA Cup Final and it helped carry the Dons to an unlikely victory.

England eclipsed by Charlton's Ireland

Houghton and Aldridge lined up in the Republic of Ireland side which qualified for the 1988 European championships. England made it to Germany too, and the two countries met in the opening match of the group stage. Houghton gave the Republic a 1-0 win and although both went out of the competition it was Jack Charlton's men who emerged with more credit. England also lost to eventual finalists the USSR and Holland to finish as wooden spoonists.

A chink of light in a gloomy season for England came in April, when 17-year-old Alan Shearer hit a hat-trick for Southampton against Arsenal, the youngest player ever to do so in the First Division.

Above: Gary Lineker takes a tumble whilst playing for England, having been fouled by Scotland's Richard Gough in 1988. After a spell at Barcelona, Lineker returned to England to join Spurs in the summer of 1989.
Opposite top right: Peter Beardsley of Liverpool battles with Arsenal's Tony Adams in a title showdown which saw the Gunners come out on top.
Opposite top left: Floral tributes in the Anfield goalmouth commemorating those killed at Hillsborough on April 15 1989.

Arsenal's last gasp championship

Liverpool had Ian Rush back in their ranks in 1988-89. Rush scored 14 goals in his season at Juve but failed to settle. He returned for a season which saw the Reds engaged in a terrific championship battle with Arsenal. At the end of February Liverpool were 8th, 19 points behind the table-topping Gunners. On 26 May Arsenal came to Anfield for the title showdown. Liverpool had eaten away at Arsenal's lead and it was they who held the advantage. Arsenal, who had not won at Anfield for 15 years, needed a victory by two goals to take the title. After a goalless first half, Nigel Winterburn struck an indirect free-kick which Liverpool protested had gone straight into the net. The referee judged that it brushed Alan Smith's head and the goal was given. With seconds to go Michael Thomas burst into the box and flicked the ball past Grobbelaar to give Arsenal the 2-goal margin they needed.

Hillsborough
Second in the league and a 3-2 extra-time win over Everton in the second Merseyside FA Cup Final represented another fine season for Liverpool. But footballing matters had become irrelevant after the events at Hillsborough on 15 April. The eagerly awaited FA Cup semi-final clash with Nottingham Forest was six minutes

old and it became clear that there was a tragedy unfolding in the Leppings Lane end. Gates were opened to prevent a crush outside and a mass of fans surged into a part of the ground that was already packed. Perimeter fencing meant that there was no easy outlet. 94 supporters were killed, and the toll rose to 95 a few days later. Tony Bland remained in a coma for four years before his life-support machine was switched off. Lord Justice Taylor was commissioned to head an inquiry into the worst tragedy in British sporting history.

The sportsmanship shown in both the FA Cup Final and the championship decider gave rise to cautious optimism.

The Taylor Report
In the wake of the tragedy there had been no appetite to complete the competition and an abandonment was considered. But both Liverpool and the bereaved families came to regard the winning of the trophy as a tribute to those who had lost their lives.

In the 1980s the game had been tarnished by hooliganism and touched by tragedy, yet it ended on a note of dignity. The sportsmanship shown in both the FA Cup Final and the championship decider gave rise to cautious optimism. The game would endure; but as football moved into a new decade the Taylor Report would be a damning indictment of the conditions in which the fans were expected to watch their heroes perform.

1990-2005
A Premier League

At the start of the 1990s football came in for some harsh criticism. The Taylor Report was scathing about the dilapidated state of the country's stadia. For too long an ethos of "make do and mend" had prevailed. Those days were now over. The prospect of another Hillsborough was unthinkable and intolerable. The report recommended that terraces should be phased out, a view which immediately won government backing.

Above: England on the pitch ready to play Germany in the 1990 World Cup semi-final. With the score at 1-1 after extra time, England lost the game on penalties.
Above: Opposite: Stuart Pearce, who famously missed his penalty against Germany in the World Cup scores from this free kick to give Nottingham Forest the lead in the 1991 Cup Final against Spurs.

The Taylor Report

First and Second Division clubs were required to have all-seater stadia by the start of the 1994-95 season, with lower league clubs following suit by the end of the decade. The cost of improved facilities would be high - running into hundreds of millions - but the cost of doing nothing would be infinitely higher.

The Taylor Report also addressed the hooligan problem and the part played by alcohol in the appalling scenes that had blighted the game. A compulsory ID scheme was considered but rejected. Policing and ticket arrangements needed reviewing. While perimeter fencing which represented a threat to safety ought to be removed, harsh penalties were recommended for unwarranted pitch invasions.

The changing face of football

The construction of fabulous new grounds such as the Reebok, the Stadium of Light and Pride Park took football into a new era. New facilities such as these would show Wembley in a poor light. By the end of the decade plans would be under way for a new flagship stadium in the capital.

If the face of football was changed with the redevelopment and upgrading of grounds, a shift of equally seismic proportions occurred with the establishment of a Premier League. This coincided with the arrival of satellite broadcasters, who saw football as the main driver for their fledgling business. The game became polarised as never before. At the top level inflation in transfer fees, wages and ticket prices was rampant; meanwhile, the demise of Aldershot, the first league club to go out of business for thirty years, showed that the vast sums of money in the game were not filtering down to the basement.

Clubs were required to have all-seater stadia by the start of the 1994-95 season.

Merchandise and brand

There was a price to be paid for improved facilities and multi-million-pound TV rights deals, and in the end it was the fans who had to put their hands in their pockets. There were fears that die-hard fans would be priced out of the game and that the sport was undergoing a gentrification process, a return to the kind of constituency it had had in the nineteenth century. Perhaps more worryingly, the clubs did not seem to mind. Middle-class supporters with large disposable incomes were highly desirable to clubs which had a product to sell. Nor was the product simply football. Replica strips and all manner of domestic goods bearing the club brand went on sale. Fans could even get financial services from their clubs as football exploited every possible income stream.

A glorious era coming to an end

On the pitch the decade began with yet another league triumph for the team of the 80s. Liverpool rounded off their season with a 6-1 win at Coventry, though the club's eighteenth championship had already been secured by then.

The team that had suffered most heavily at hands of the Red machine was Crystal Palace, who were on the receiving end of a 9-0 mauling in the early part of the season. There must have been trepidation among Palace fans as the team faced Liverpool again in the FA Cup semi-final at Villa Park. It was a remarkable game and a turning point for Liverpool. Andy Gray equalised to make it 3-3 in the 90th minute, and Alan Pardew headed Palace into the Final in extra time. A glorious era was coming to an end. Over the next few seasons Liverpool would show flashes of their brilliant best, but these would be punctuated by many inept performances. The strong defence of days gone by would become quite porous and Liverpool would be relegated to the role of just another member of the chasing pack.

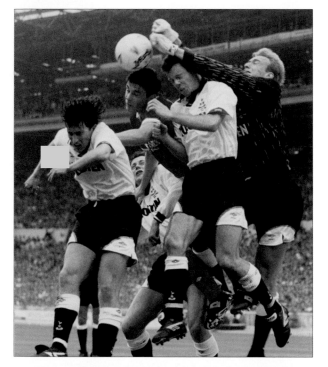

Ferguson's job on the line

After beating Liverpool, Palace went on to face the team which was to assume the mantle that had been worn by the Reds for so long. Manchester United had finished 11th and 13th in the past two seasons, and it was said that after four years in charge Alex Ferguson's job was on the line. A Mark Hughes' goal salvaged a replay for United, and Lee Martin scored the goal which brought Ferguson his first piece of silverware.

Italia '90

Before England went to the World Cup in Italy, manager Bobby Robson announced that he would be quitting to return to club management with PSV Eindhoven. Robson's team topped their group, albeit with a one-goal win over Egypt and draws against the Republic of Ireland and Holland. A superb David Platt volley late in extra time accounted for Belgium in the second round. By then it was clear that the team's precocious young midfielder, Paul Gascoigne, was the star turn. "Gazza" had become the country's first £2 million footballer when he moved from Newcastle to Spurs in 1988. At Italia '90 the raw talent blossomed and he proved that he was a great showman as well as a great player.

Platt's superb volley late in extra time puts England into the World Cup quarter-final.

England beaten on penalties

Against Cameroon in the quarter-final England were trailing 2-1 with time running out. Lineker was brought down in the box and converted the penalty to take the match into extra time. It was a case of deja-vu, and Lineker's second spot-kick set up a semi-final clash with West Germany. That match will long be remembered for the tears Gascoigne shed after a rash tackle earned him a booking which would have kept him out of the final. In the end that was academic. An Andreas Brehme free-kick took a wicked deflection and looped over Shilton to put the Germans ahead. Lineker equalised and the game went to penalties. Pearce and Waddle both missed and England were out. There was the consolation of the Fair Play award and the fact that the team had provided rich entertainment and no small amount of drama.

Power Struggle

1990-91 saw the beginnings of a power struggle at the top of the game. Relations between the FA and Football League had never been particularly warm, and when the League suggested that the game should be unified under a single umbrella, the response amounted to exactly the opposite. The FA's blueprint for the future was the establishment of a premier division. This would be the game's gold standard, and would help to improve the fortunes of the national team. Unsurprisingly, the Football League was horrified at the prospect of the glamour clubs seceding in this way. They went to court to challenge the legality of the FA's proposals but found they had no case.

The end of the UEFA ban

This season marked the end of the UEFA ban on English clubs, although Liverpool received a further year's penalty. The 6-year ban was said to have put English football down the pecking order in relation to the other traditional powerhouses on the Continent. That didn't stop Manchester United from lifting the Cup Winners' Cup. The 2-1 victory over Barcelona in Rotterdam must have been particularly pleasing for Mark Hughes. His brief spell at the Nou Camp had been a nightmare, and a superb winning goal from a narrow angle showed Barca what an in-form "Sparky" could do. This victory meant that Alex Ferguson joined a select group of managers to have won a European trophy with two different clubs.

Arsenal's title

United had been deducted a point in the league following a brawl in their clash with Arsenal at Old Trafford in October. The Gunners were docked two points, but neither penalty proved costly in the shake-up. United finished 6th, while Arsenal still ended the campaign seven points clear of Liverpool at the top.

Liverpool had started the season the stronger, recording ten straight wins. The turning point came in a 5th round FA Cup-tie against Everton. After a goalless draw at Anfield, the two teams met at Goodison. The game ended 4-4, highlighting the fact that Liverpool were still potent up front but far from secure at the back. The following day Kenny Dalglish announced his resignation, citing the strain of the job. The man appointed in his place was an Anfield thoroughbred but he didn't come from within. Graeme Souness was persuaded to leave Rangers and take over the reins at the club he had captained with such distinction

Opposite top: Paul Gascoigne with Steve Sedgeley and Gary Mabbutt celebrating Spurs 3-1 victory over Arsenal in the semi-final of the FA Cup in 1991 played at Wembley. The following month Tottenham secured the Cup with a 2-1 win over Nottingham Forest.
Opposite middle: Spurs' Eric Thorsvedt punches clear in the hard-fought contest that went into extra time.
Opposite bottom: Gary Mabbutt holds the trophy aloft.
Left: Steve Nicol, Bruce Grobbelaar and Ian Rush with the FA Cup in 1992.

Arsenal set defensive standard

Although Liverpool maintained their position as league runners-up in 1992, the writing was on the wall. The Reds conceded 40 goals and lost eight games; Arsenal were defeated only once and let in just 18 goals. George Graham had paid QPR £1.3 million for David Seaman the previous summer, a record for a goalkeeper. He took his place behind Adams, Bould, Dixon and Winterburn to form a defensive unit that would set the standard for defensive meanness.

Arsenal faced Spurs in the FA Cup semi-final, the first to be staged at Wembley. Gascoigne stole the show with a stunning 35-yard free-kick, setting up a marvellous 3-1 win. Gazza was again centre stage in the final, against Nottingham Forest, but this time for the wrong reasons. He had already put in a couple of rash tackles when he challenged Gary Charles on the edge of the Spurs area. Gascoigne conceded the free-kick but it was he who came off worse. He suffered knee ligament damage which was to put him out of action for months. Stuart Pearce rubbed salt into Spurs' wounds by scoring from the free-kick after Gazza was stretchered off. Paul Stewart hit an equaliser and although Spurs' winner came via a deflection off Des Walker in extra-time, the better team won.

Alan Shearer

In November 2002, Alan Shearer scored his 100th Premiership goal for his home city club, Newcastle United, and became the first player to achieve this landmark at two clubs, the other being Blackburn Rovers. No wonder that after the 2002-3 season, he was named Player of the Decade - a sweet moment for a striker who had retired from international football after Euro 2000 to make way for younger blood, but can still produce magic in the box.

His career began as a teenager in 1988 with Southampton, who had been tipped off by a North East scout. Blackburn secured him in the summer of 1992 for a British record transfer of £3.6 million, and Shearer's deadly finishing helped the club to win the Championship three years later. When Rovers signed Chris Sutton from Norwich, the celebrated "SAS partnership" began. He returned to Newcastle in 1996 for a £15 million fee. Shearer won the first of his 63 caps in February 1990, coming off the bench to score against France. It was the first of a 30-goal haul, putting him joint-fifth in the all-time list. Before the end of the 2004-05 season the Toon Army received the welcome news that their talisman had agreed to stay on for one more campaign. It represented a final opportunity for Shearer to bring silverware to St James' Park, while on a personal level he had Jackie Milburn's record 178 league goals within his sights.

Gazza to Lazio

Lazio had already been chasing Gascoigne's signature, and the deal was finally done in June 1992. It would be six years before Gazza would return to the domestic game. His time in Italy, and subsequently with Glasgow Rangers, would show him in every possible light: flashes of genius one minute, pressing the self-destruct button the next and everything done in his inimitably impish way. Injuries didn't help, but for a player of his gifts there should have been a greater return than his 1992 FA Cup winners' medal with Spurs. That would remain his only honour in the English game.

Top: The Arsenal faithful trudge through the rain on the way to the towering new stand at Highbury, in December 1993.
Above: Paul Merson (right) celebrating an Arsenal goal. The Gunners won the championship in the 1990-91 season by seven points. Liverpool were second and United a distant sixth.
Opposite above: Manchester United players following their championship in the 1993-94 season. It was the end of the first full season at the club for Eric Cantona (third from the left).

Eric Cantona

Of all the brilliant players from overseas that found their way into the English game in the 1990s Eric Cantona stands alone as the player who has had the most influence on the teams he played for. Having just helped Marseille to win the French Championship, he joined Leeds halfway through the 1991-92 season. Cantona's success continued as the Yorkshire club went on to win their first championship since the heady days of the 1970s, in what was the final year of the League system before the introduction of the Premier League. Leeds fans were shocked when Howard Wilkinson sold the 26-year-old to rivals Manchester United in November 1992.

Four championships and two Doubles

With his incredible vision and majestic touch, and his trademark upturned collar, Cantona performed complex skills with apparent ease. The Old Trafford faithful took him to their hearts and chanting 'Oo-ah-Cantona' in praise of their hero became a trademark of the fans. Cantona went on to win four championships with United, including the Double on two occasions. The second of those came in 1996, when he scored the goal that beat Liverpool in an exciting FA Cup Final. At the end of the 1995-96 season Cantona was named Footballer of the Year for his superb performances during that campaign.

Unfortunately, in the 1994-95 season, Cantona showed the other side to his character. His kung fu-style kick at a fan after being sent off at Crystal Palace in January 1995 earned him an eight-month ban. It was not the first time Cantona had run into disciplinary problems. His career was punctuated with arguments with players and managers alike, including run-ins with national team coaches, without which he would certainly have won more than 44 caps for France.

To the dismay of United fans Cantona announced his retirement from football at the end of the 1996-97 season, when he was just 30 years old.

Wilkinson's Leeds win the championship

Leeds were the last winners before the new Premiership era got under way. Howard Wilkinson's side had won promotion in 1990 and finished 4th in their first season back in the top flight. In 1991-92 Leeds held off the challenge of Manchester United to bring the club their first championship since 1974. Gordon Strachan, who had joined the club from Manchester United in 1989 for just £300,000, had been in sparkling form, despite turning 35 during the season. Alongside him in midfield were Batty, McAllister and Speed, giving a blend of youth and experience, finesse and steel. Midway through the season Wilkinson added more flair by bringing in the controversial French star Eric Cantona. 25-year-old Cantona had had a string of clubs and several run-ins with the authorities in France. He briefly turned his back on the game but decided to start afresh on the other side of the Channel. Sheffield Wednesday boss Trevor Francis had a look at him, but as he vacillated, Howard Wilkinson stepped in to offer terms.

Cantona's Gallic flair

The honeymoon would not last much beyond securing the championship as far as the club was concerned. For the fans it was a different matter. They warmed to the Gallic flair and air of arrogance Cantona showed on the field. The chant "Oo-ah-Cantona" rang round the Elland Road terraces, but not for long. By the end of the year Cantona had moved to Old Trafford for just £1 million. Over the next five years the Frenchman would become the pivotal player in Ferguson's dream team.

Ryan Giggs

Ryan Giggs burst onto the footballing stage just as the Premiership was coming into being. On his debut in 1991, he was the first of Manchester United's brilliant youth side to become a regular in the first team. His amazing speed, superb control and awe-inspiring dribbling immediately invited comparisons with the great George Best. But Giggs has managed to avoid many of the pitfalls and temptations that lured Best. Instead he has preferred to impress on the pitch, and in the past decade has helped United to dominate the domestic scene, including winning the Double on three occasions. One of those occasions came in 1999, when United also lifted the European Cup, more than thirty years after their first win in the prestigious competition.

When he won his first cap at the age of 17 years 332 days, Giggs became Wales' youngest-ever international.

United do the Double

Opposite above: Eric Cantona in an aerial duel against Chelsea in the 1994 Cup Final. His two spot kicks helped win the trophy, to make Manchester United only the fourth team to do the Double in the twentieth century.

Opposite below: Following the Taylor Report, clubs were required to have all-seater stadia by the start of the 1994-95 season. Old Trafford, seen here, was in its final phase of development. The Stretford End would now seat 9,600 spectators.

Left: Track-suited Terry Venables demonstrating his craft as a master coach with his Tottenham players in 1992.

Roy Keane

It is Roy Keane that Sir Alex Ferguson points to as the most influential of all the superstars that have made Manchester United the dominant force in English football since the inception of the Premiership.

But it was Brian Clough who spotted Keane's potential when he was playing for Cobh Ramblers in the Irish League. Clough paid just £10,000 to take the Irishman to Nottingham Forest in what must rank as one of the bargains of all time. In 1993 Keane moved to Old Trafford from Forest and, at United, his fierce competitiveness, tireless running and great technical ability have enabled him to develop into one of the most complete midfielders in world football. He took over as the driving force in midfield from Bryan Robson, who was a tough act to follow. Since joining United at the age of 21, his footballing skills and superb leadership skills have eaned him the captain's position and as such he has helped guide the team in their unprecedented run of success in recent years. In the five seasons between 1996 and 2001, United conceded the Premiership title just once when Arsenal won in 1997-98. Many people have pointed out that during that season Keane missed most of the campaign through injury.

World Cup 1994

On the international front, Keane excelled as part of the Republic of Ireland team in the 1994 World Cup in the USA, where the team progressed respectably before being knocked out by Holland. Although the team failed to qualify for France in 1998, Keane was regarded as a key figure for the Republic's chances in Japan and Korea, 2002. The infamous bust-up between Keane and manager Mick McCarthy meant that Keane was back home before the tournament even started.

Despite the fracas of the World Cup in the summer, 2002-03 saw Keane at his best, driving United on towards yet another title when it looked certain to go to Arsenal for the second successive season. Meanwhile, the arrival of Brian Kerr as the new Republic of Ireland manager prompted Keane to change his mind and return to the international stage.

Souness makes changes

The 1992 FA Cup went to Liverpool, who beat Sunderland 2-0 in the final. Souness had been busy in the transfer market, not all of his deals finding favour with the fans. Beardsley and Staunton left for Everton and Villa respectively. In came Mark Walters from Rangers and the Derby pair, Mark Wright and Dean Saunders. Michael Thomas, the man who had broken Liverpool fans' hearts in 1989, arrived from Arsenal. Thomas hit one of the goals that beat Sunderland. The other came from Rush, a record fifth goal for the Welshman in FA Cup finals.

For Souness, who had suffered a mild heart attack and was recovering from a bypass operation, FA Cup victory in 1992 would be a false dawn; it would be Liverpool's only trophy in his three-year reign.

Taylor's England reign

Graham Taylor had been appointed England manager after the 1990 World Cup. His achievements at Watford and Aston Villa had been considerable. He had taken Villa from 17th in 1989 to runners-up the following year. Qualification for the 1992 European Championship was secured, although not without the odd moment of disquiet. A late Gary Lineker goal in Poland gave England the point they needed to edge out the Republic of Ireland. That strike was Lineker's 48th for England, one short of Bobby Charlton's record. After goalless draws against Denmark and France, Lineker's third chance to equal the record came against hosts Sweden, a game which England needed to win to progress. David Platt volleyed England into an early lead but Sweden hit back to win 2-1. Taylor substituted Lineker with half an hour to go, a decision which mystified many onlookers. It was to be his last game in an England shirt. Taylor came in for fierce criticism for his team selection and tactics. ·A country which had reached the last four at Italia '90 had finished bottom of their group in the European Championship two years later.

Top: Manchester United celebrate after beating Liverpool in the 1996 Cup Final. Eric Cantona's stunning strike was the difference between the teams.
Above: Paul Scholes turning away from Van Bommel in a friendly international against Holland.
Opposite below: Ian Rush replaces Stan Collymore for Liverpool in the 1996 Cup Final against Manchester United.
Opposite above: Republic of Ireland's Roy Keane brings down Holland's Marc Overmars during a World Cup qualifying game.

Milestones 1990-2005

1990 Fourteenth World Cup held in Italy; England after losing in the semi-finals to eventual winners West Germany, ended up 4th by losing to Italy in the 3/4 place play-offs

UEFA lifts its ban on English clubs – Manchester United and Aston Villa join European competitions

FA rules that a professional foul should be a sending-off offence

1991 Manchester United wins the European Cup Winners' Cup

Artificial pitches withdrawn from First Division

1992 The Premier League comes into being with 20 member clubs; the Football League reduced to 71 clubs in three leagues

BskyB win exclusive rights to broadcast Premier League matches

Blackburn buy Alan Shearer for a then record of £3.6 million from Southampton followed by another record buy of Chris Sutton for £5 million, both buys helped Blackburn to win the 1994-5 Premiership title

1993 George Graham, Arsenal manager, banned for a year following irregular payments made to him

Alex Ferguson becomes first manager to win Scottish and English leagues, with Aberdeen and Manchester United respectively

1994 Tottenham Hotspur fined and banned from the FA Cup following charges of financial irregularities

Arsenal wins the European Cup Winners' Cup

Fifteenth World Cup held in USA; Brazil win in an event which saw England fail to qualify for the tournament

Bobby Charlton knighted for services to football

1995 Stan Collymore is transferred from Nottingham Forest to Liverpool for a record British fee of £8.5m

The Bosman Ruling allowed freedom of movement for players out of contract

Arsenal manager George Graham is dismissed due to accusations of financial irregularities, despite helping Arsenal win six trophies since he took over in 1986. Frenchman Arsene Wenger takes over as Arsenal manager

Goalkeeper Bruce Grobbelaar is arrested on suspicion of match-fixing together with Wimbledon players Hans Segers and John Fashanu but all three were subsequently cleared by the High Court

1996 Alan Shearer transferred between Blackburn and Newcastle for a British record of £15m

Peter Shilton becomes the first player to complete 1000 league appearances

Euro '96 – England host the European Championships losing 6-5 to Germany on penalties in the semi final as Gareth Southgate misses a sudden-death penalty

1998 Sixteenth World Cup held in France – the home side won while England lost 3-4 on penalties to Argentina in the second round, with David Batty and Paul Ince missing their penalties

Arsenal wins the Double after taking the Premiership title and defeating Newcastle 2-0 in the FA Cup

Chelsea wins European Cup Winners' Cup, the League Cup and the European Super Cup under the leadership of player-manager Gianluca Vialli

Notts County become the first team to play over 4000 league games on 10th January against Rochdale

1999 Alex Ferguson and Geoff Hurst knighted for services to football

Manchester United wins an unprecedented treble – the FA Cup, European Cup and the Premier league title

2000 England appoint Sven Goran Eriksson as the new manager, the first non-English person to hold the post

Last match at Wembley Stadium before it closed prior to demolition to make way for a new stadium

2001 Manchester United pays £19m to PSV Eindhoven for Ruud van Nistelrooy and £28m to Lazio for Juan Veron

2002 Seventeenth World Cup is held jointly in Korea and Japan; England lost 2-1 to eventual winners Brazil in the quarter Finals

2003 England captain in the seventeenth World Cup, David Beckham is awarded an OBE shortly before his surprise £24.5 million transfer to Real Madrid from Manchester United

2004 Fifa celebrates its centenary

Greece wins the European Championship, staged in Portugal

2005 Liverpool wins the Champions League.

Below: Paul Scholes
Opposite: Gianfranco Zola

The Premier League

1992-93 ushered in the new era of the Premier League. Squad numbers were introduced and players' shirts sported their names. Sponsorship was now big business, and Carling put their name - and money - into the new venture. Only nine fixtures on the opening Saturday showed that one of the game's great traditions was no longer set in stone. BskyB wanted football to fit in with its schedule, rather than the other way round. It was a case of he who pays the piper calls the tune.

Manchester United were the inaugural Premiership champions. Ferguson's side romped home 10 points clear of the pack to bring the league crown to Old Trafford for the first time since 1967. Arsenal were left languishing in mid-table, while Liverpool could finish only 6th, failing to qualify for Europe for the first time in 30 years. The Gunners did have the consolation of winning both cups, beating Sheffield Wednesday in each of the finals. Bit-part player Steve Morrow scored the winner in the League Cup final, and suffered a broken arm after Tony Adams hoisted him aloft and then dropped him. It was another fringe player, Andy Linighan, who headed a dramatic winner in the FA Cup final, which went to a replay.

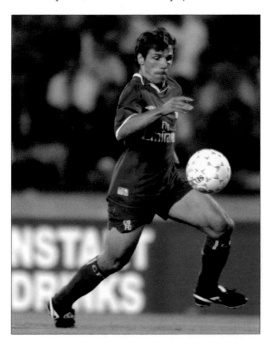

Keane joins United
United added Roy Keane to their ranks for the defence of their title. His arrival from Nottingham Forest for a British record £3.75 million made the United side even more formidable. This time they went one better, finishing eight points clear of Blackburn in the title race, and completing the double with an FA Cup victory over Chelsea.

The national team's fortunes went from bad to worse. Defeats against Norway and Holland left England needing to beat minnows San Marino by seven goals and hope that Holland lost in Poland. England started disastrously, conceding a goal in under ten seconds, which was believed to be an international record. The team recovered to win 7-1 but that was of little consequence as Holland got the win they needed. England had failed to qualify for the World Cup for the first time since 1978. Taylor, who had come in for some vitriolic criticism in the press, fell on his sword.

Venables replaces Taylor
Terry Venables was named as his successor. Venables had been ousted from White Hart Lane in a power struggle with chairman Alan Sugar, a dispute that was being played out in the High Court. With England hosting Euro '96, Venables had no immediate concerns of getting his England side through a competitive series. Graeme Souness's immediate concern was in finding another job as the Liverpool board finally lost patience. He became the first Liverpool manager to be shown the door since the 1950s. The club reverted to their tried and trusted system of appointing from within, Roy Evans being given the task of bringing back the glory days.

George Graham's record
Manchester United's first European Cup campaign since 1967-68 came to an abrupt end as they were beaten by Galatasaray in the Second Round. It was left to Arsenal to fly the flag for England in the 1993-94 European Cup Winners' Cup, and they did so in fine style. An Alan Smith goal was enough to beat Parma in the final, and although George Graham's side wasn't known for champagne football, six trophies in eight years told its own story.

The following season Graham nearly made it seven when they reached the final again. A freak 50-yard lob by ex-Spurs player Nayim won the match for Real Zaragoza seconds before the end of extra time.

Sutton and Shearer lead Blackburn to the title

The 1994-95 championship went to the wire. Kenny Dalglish's Blackburn, spearheaded by the SAS - Sutton and Shearer - went to Anfield on the last day of the season needing a victory to be sure of the title. Anything less could let in United, who were at West Ham. A last-minute goal by Jamie Redknapp looked to have spoiled Blackburn's party, until news came through that United had been held to a goalless draw. Blackburn thus claimed their first championship since 1914.

Newcastle go close

United reclaimed top spot in 1995-96, reeling in Kevin Keegan's Newcastle side, who had held a 12-point advantage early in the New Year. The two clubs would finish in the same positions the following season, Alex Ferguson having a distinct edge in the battle of wits that accompanied the onfield skirmishes.

In February 1995 it was revealed that George Graham had received illegal payments in transfer deals brokered by the agent Rune Hauge. Graham's track record couldn't help him; he was sacked by Arsenal and given a one-year ban by the FA. Allegations that Bruce Grobbelaar was involved in match-fixing at the behest of a Far East betting syndicate also hit the headlines. As recently as 1990, Swindon Town had been denied promotion to Division One after being found guilty of betting on the outcome of matches they were involved in.

In January 1995 the game was further tarnished when Eric Cantona lashed out at a fan with a kung fu-style kick after being red carded at Crystal Palace. He received an eight-month ban and a community service order. Arsenal's Paul Merson revealed that he had a drug problem, while team-mate Tony Adams had already served a prison sentence for drink-driving. All three players showed that rehabilitation was possible. In Cantona's case he returned to hit the goal which beat Liverpool in the 1996 FA Cup final. United had won the double again and the Frenchman was named Footballer of the Year.

"Football's Coming Home"

Euro 96 provided welcome relief from a lot of unseemly publicity. The fans sang "Football's Coming Home" and England gave the country something to smile about. A piece of Gascoigne magic helped the team to a 2-0 win over Scotland, and a 4-1 demolition job on the Dutch masters sent the country into a fever of anticipation. David Seaman was the hero in the penalty shoot-out victory over Spain in the quarter-final. When Alan Shearer scored after two minutes against Germany in the semis it looked as if England might go all the way. But the Germans levelled and the two countries went into a shoot-out for the second time in a major tournament. Gareth Southgate had been immaculate in central defence but his spot-kick was saved, leaving Moller to score the goal which put England out.

Paul Gascoigne

Problems with alcohol, injuries and his weight jinxed one of the most dazzling midfield players England has ever seen. "Gazza" grabbed the headlines for both self-destructive behaviour and brilliance. It was a tragedy for him, and for England, that he lacked the mental strength to match his mazy dribbling and slide-rule passes – a great footballing talent was squandered.

A Geordie full of laddish humour, he quickly made an impact at Newcastle United, which he joined in 1985 at 17. Terry Venables paid a record £2 million to bring the prodigious talent to Tottenham Hotspur in 1988. But in the 1991 FA Cup Final, having scored some fabulous goals on the road there, including a blinding 35-yard free-kick against the Gunners in the semi-final, Gascoigne recklessly fouled Forest's Gary Charles and injured his own cruciate ligament, which put him out of the game for a season.

National hero

Italia 90 had seen him emerge as a national hero, with the fans loving his heartfelt emotion when England went out to West Germany on penalties in the semi-final as much as they'd admired his moments of inspirational genius. He returned to Italy in 1992 for three difficult and injury-beset years at Lazio, but came back to Britain in 1995 for a renaissance at Glasgow Rangers, helping them to the Scottish title with 14 league goals in his first season and becoming Scotland's Footballer of the Year.

Euro 96, held in Britain, was a stage on which Gascoigne shone, and he scored a memorable goal against Scotland – one of the best of the championship. It was to be his high-water mark, for Glenn Hoddle left him out of the England squad for France 98, and he would never play for his country again.

Erratic in fitness and performance, Gazza's subsequent career, via Middlesbrough in 1998 and briefly Everton, has seen him unsigned at home and desperately trying to keep his place in China. It would be wonderful if he made a spectacular comeback, but sadly it now seems beyond him.

Opposite right: One of the most dramatic moments of Euro '96 when Stuart Pearce scored against Spain. After blasting the kick into the corner, he roared with delight. Pearce had missed from the spot when England were knocked out of the 1990 World Cup semi-finals by West Germany. Above: Teddy Sheringham shares the moment with an emotional Pearce.
Opposite left: Sheringham and Gascoigne celebrate after the midfielder's stunning goal clinched England's victory over Scotland in Euro '96.

League Division One and Premiership 1990-2005

1989-1990

1	Liverpool	79
2	Aston Villa	70
3	Tottenham Hotspur	63
4	Arsenal	62
5	Chelsea	60
6	Everton	59
7	Southampton	55
8	Wimbledon	55
9	Nottingham Forest	54
10	Norwich City	53
11	Queen's Park Rangers	50
12	Coventry City	49
13	Manchester United	48
14	Manchester City	48
15	Crystal Palace	48
16	Derby County	46
17	Luton Town	43
18	Sheffield Wednesday	43
19	Charlton Athletic	30
20	Millwall	26

1990-91

1	Arsenal	83
2	Liverpool	76
3	Crystal Palace	69
4	Leeds United	64
5	Manchester City	62
6	Manchester United	59
7	Wimbledon	56
8	Nottingham Forest	54
9	Everton	51
10	Tottenham Hotspur	49
11	Chelsea	49
12	Queen's Park Rangers	46
13	Sheffield United	46
14	Southampton	45
15	Norwich City	45
16	Coventry City	44
17	Aston Villa	41
18	Luton Town	37
19	Sunderland	34
20	Derby County	24

1991-92

1	Leeds United	82
2	Manchester United	78
3	Sheffield Wednesday	75
4	Arsenal	72
5	Manchester City	70
6	Liverpool	64
7	Aston Villa	60
8	Nottingham Forest	59
9	Sheffield United	57
10	Crystal Palace	57
11	Queen's Park Rangers	54
12	Everton	53
13	Wimbledon	53
14	Chelsea	53
15	Tottenham Hotspur	52
16	Southampton	52
17	Oldham Athletic	51
18	Norwich City	45
19	Coventry City	44
20	Luton Town	42
21	Notts County	40
22	West Ham United	38

1992-93

1	Manchester United	84
2	Aston Villa	74
3	Norwich City	72
4	Blackburn Rovers	71
5	Queen's Park Rangers	63
6	Liverpool	59
7	Sheffield Wednesday	59
8	Tottenham Hotspur	59
9	Manchester City	57
10	Arsenal	56
11	Chelsea	56
12	Wimbledon	54
13	Everton	53
14	Sheffield United	52
15	Coventry City	52
16	Ipswich Town	52
17	Leeds United	51
18	Southampton	50
19	Oldham Athletic	49
20	Crystal Palace	49
21	Middlesbrough	44
22	Nottingham Forest	40

1993-94

1	Manchester United	92
2	Blackburn Rovers	84
3	Newcastle United	77
4	Arsenal	71
5	Leeds United	70
6	Wimbledon	65
7	Sheffield Wednesday	64
8	Liverpool	60
9	Queen's Park Rangers	60
10	Aston Villa	57
11	Coventry City	56
12	Norwich City	53
13	West Ham United	52
14	Chelsea	51
15	Tottenham Hotspur	45
16	Manchester City	45
17	Everton	44
18	Southampton	43
19	Ipswich Town	43
20	Sheffield United	42
21	Oldham Athletic	40
22	Swindon Town	30

1994-95

1	Blackburn Rovers	89
2	Manchester United	88
3	Nottingham Forest	77
4	Liverpool	74
5	Leeds United	73
6	Newcastle United	72
7	Tottenham Hotspur	62
8	Queen's Park Rangers	60
9	Wimbledon	56
10	Southampton	54
11	Chelsea	54
12	Arsenal	51
13	Sheffield Wednesday	51
14	West Ham United	50
15	Everton	50
16	Coventry City	50
17	Manchester City	49
18	Aston Villa	48
19	Crystal Palace	45
20	Norwich City	43
21	Leicester City	29
22	Ipswich	27

1995-96

1	Manchester United	82
2	Newcastle United	78
3	Liverpool	71
4	Aston Villa	63
5	Arsenal	63
6	Everton	61
7	Blackburn Rovers	61
8	Tottenham Hotspur	61
9	Nottingham Forest	58
10	West Ham United	51
11	Chelsea	50
12	Middlesbrough	43
13	Leeds United	43
14	Wimbledon	41
15	Sheffield Wednesday	40
16	Coventry City	38
17	Southampton	38
18	Manchester City	38
19	Queen's Park Rangers	33
20	Bolton Wanderers	29

1996-97

1	Manchester United	75
2	Newcastle United	68
3	Arsenal	68
4	Liverpool	68
5	Aston Villa	61
6	Chelsea	59
7	Sheffield Wednesday	57
8	Wimbledon	56
9	Leicester City	47
10	Tottenham Hotspur	46
11	Leeds United	46
12	Derby County	46
13	Blackburn Rovers	42
14	West Ham United	42
15	Everton	42
16	Southampton	41
17	Coventry City	41
18	Sunderland	40
19	Middlesbrough	39
20	Nottingham Forest	34

1997-98

1	Arsenal	78
2	Manchester United	77
3	Liverpool	65
4	Chelsea	63
5	Leeds United	59
6	Blackburn Rovers	58
7	Aston Villa	57
8	West Ham United	56
9	Derby County	55
10	Leicester City	53
11	Coventry City	52
12	Southampton	48
13	Newcastle United	44
14	Tottenham Hotspur	44
15	Wimbledon	44
16	Sheffield Wednesday	44
17	Everton	40
18	Bolton Wanderers	40
19	Barnsley	35
20	Crystal Palace	33

1998-99

1	Manchester United	79
2	Arsenal	78
3	Chelsea	75
4	Leeds United	67
5	West Ham United	57
6	Aston Villa	55
7	Liverpool	54
8	Derby County	52
9	Middlesbrough	52
10	Leicester City	49
11	Tottenham Hotspur	47
12	Sheffield Wednesday	46
13	Newcastle United	46
14	Everton	43
15	Coventry City	42
16	Wimbledon	42
17	Southampton	41
18	Charlton Athletic	36
19	Blackburn Rovers	35
20	Nottingham Forest	30

1999-2000

1	Manchester United	91
2	Arsenal	73
3	Leeds United	69
4	Liverpool	67
5	Chelsea	65
6	Aston Villa	58
7	Sunderland	58
8	Leicester City	55
9	West Ham United	55
10	Tottenham Hotspur	53
11	Newcastle United	52
12	Middlesbrough	52
13	Everton	50
14	Coventry City	44
15	Southampton	44
16	Derby County	38
17	Bradford City	36
18	Wimbledon	33
19	Sheffield Wed	31
20	Watford	24

2000-01

1	Manchester United	80
2	Arsenal	70
3	Liverpool	69
4	Leeds United	68
5	Ipswich Town	66
6	Chelsea	61
7	Sunderland	57
8	Aston Villa	54
9	Charlton Athletic	52
10	Southampton	52
11	Newcastle United	51
12	Tottenham Hotspur	49
13	Leicester City	48
14	Middlesbrough	42
15	West Ham United	42
16	Everton	42
17	Derby County	42
18	Manchester City	34
19	Coventry City	34
20	Bradford City	26

	2001-02			2002-03			2003-04			2004-05	
1	Arsenal	87	1	Manchester United	83	1	Arsenal	90	1	Chelsea	95
2	Liverpool	80	2	Arsenal	78	2	Chelsea	79	2	Arsenal	83
3	Manchester United	77	3	Newcastle United	69	3	Manchester United	75	3	Manchester United	77
4	Newcastle United	71	4	Chelsea	67	4	Liverpool	60	4	Everton	61
5	Leeds United	66	5	Liverpool	64	5	Newcastle United	56	5	Liverpool	58
6	Chelsea	64	6	Blackburn Rovers	60	6	Aston Villa	56	6	Bolton Wanderers	58
7	West Ham United	53	7	Everton	59	7	Charlton Athletic	53	7	Middlesbrough	55
8	Aston Villa	50	8	Southampton	52	8	Bolton Wanderers	53	8	Manchester City	52
9	Tottenham Hotspur	50	9	Manchester City	51	9	Fulham	52	9	Tottenham Hotspur	52
10	Blackburn Rovers	46	10	Tottenham Hotspur	50	10	Birmingham City	50	10	Aston Villa	47
11	Southampton	45	11	Middlesbrough	49	11	Middlesbrough	48	11	Charlton	46
12	Middlesbrough	45	12	Charlton Athletic	49	12	Southampton	47	12	Birmingham	45
13	Fulham	44	13	Birmingham City	48	13	Portsmouth	45	13	Fulham	44
14	Charlton Athletic	44	14	Fulham	48	14	Tottenham Hotspur	45	14	Newcastle	44
15	Everton	43	15	Leeds United	47	15	Blackburn Rovers	44	15	Blackburn Rovers	42
16	Bolton Wanderers	40	16	Aston Villa	45	16	Manchester City	41	16	Portsmouth	39
17	Sunderland	40	17	Bolton Wanderers	44	17	Everton	39	17	West Bromwich A	34
18	Ipswich Town	36	18	West Ham United	42	18	Leicester City	33	18	Crystal Palace	33
19	Derby County	30	19	West Bromwich A	26	19	Leeds United	33	19	Norwich	33
20	Leicester City	28	20	Sunderland	19	20	Wolverhampton W	33	20	Southampton	32

Emile Heskey beats Johan Mjallby in the air during a friendly international match against Sweden.

FA Cup Finals 1990-2005

1990	Manchester United	v	Crystal Palace	3-3 (1-0)
1991	Tottenham Hotspur	v	Nottingham Forest	2-1
1992	Liverpool	v	Sunderland	2-0
1993	Arsenal	v	Sheffield Wednesday	1-1 (2-1)
1994	Manchester United	v	Chelsea	4-0
1995	Everton	v	Manchester United	1-0
1996	Manchester United	v	Liverpool	1-0
1997	Chelsea	v	Middlesbrough	2-0
1998	Arsenal	v	Newcastle United	2-0
1999	Manchester United	v	Newcastle United	2-0
2000	Chelsea	v	Aston Villa	1-0
2001	Liverpool	v	Arsenal	2-1
2002	Arsenal	v	Chelsea	2-0
2003	Arsenal	v	Southampton	1-0
2004	Manchester United	v	Millwall	3-0
2005	Arsenal	v	Manchester United	0-0
				(aet)
			Arsenal won 5-4 on penalties	

Arsene Wenger

The choice of this quietly spoken, cerebral polyglot raised a few eyebrows among Arsenal fans when he was named as the man to take over from Bruce Rioch in September 1996. But Wenger was a very experienced coach, well known and respected within footballing circles. In 1981 he became youth coach at Strasbourg, the club he had played for. He then had spells at Cannes and Nancy, but it was when he joined Monaco that he started to make a name for himself. He won the French league with Monaco in 1988, his attractive side including the mercurial talents of Glenn Hoddle and Chris Waddle. In 1997-98, less than two years after arriving at Highbury, Wenger masterminded a famous League and Cup Double. He repeated the feat in 2001-02, and it looked as if his outstanding team had taken Manchester United's mantle as the best in the Premiership. Arsenal looked on course for a third Double in five years in 2002-03, but the team faltered after a blistering start. The Gunners had to be content with runners-up to United, though they retained the FA Cup with a victory over Southampton.

Middle: Two England managers show the strains of the job. Glen Hoddle (right) who took England to the World Cup finals in France 1998 only to see his team bow out following another penalty shoot-out and Kevin Keegan (left) who replaced him for the unsuccessful campaign of Euro 2000. England had let a vital two-goal lead slip in their opening match against Portugal, losing 3-2.
Opposite: Chelsea celebrating after beating Middlesbrough 2-0 in the 1997 Cup Final.
Top: Arsene Wenger achieved the Double with Arsenal in only his second season in charge of the team. David Seaman (top right) was England's first choice keeper and fundamental to the Gunners' success.
Above: David Beckham sets a fashion trend in boots that were to become his hallmark.

The Bosman ruling

Jean-Marc Bosman had never set Belgian football alight, let alone the world. But when he took his club Liege to the European Court of Justice on the issue of freedom of contract, he secured a ruling that was to have profound implications for all clubs. From now on contract negotiations - and an eye on the clock - would become of paramount importance when it came to a club's balance sheet. Few businesses had to contend with multi-million pound assets disappearing overnight, but that wasn't far from the case post-Bosman.

Wenger joins Arsenal

Many Arsenal fans scratched their heads when Arsene Wenger was named as the man to take over at Highbury in 1996, following Bruce Rioch's brief tenure. Wenger couldn't prevent United from taking the title again in his first season, but in 1997-98 he led the Gunners to the Double. It was to be the start of a long battle for supremacy in the domestic game, one involving psychological warfare as well as battles on the field.

Hoddle at the England helm

Terry Venables had announced before Euro 96 that he would be standing down to devote his energies to sorting out his legal and business affairs. Chelsea's Glenn Hoddle was installed as the new supremo; at 38 he became the youngest ever England manager. Hoddle's first test came at France '98. England scraped into the finals, looking far from impressive. A defeat against Romania at the group stage didn't prove costly as it was sandwiched between victories over Tunisia and Colombia. Michael Owen had come off the bench to score against Romania and the clamour among fans for him to start in the second-round match against Argentina was deafening. Hoddle had taken the brave decision to leave Gascoigne out of his final 22; the decision to play Owen was far easier. The 17-year-old Liverpool prodigy scored the goal of the tournament to put England 2-1 ahead. Argentina levelled, and after David Beckham was red-carded for a petulant kick at Diego Simeone it looked to be slipping away from England's grasp. Sol Campbell thought he'd given 10-man England a 'golden goal' winner with a towering header in extra time. It was ruled out for an infringement and England suffered yet another penalty shoot-out exit. Paul Ince and David Batty were the unlucky men to miss from the spot on this occasion.

Liverpool prodigy scores the goal of the World Cup.

United crowned champions of Europe

Above: United fans swarm the streets of Manchester in celebration of their team's victory, after beating Bayern Munich 2-1 in the European Cup Final in Barcelona.
Opposite below: Alex Ferguson proudly parades the European Cup at Manchester Airport.

In the domestic game the United bandwagon rolled on. Ferguson's men reclaimed the title in 1999, the first in a hat-trick of championships that would equal Liverpool's feat of the 1980s. European Cup success was still proving elusive, however, a 1997 semi-final defeat by Borussia Dortmund being the nearest United had come to repeating the club's achievement under Busby. In May 1999 the coveted trophy was finally claimed, and in dramatic fashion. United entered the tournament as runners-up, but while Arsenal faltered in their group matches, United emerged to dispose of Inter Milan and Juventus at the knockout stage. A 32-match unbeaten run had carried the club to yet another domestic double and to the Champions' League final, against Bayern Munich in Barcelona. Trailing 1-0 with a minute to go, Sheringham scored to give United a lifeline. Seconds later Sheringham flicked on a Beckham corner and Solskjaer stabbed the ball into the roof of the net.

Alex Ferguson

Alex Ferguson arrived at Old Trafford in 1986 with an impressive record from his eight years at Aberdeen. He succeeded in breaking the Celtic-Rangers stranglehold on Scottish football, winning the championship three times and the Scottish Cup on four occasions. He also guided the Dons to a famous European Cup Winners' Cup victory over Real Madrid, beating the mighty Spanish side 2-1 in the Final in Gothenburg. He had a brief spell as caretaker manager of Scotland following the death of Jock Stein.

Youth system bears fruit

Ferguson then turned his attention to making Manchester United a powerhouse in England's top flight at a time when Liverpool were the undisputed top dogs. Fortunes in the early days were mixed. His team lifted the FA Cup in 1990 and followed it up with a victory over Barcelona in the European Cup Winners' Cup Final the following year. Shortly afterwards the youth system in which Ferguson had invested so heavily began to bear fruit. Players of the stature of Giggs, Beckham, Scholes and the Neville brothers progressed to the senior side. Ferguson also made some astute signings, notably Peter Schmeichel and Eric Cantona, who together cost just £1.5 million. Ferguson's side proved irresistible, winning the inaugural Premiership title in 1993. A league and Cup Double followed in 1994, and again in 1996. But the crowning moment came in 1999, when Ferguson added the European Cup to his sizeable haul of domestic trophies. He announced that 2002 would be his final season, but had a change of heart and took United to yet another championship in 2002-03.

Sven-Goran Eriksson

After Terry Venables, Glenn Hoddle and Kevin Keegan had come and gone in a relatively short space of time, FA administrators took the unprecedented step of appointing Sven-Goran Eriksson as national team boss, the first overseas incumbent. The decision angered some, while others praised the farsightedness of bringing in a man with an excellent record as a coach. Eriksson hit the headlines in 1982, when he took IFK Gothenburg to the UEFA Cup Final. His team beat Valencia and Kaiserslautern along the way and Hamburg in the Final, becoming the first Swedish side to lift a European trophy. Eriksson was back there again in 1983, this time with Benfica. On this occasion he finished on the losing side, Anderlecht coming out on top over the two legs.

Lazio's first championship for 26 years

Eriksson won three championships with Benfica and made it to the 1990 European Cup final, where his team lost 1-0 to the all-conquering AC Milan. Serie A beckoned next and Eriksson had spells at Roma, Fiorentina and Sampdoria before joining Lazio in 1997. His first season with the Rome club was a rollercoaster. The team won the Italian Cup, fell away in the league and went down 3-0 to Inter in the UEFA Cup final. In 2000 he delivered the Serie A title, Lazio's first championship for 26 years. He was appointed England manager the following year, when the team was in a precarious position in the World Cup qualifying campaign. He galvanised the team, taking England to the top of their group with results including a memorable 5-1 win in Germany. He got England out of the "Group of Death" in Japan and Korea and the team beat a good Danish side before going out to eventual winners Brazil. Eriksson's men also fell at the quarter-final hurdle at Euro 2004, going out on penalties to hosts Portugal. It was widely seen as a missed opportunity, increasing the pressure on the team to go at least one better at the 2006 World Cup.

Eriksson silences his critics

There was another England-Germany clash at Euro 2000 as the countries were drawn together at the group stage. A Shearer goal gave England victory, but both countries made an early exit. England had let a two-goal lead slip in their opening match against Portugal, losing 3-2. They also led Romania 2-1 in their final match but again failed to press home the advantage and were on the receiving end of another 3-2 defeat.

Failure to qualify for the latter stages led Kevin Keegan to question his ability at the highest level. He stood down with qualification for the 2002 World Cup in Japan and Korea hanging in the balance. The FA looked further afield for their next appointment. Sven-Goran Eriksson was not a universally popular choice, despite his excellent credentials. He silenced many of his critics with a stunning 5-1 win in Germany in September 2001, a result which got England's World Cup campaign back on track.

"Group of Death"

Eriksson succeeded in getting the country out of the "Group of Death", a Beckham penalty against Argentina exorcising the ghost of France '98. A comfortable win over Denmark followed, but England went down to favourites Brazil in the quarter-final. Ronaldinho's 35-yard free-kick floated over Seaman's head for the winning goal, leading many to speculate on his future for both Arsenal and England.

Above: The scoreboard records the moment - England's great victory over rivals Germany after having lost the home game of the World Cup qualifying group at Wembley 1-0.

David Beckham

David Beckham has been a villain and he has been a hero. After a bad-tempered kick on Diego Simeone in England's 1998 World Cup clash with Argentina, he was cast as the villain of the piece. But, by the end of the 2002 World Cup, he was universally regarded as England's new hero. His artistry on the ball, superb distribution and the quality of his dead-ball kicks were always acknowledged – what he had gained in the intervening years was a greater maturity and outstanding leadership skills.

When he was still a youngster, Beckham won an award at a Bobby Charlton Soccer Skills school and had trials with his local club, Leyton Orient, but it was Manchester United who signed him just after his 16th birthday. Although he made his debut in a League Cup tie against Brighton in September 1992, Alex Ferguson nurtured his young star carefully and it wasn't until April 1995 that he gave Beckham his Premiership debut. The following season he established himself in United's midfield and in September 1996 Glenn Hoddle gave him a place in the England team.

Three successive Premiership titles

Beckham was a key figure in United's celebrated Treble-winning team of the 1998-99 season. During the Champions League campaign, United played Inter Milan, a game that was billed as the return clash between Beckham and Simeone. It was less than a year since the infamous World Cup incident but Beckham gave a superb performance, the two players swapped shirts at the end of the game and the victory went to United. At the end of that season, Beckham was narrowly beaten by Rivaldo for the World Footballer of the Year award.

'Becks' was instrumental in helping United to their third successive Premiership title in 2001. In October of the same year it was his stunning free-kick in the closing seconds of the game against Greece which reserved England's place at the 2002 World Cup in Japan and Korea.

His service in that World Cup meant that Beckham had a virtually unassailable position as England captain during the 2002-03 season, yet he was unsure of a place in United's starting line-up. After much speculation on his future, in June 2003 Beckham signed a £25 million deal to take him to Real Madrid, the team that knocked United out of that season's Champions Cup.

Gunners Double Up

In 2001-02 Arsenal won their second Double under Wenger and the third in the club's history. The Gunners began the 2002-03 season like an express train and Wenger tentatively suggested that his side was capable of going through the season unbeaten. Clubs in the chasing pack, looking to strengthen, had the new transfer arrangements to contend with. After the start of the season the 'window' would not be open to further deals until January. Arsenal faltered in the second half of the season and in the end they had to settle for retaining the FA Cup and the runners-up spot in the league. United, by contrast, went on a blistering run in the new year to claim their 8th Premiership title in 11 seasons. There was also the prospect of a second European Cup Final appearance, this time at Old Trafford. United managed to beat holders Real Madrid in the home leg of their quarter-final clash, but the damage had already been done at the Bernebeu.

The season ended with the England captain departing to join the team that had knocked United out of the European Cup. David Beckham's name had been linked with several clubs when it became clear that United were prepared to let him go. Real Madrid were one of the few clubs who could afford the £25 million fee as the inflationary bubble had undoubtedly burst. A significant part of Beckham's fee was for the acquisition of a unique brand; Real would expect to recoup the outlay in the sales of merchandise as well as in his contribution on the pitch.

Michael Owen

Since he electrified first the Premiership, then the world, in the 1997-98 season, Michael Owen has continued to rewrite the record books. By the end of the 2004-05 season Owen had notched 32 international goals, standing fourth in the all-time list of England marksmen. Averaging almost a goal every other game, he remains on course to achieve his aim of 50 goals in 100 appearances for his country. Owen was the star of Liverpool's Youth Cup-winning side in 1996. Roy Evans handed him his Premiership debut at Wimbledon at the end of the 1996-97 season, and the 17-year-old immediately notched his first senior goal. He scored 30 more in the 1997-98 season, earning him the PFA Young Player of the Year award, and more significantly an England call-up. When, in February 1998, he lined up against Chile, Owen became the youngest England player of the century; at 18 years 59 days he took the record previously held by Duncan Edwards. Shortly afterwards, he became the youngest player to score for England when he netted a goal against Morocco in a World Cup warm-up match.

Goal of the tournament

England manager Glenn Hoddle took him to the World Cup in France 1998, but not as first-choice striker. Owen changed that after he came off the bench to score against Romania. In the second round clash with Argentina he won a penalty, then struck the goal of the tournament.

Owen's glittering career has presented numerous highlights, including a stunning two-goal tally to seize the FA Cup from Arsenal in 2001, and the marvellous hat-trick in the 5-1 demolition of Germany in a World Cup qualifier four months later. It was such performances which earned him the 2001 European Footballer of the Year award, the first British player to achieve that honour since Kevin Keegan in 1979. He celebrated, in true Owen style, by striking his hundredth goal for Liverpool in the same month.

His second World Cup in Japan and Korea in 2002 brought him goals against Denmark and Brazil. And the penalty he won in the game against Argentina in the 'Group of Death' was instrumental in England's momentous defeat of their historic rivals.

In the summer of 2004 Owen left Anfield to join Beckham at Real Madrid. His first season at the Bernebeu was a frustrating one. His goal return in relation to minutes on the pitch was excellent, but fierce competition and a considerable amount of time on the bench prompted speculation of an early return to the Premiership.

Football's finances

The financial correction that had occurred since the heady days of the 1990s was stark. The collapse of On Digital showed that football was not a cash cow that could be milked at all levels. Leeds fans watched their Champions League semi-final side of 2001 disintegrate before their eyes, hard proof that gambling on a seat at European football's top table was a high-risk strategy.

The parlous state of football's finances meant that even Champions League qualification was not necessarily a passport to a land of milk and honey. On the final day of the 2002-03 season Chelsea beat Liverpool to secure the fourth Champions League spot. Less than two months later chairman Ken Bates sold his majority shareholding to Russian oil billionaire Roman Abramovich. In seven seasons Chelsea had never finished out of the top six in the Premiership, had twice lifted the FA Cup and also won the Cup Winners' Cup. And yet the club was £80 million in debt and Bates admitted that pockets deeper than his were needed to take Chelsea forward.

Thierry Henry

Early in the 2002-03 season Arsenal fans had good reason to celebrate when Thierry Henry committed himself to Highbury for as long as the club wanted him. His superb form on the field helped him towards his winning of the prestigious Player of the Year award in April 2003.

Just four years earlier Henry had been languishing at Juventus; he was neither assured of a first-team place, nor enjoying his football. An £11-million offer from Arsenal's Arsene Wenger in August 1999 and the Turin club was happy to let him go. For Henry it was a chance to revitalise his career. Wenger knew exactly what he was getting – he had signed Henry as a teenager when he was coach at Monaco. As a top junior sprinter, with the ball skills to match, Henry was set to make a huge contribution to the modern game. He started out as a speedy winger, but Wenger made the inspired decision to play him in a central role at Arsenal. At first, even Henry himself wasn't convinced, but in his time at Highbury, he has proved to be one of the most lethal central strikers in world football.

World Cup 1998

It was in his home country, playing for his home nation that Henry broke through onto the international stage. In the World Cup in France in 1998, he hit three goals in the group matches, but missed out on a starting place in the final. A sending-off against Uruguay rounded off an awful tournament for both Henry and France in the 2002 World Cup. However, next time around, in Germany in 2006, he will be only 28; there will be many more opportunities for talented Thierry Henry to make his mark on the biggest stage.

Arsenal match Invincibles

Even established Premiership sides now had to strike a balance between sound investment and over-commitment. For Leeds it was all too late; a string of stars had been sold at knockdown prices and the team propped up the division in 2003-04.

Chelsea, backed by Abramovich's personal fortune, was the one club able to buck the trend. Coach Claudio Ranieri spent over £100 million on a crop of international stars, players of the stature of Makelele, Duff, Crespo and Mutu. Inevitably there were accusations of trying to buy success, and for most of the 2003-04 season it looked as if the strategy was going to bear fruit. Chelsea stayed with the scorching pace set by Arsenal longest, but in the end not even Ranieri's all-stars could match the brilliance of Arsene Wenger's team. The Gunners completed their league programme unbeaten, a feat not achieved in English football's top flight since 1888-89, when Preston's Invincibles won the inaugural League Championship.

Chelsea took revenge over their London rivals with a quarter-final victory in the Champions League, but went down to Monaco in the semis. By most standards Chelsea had had a successful season, but the lack of silverware meant that football's worst-kept secret was finally revealed: out went Ranieri and in came Jose Mourinho, who had just steered Porto to Champions League victory, following a UEFA Cup triumph over Celtic in 2003.

Manchester United was among Porto's scalps in the latter's Champions League campaign. United also trailed in a distant third in the Premiership, 15 points behind Arsenal. Ferguson's side did win the FA Cup semi-final clash between the two giants, and a comfortable 3-0 victory over Millwall in the final gave United their 11th victory in the competition, stretching the club's lead at the top of the all-time list.

Changes at Anfield

The fact that Chelsea had managed to break the Manchester United-Arsenal duopoly in 2003-04 undoubtedly helped to bring down the curtain on Gerard Houllier's reign at Anfield. Liverpool fans saw their team secure Champions League football by finishing fourth in the Premiership, but with a 28-point gulf separating the Reds from Arsenal. In terms of points Liverpool were closer to the relegated clubs, having finished just 26 points ahead of Leeds, Wolves and Leicester. The man charged with bringing the glory days back to Anfield was Rafael Benitez, who had just completed a Primera Liga-UEFA Cup double with Valencia.

Euro 2004

Opposite above left: Frank Lampard celebrates his goal against France with Wayne Rooney.
Opposite above right: Wayne Rooney celebrates a goal with David Beckham during the 4-2 defeat of Croatia.

Euro 2004

With domestic matters settled, there was the usual pre-tournament mood of buoyant optimism as England departed for Portugal. There was almost a dream start as Sven Goran Eriksson's men led holders and favourites France through a Frank Lampard header in their opening group fixture. Two injury-time goals from Zidane meant that England emerged with considerable credit but no points.

A comfortable 3-0 win over Switzerland followed, Wayne Rooney grabbing a brace and becoming the youngest scorer in the competition's history. That record was taken a few days later by Switzerland's Johan Vonlanthen, but with two more goals in the 4-2 victory over Croatia, it was Rooney's name that was on everyone's lips. He headed the list of the tournament's marksmen and the impact he had made was compared with Pele's debut on the world stage at the 1958 World Cup.

England qualified for the quarter-finals behind France, the first time that the country had reached the knockout stage of the competition on foreign soil.

The team got off to a dream start against hosts Portugal, Michael Owen silencing his critics with a brilliant strike after three minutes. It was his 26th goal in his 60th appearance in an England shirt. Rooney limped out with a broken metatarsal midway through the first half, and as the game wore on England fought an increasingly rearguard action. With seven minutes to go the hosts equalised through substitute Helder Postiga, who had all too rarely found the back of the net when turning out for Spurs. There were shades of France '98 as Sol Campbell thought he'd headed England into the semis in the dying seconds, but the Swiss referee spotted an infringement and the game went to extra-time.

Rui Costa's ferocious strike in the second period was cancelled out when Lampard pounced on a knockdown to score his third goal of the tournament. After 120 minutes the teams were locked at 2-2.

Beckham capped a hugely disappointing tournament by blazing over in the penalty shoot-out. Rui Costa did the same to level matters and it went to sudden death. Portuguese 'keeper Ricardo saved from Darius Vassell and then slotted home the decisive spot-kick. In reaching the last eight, and thus only matching the performance at the 2002 World Cup, Euro 2004 was widely regarded as a missed opportunity for England.

Triumphs for Chelsea and Liverpool

2004-05 will be remembered as the season when Manchester United and Arsenal, between them winners of the Premiership title in 11 of the previous 12 years, could do nothing to stop the Chelsea juggernaut. Jose Mourinho's men didn't quite manage to emulate Arsenal's achievement of the previous campaign – defeat at Manchester City prevented that - but it was still a record-breaking season. 29 wins and 95 points eclipsed the previous marks, while Petr Cech's 1025 minutes without conceding broke Peter Schmeichel's record for shut-outs. Chelsea shipped just 15 goals, two fewer than Arsenal in 1998-99. The meanest defence in the land was marshalled by the outstanding John Terry, who edged Frank Lampard for the PFA Player of the Year award, the first defender to be thus honoured since Paul McGrath in 1993. The title came in Chelsea's centenary, and exactly 50 years after Ted

Drake delivered Chelsea's only other championship.

The Carling Cup also went to Stamford Bridge, Chelsea beating Liverpool in the final. Rafael Benitez's erratic side saved its best performances for Europe. With Utd and Arsenal both out of the Champions League at the last 16 stage, Liverpool scored excellent wins over Bayer Leverkusen and Juventus to set up a semi-final clash with Chelsea. It was billed as the biggest game in the history of English club football, and also saw the reigning Champions League and UEFA Cup-winning managers go head to head. A Luis Garcia goal at Anfield settled the issue. Liverpool, who would finish 37 points adrift of the champions, were through to their sixth European Cup final on the 20th anniversary of the Heysel tragedy.

Gerrard leads Reds' revival

Opponents AC Milan were favourites in Istanbul, and odds of 300-1 against the Reds were being quoted at half-time, by which time they were three goals down. Steven Gerrard led from the front as Liverpool fought back to take the game to penalties, and two Dudek saves in the shoot-out saw Liverpool complete the greatest ever comeback in a European final. Their fifth win in the

Left: An elated Frank Lampard scores against Bolton Wanderers. The 2-0 victory makes Chelsea winners of the Barclays Premiership for 2004/2005.
Above: Jose Mourinho, winner of the Premiership at his first attempt.
Opposite: Liverpool's captain, Steven Gerrard, holds the trophy as teammates celebrate after the UEFA Champions League Final at the Ataturk Olympic Stadium in Turkey.

competition meant that the cup would stay at Anfield. Arsenal beat Man Utd in the Premiership runners-up race, Arsene Wenger maintaining his record of never finishing outside the top two. Third spot for the second year running represented Utd's 'worst' performance since the inception of Premiership, and came amid the uncertainties created by Malcolm Glazer's take-over of the club.

Gunners win Cup Final shoot-out

Arsenal and Utd's only hope of silverware rested on the FA Cup, and they met in the final. Utd did everything but score, but after a goalless 120 minutes Lehmann's save from Scholes meant that the Gunners won the first Cup Final shoot-out.

Everton, widely tipped as relegation candidates, secured the fourth Champions League spot, earning David Moyes the Manager of the Year award. Everton lost Rooney just before start of season, and the influential Gravesen in January, but still secured the club's first European Cup campaign for 34 years. Fifth place Liverpool had to sweat on a dispensation to be allowed to defend their Champions League crown, while Bolton fans looked forward to European football for first time in the club's history.

On the final day of the season the relegation dogfight provided the greatest drama. It was perm three from four to go down, and at various times Norwich, Crystal Palace, Southampton and West Brom all occupied the vital 17th place. The Baggies were the only side to win, a 2-0 victory over Portsmouth guaranteeing Premiership football for Bryan Robson's men. Eight points adrift at the foot of the table at Christmas, West Brom made Premiership history by surviving the drop. For Southampton it was the end of a 27-year run in the top flight.

In the Championship, Wigan Athletic won automatic promotion as runners-up to Sunderland. Elected to the league at end of 77-78 season, Wigan had been bought in 1995 by Dave Whelan, 68-year old founder of the JJB sportswear empire. His money, together with Paul Jewell's shrewd management, had produced a fairytale rise to the top. Alan Pardew, much castigated by West Ham fans, answered his critics by taking the Hammers back to the Premiership via the play-offs.

Champions of Europe: Liverpool teammates celebrate at the end of UEFA Champions League Final.

Acknowledgements

The photographs in this book are from the archives of the *Daily Mail*.
Particular thanks to
Steve Torrington, Dave Sheppard, Brian Jackson, Alan Pinnock, Richard Jones and all the staff.

The following photographs are Copyright 2003 Topham Picturepoint:
Pages: 9;10 (T&B);11;12;13;14;15;18;23;27;32.

Thanks also to
Cliff Salter, Richard Betts, Peter Wright, Trevor Bunting, Alice Hill, Simon Taylor, Gareth Thomas, Jane Hill,
Carol Salter, Corinne Hill, Jim Carpenter, Maureen Hill, Harry Nettleton, Tom Nettleton,
Matthew Nee and Duncan Hill
Design by John Dunne.